ASKING the RIGHT QUESTIONS

THIRD Edition

ASKING the RIGHT QUESTIONS

THIRD Edition

Tools for
COLLABORATION
and
**SCHOOL
CHANGE**

SCHOOL

CLASSROOM

DISTRICT

Edie L. Holcomb
Foreword by
Shirley M. Hord

CORWIN PRESS
A SAGE Company

For information:

Corwin Press
A SAGE Company
2455 Teller Road
Thousand Oaks, California 91320
www.corwinpress.com

SAGE Ltd.
1 Oliver's Yard
55 City Road
London EC1Y 1SP
United Kingdom

SAGE India Pvt. Ltd.
B 1/I 1 Mohan Cooperative Industrial Area
Mathura Road, New Delhi 110 044
India

SAGE Asia-Pacific Pte. Ltd.
33 Pekin Street #02-01
Far East Square
Singapore 048763

Printed in the United States of America

Library of Congress Cataloging-in-Publication Data

Holcomb, Edie L.
Asking the right questions: tools for collaboration and school change/Edie L. Holcomb.—3rd ed.
    p. cm.
Includes bibliographical references and index.
ISBN 978-1-4129-6274-2 (hardcover w/cd)
ISBN 978-1-4129-6275-9 (pbk. w/cd)

  1. Group work in education—United States. 2. Team learning approach in education—United States. 3. Educational change—United States. 4. School management and organization—United States. I. Title.

LB1032.H64 2009
371.39'5—dc22

This book is printed on acid-free paper.

08   09   10   11   12   10   9   8   7   6   5   4   3   2   1

Acquisitions Editor:	Arnis Burvikovs
Associate Editor:	Desirée Enayati
Production Editor:	Melanie Birdsall
Copy Editor:	Teresa Herlinger
Typesetter:	C&M Digitals (P) Ltd.
Proofreader:	Caryne Brown
Indexer:	Molly Hall
Cover Designer:	Rose Storey
Media Editor:	Peggie Howard

Contents

List of Figures

List of CD-ROM Contents

Introduction

1. Asking the Right Questions
Figures
School Change as Inquiry
Matrix of Tools for *Asking the Right Questions*
A Tool for Team Training
Fill-In Forms
School Change as Inquiry Template
Matrix of Tools for *Asking the Right Questions* Template
Answer Key
Discussion Guide

2. Answering the "Where Are We Now?" Question
Figures
Histogram of Student Achievement
Histogram of Disaggregated Student Achievement
Run Chart of Reading Scores
Symbolic Display of Student Demographics: Race
Symbolic Display of Student Demographics: Socioeconomics
Symbolic Display of Student Success: Race
Symbolic Display of Student Success: Socioeconomics
Flowchart for an Initiative
Continuum of Site-Based Shared Decision Making
Site-Based Decision Making
High School Leadership Structure
Restructuring Options: Status Quo
Restructuring Options: Option A
Restructuring Options: Option B
Restructuring Options: Option C
New Organizational Structure
Answer Key
Discussion Guide

Foreword to the Third Edition

It you don't have a hammer,

A shoe will do.

The brief comment, above, initiated the Foreword to the first edition (1996) of Edie Holcomb's book, *Asking the Right Questions.* In the Foreword to the second edition (2000), this myth was dispelled. In this third iteration of *Asking the Right Questions*, it is timely to bury (deeply) the above-stated idea. As Holcomb points out, the standards movement and the requirements of No Child Left Behind legislation make it abundantly necessary to gain clarity about our goals for school improvement, and thus, increased successful learning outcomes for students. Any old shoe *won't* do. Fortunately, Holcomb provides us with a broad array of tools and techniques, and a wide range of tactics and strategies to support and guide our efforts at increasing the effectiveness of our schools.

An additional expansion in this third edition is the attention given to the confluence of classroom, school, and district office. In this book, these three entities are treated as collaborators who work in tandem in the pursuit of school change and improvement. No longer is there the we–they separation of the school and district staff; instead there are sense-making suggestions for the roles that each plays and the tools required for effectively enacting those roles.

A quick review of the table of contents reveals the richness of what is found between the covers of this book. Would-be school improvers, as well as experienced change agents, will delight in even a quick scan of possibilities, for each will find excellent ideas and actions to employ in his or her work. Holcomb has enhanced her prior volumes, to the benefit of all school change leaders, whether they are internal to the school or district or externally situated. Of special note is her reference to or framing of the book's tools for the adoption and implementation processes upon which true change will occur. Six strategies identified consistently in the school improvement and reform literature undergird the implementation process and are given attention (Hall & Hord, 2006):

1. Create and articulate a shared vision of the change

2. Plan for adopting and implementing the change, and provide resources

3. Invest in training and professional development

4. Check progress

5. Provide continual assistance

6. Create a context conducive to change

Four of these six strategies are given life through the tool of Innovation Configuration (IC) Maps. The IC Map, described and carefully explained by Holcomb (see Chapter 5), is actually the written-down vision of the change as it is imagined when the change is implemented in a high-quality way in classrooms or the school, or whatever its intended context. The IC Map tool is further used as a guide for developing a plan for implementation and for identifying resources needed. The map provides the professional developer with information needed for the design and delivery of training and professional learning of those who will be implementing the change. In turn, the IC Map may be used to monitor or assess progress of individuals (and through aggregation, groups) as they develop the knowledge and skills to use the change effectively. The utility of this tool cannot be overestimated, for it provides clarity to both the leaders of a change/school improvement effort and the individual implementers of it. The IC Map is but one example of the practical and quality tools, strategies, and approaches the reader can expect from this volume.

Holcomb herself has been a campus leader of school reform and has experienced the process at the personal and practical levels. These experiences encompass a wide range of roles and responsibilities. For example, she has supported the development of others, preparing them for the leadership role. In these efforts, she has developed professional development materials and activities and has shared her expertise in a variety of formats and venues, nationally and internationally.

She has been in the vineyard as a school practitioner leading change. She has also been a school change trainer, supporting the process from a managerial perspective. Always a student of the research literature, she enhances her experiential knowledge base with the study results of researchers' rigor and precision. Her experiences and perspectives of the world have contributed to her thoughtful advice and counsel. As an insider and an outsider—she has been in both places—Holcomb offers us this rich manuscript, contributing to our resources and to the measurable probability of successful school change.

At their work table, all persons who have responsibility for guiding schools to increased effectiveness, from both the campus and district levels, should have this volume dog-eared and sticky noted. They will find much of value to "mark" in this book.

—Shirley M. Hord
Scholar Emerita, Retired
Southwest Educational Development Laboratory (SEDL)
Austin, Texas

Preface to the Third Edition

My mission
   is to increase student achievement
      by teaching and modeling skills and processes
   that empower those who care
      to make decisions and implement change.

That personal mission statement was written from the heart almost 15 years ago and has sustained its relevance and rigor to challenge my practice all this time.

But that doesn't mean I've always had the right skill or process on the tip of my tongue. Take, for example, the early morning when a jangling phone interrupted my wake-up routines. I grabbed a towel with one hand and the phone with the other. An unfamiliar voice on the other end asked, "Is this the Edie Holcomb who's been consulting with the Restructuring Committee?" As I acknowledged that identity, mental red lights and alarm bells kicked in, full force. The Restructuring Committee was going quite well, but there are always those who don't want to "re-" anything. Is it a reporter? A board member? A misinformed nonparticipant? The caller continued. "Well, my name is 'John Smith.' I'm on the scheduling committee at our high school, and we've been studying a four-period day, and that's what we want to recommend to the whole faculty. But there's going to be a lot of resistance, and I was told you know a lot of group processes, and I'm wondering if you could recommend the approach that would work best." The relief that it wasn't the media was followed by sheer panic as my mental screen went absolutely blank. I fumbled with some general suggestions as I also fumbled with how to manipulate paper and pen without losing anything else I was grasping. After capturing the vital information so I could return his call later in the day, I asked myself, "If I'm the Edie Holcomb who knows a lot of group process techniques, why can't I think of a single one when I'm caught off guard like that? I need a 'cheat sheet' to hang by every phone in my house and office so I can *remember* what I know when I get these unexpected phone calls!"

A few days later, at a table littered with coffee cups and cookie crumbs, an apprehensive group of principals was wrestling with the role changes occurring as a result of the district's latest mandate for site-based management.

(The previous swing of the pendulum had been 12 years ago, and many principals had not shared that experience.) Official job descriptions and evaluation systems had remained unchanged for two decades, but every building was now to form a school council, and the administrators would be held responsible for its success. Even those most optimistic, cheering up the others with the potential for greater autonomy and authentic shared decision making, wondered whether they had the knowledge and skills to pull it off this time. One voice rose above the rest:

> I'm supposed to form this team, and I don't even know who should be on it or what it should do. No one in my school—not even me—has ever been to a workshop on teamwork. We need some training first, but we have to start without it. What we need is an outline of the steps we have to take and some tools to involve people, then learn the rest as we go.

In response, I went to the easel and began to sketch an outline, which has evolved into the matrix in Figure 1.2. As I continued to work with this group and others, my friend Barb Furlong insisted that there was a "big need for help like this" and that I should write it down and get it published. So I drafted an outline and sent it off to Gracia Alkema, the president of Corwin Press at that time. I had been reviewing manuscripts for Corwin Press, and Gracia had been nagging me to write one of my own. The first edition was an attempt to help others, but it might never have happened without the helpful push from these two wonderful women.

Debates about site-based management and questions about its relationship to student learning continued to simmer. Central office colleagues wondered about their roles and responsibilities and worried about curriculum chaos and instructional improvement. So the second edition included more tools and examples to clarify district and school roles, and how to create decision-making structures within the school.

Meanwhile, the role of the federal government was billowing up into the mushroom cloud of No Child Left Behind. Authentic goal setting was giving way to externally calculated and imposed benchmarks to assure adequate yearly progress or be wiped out of existence in 2014. Some authors began to question the relevance of mission statements and school improvement plans, emphasizing the importance of teachers working in collaboration through various forms of professional learning communities. As the stress increased, so did the need for clarity and coherence about roles and responsibilities (what to do) and group norms and process skills (how to do it).

WHAT IS NEW IN THE THIRD EDITION

This third edition of *Asking the Right Questions* still focuses on the school as the unit of change but attends more to the three levels that create the context and impact effectiveness: the district, the school, and the classroom. New tools have been added, including Symbolic Displays, Innovation Configuration Maps, the

Priority Grid, and Open Space Technology. More examples from the field range from focusing on instruction to prioritizing for school construction. There is a new set of questions that shape practice (Chapter 7) and three questions for examining school and district improvement plans: Is our plan powerful? Are we working our plan? Is our plan working? As a contrast, there is also a segment on the *wrong* questions. A new feature is the "Answer Key" at the end of each chapter, which highlights the main points to remember.

The more things change, the more they stay the same. We still need to remember all the things we learned in Kindergarten and play together nicely in the sandbox. And I still find my "cheat sheets" (Figures 1.1 and 1.2) helpful for diagnosing the struggle a group is experiencing and choosing skills and processes that may move them forward.

This book does not pretend to contribute a vast repository of new knowledge to the field of organizational development and school change. That knowledge is readily available, and some helpful sources are listed in the References and Further Reading. What this book adds are practical tips and stories of application and implementation from educational settings.

Asking the Right Questions: Tools for Collaboration and School Change has found a unique niche as a synthesizer of skills often learned in isolated fragments and of processes that now compete for the "one best way" award. It is neither a scholarly tome on change research nor an exhaustive compendium of detailed exercises defended with academic rationale. This is simply a "what can I do with my group on Monday with the skills I already have" guide for leaders of district and school teams, whether laypersons or experienced educators. It's about empowering those who care to make decisions and implement change.

Acknowledgments

The first edition of this book was dedicated to the memory of my minister father, Warren E. Holcomb, who continued to nurture me through adulthood, providing daily demonstrations of lifelong learning and servant leadership. The second edition honored my mother, Edith, who has continued her solo journey with courage and dignity, volunteering in primary classrooms well into her 80s. Their lives continue to inspire mine—and this third edition—to seek ways in which to share and help others.

This work could not have been continued without the opportunities, assistance, and support provided by many individuals and groups. I offer apologies in advance to those I will inevitably omit and extend grateful thanks to the following:

Lee F. Olsen, my husband, research assistant, cheerleader, coach, business manager, and all-around right-hand man

Robb Clouse—for being my first Corwin Press editor and continuing to encourage me as he rose to the position of Publisher and Editorial Director

My Corwin Press team of Desirée Enayati, Melanie Birdsall, Teresa Herlinger, Rose Storey, and Peggie Howard—for their collaboration and expertise in production

Shirley Hord, scholar emerita, Southwest Educational Development Lab—for personal encouragement and for the inspiration of her persistent pursuit of school improvement and professional learning communities

Richard Rossmiller, professor emeritus, University of Wisconsin—former boss, continuing colleague, role model, and friend

Barb Furlong—for her first suggestion that I develop a chart and her insistence that I write about it

Dennis Glaeser, colleague from Wisconsin's CESA 6—for his initial draft of the five critical questions

Dave Pedersen, Jody Bublitz, Janet Kennedy, and Georgia Nisich—for technical expertise turning my scribbles and wall charts into figures

Joan Dore, Charlotte Carr, Allison Harris, and Jane Goetz—for great learning experiences in the Seattle School District

Cindy Harrison and Jan Herrera—for examples from Adams 12 Five Star District and Thornton High School in Colorado

Blane McCann, Jim Fergus, and Terri Huck—for examples from John Bullen Middle School, Kenosha, WI

Cathy Miles, New Leaders Resident, Baltimore, MD—for sharing the results of her "first fishbone"

Nana LoCicero and staff of Roosevelt Elementary School in Kenosha—for their work on an Innovation Configuration Map of writing instruction

Dan Weyrauch and staff of the future Brass Community School—for trusting me to help guide their future through reading program resolution, instructional design, strategic planning, and transition coaching

Olivia Zepeda, Gadsen School District #32, San Luis, AZ—for sharing the Innovation Configuration Map of the roles of leaders during change

Steve Clarke and staff, Bellingham High School, Bellingham, WA—for the efforts that produced the results ascribed to "Knownwell High School"

Rosalynn Kiefer, Denise Pheifer, and many others in Wisconsin ASCD—for years of collegial support

Vera Torrence, National Curriculum Director, New Leaders for New Schools—for affirming my big-picture view of leadership, teamwork, and data use in school improvement

And to many more dedicated educators in Alabama, Arizona, Arkansas, Colorado, Florida, Illinois, Indiana, Iowa, Kansas, Kentucky, Louisiana, Maine, Michigan, Minnesota, Missouri, New Jersey, New York, Ohio, Oregon, Pennsylvania, South Carolina, Texas, Virginia, Washington, Wisconsin, Guam, Canada, St. Lucia, Hong Kong, and the Philippines—for honoring me with opportunities to work and learn with you.

Your dedicated efforts on behalf of staff and students have provided examples for this book and for the professional lives of all of us.

PUBLISHER'S ACKNOWLEDGMENTS

Corwin Press gratefully acknowledges the contributions of the following individuals:

Regina S. Birdsell, Assistant
    Executive Director
Connecticut Association of Schools
Cheshire, CT

Rita Corbett, Owner/Consultant
RJC Consulting
Elgin, IL

Mary Devin, Associate Professor
Corwin Press Author
Kansas State University
Manhattan, KS

Janet Hurt, Associate
    Superintendent
Logan County Schools
Russellville, KY

Michael Keany, Director
    Long Island School
Leadership Center
Wheatley Heights, NY

Bess Scott, Principal
McPhee Elementary School
Lincoln, NE

Jeffrey Spiegel,
    Assistant Superintendent
Supervisory Administrative Unit 43
Newport, NH

Steven R. Thompson,
    Assistant Professor
Department of Educational
Leadership
Miami University
Oxford, OH

Denny R. Vincent, Consultant
Kentucky Center for School Safety
Richmond, KY

Linda Vogel, Assistant Professor
University of Northern Colorado
Greeley, CO

About the Author

 **Edie L. Holcomb** is highly regarded for her ability to link research and practice on issues related to school leadership, improvement, and reform. She holds a BS in elementary education, an MS in gifted education, and an EdS in educational administration. She received her PhD in educational administration from the University of Minnesota.

Holcomb's classroom experience includes teaching at all grade levels with heterogeneous classes, inclusion of students with multiple disabilities, and coordination of services for gifted and talented students. Her building-level administrative experience was acquired in settings ranging from affluent suburban to schoolwide Title I with racial/ethnic diversity and English Language Learners.

At the university level, Holcomb served as Associate Director of the National Center for Effective Schools, developing *School-Based Instructional Leadership*, a training program for site-based teams. As Associate Professor of Educational Administration at Wichita State University in Kansas, she coordinated the principalship course and internships, and taught applied inquiry in the field-based doctoral program.

Holcomb's central office experience occurred in districts ranging from 3,000 to 47,000 students. She is familiar with the challenges of urban education, having served as Director of Standards and Assessment and later as supervisor of 21 schools in the Seattle (WA) School District. Her current position as Executive Director of Curriculum and Instructional Services in the 23,000-student district of Kenosha, Wisconsin, just north of Chicago, will wrap up her career as a full-time practitioner.

Holcomb has provided technical assistance for implementation of school improvement efforts throughout the United States and in Canada, Guam, St. Lucia, Hong Kong, and the Philippines. She helped develop Washington State's *School System Improvement Resource Guide*, and worked with the Ohio Department of Education on its plans for technical assistance and support for districts and schools identified for improvement under No Child Left Behind. She is a faculty member of New Leaders for New Schools, a nonprofit organization committed to attracting, preparing, and supporting principals to lead challenging schools in nine major cities of the United States. Holcomb continues to assist schools and districts, consulting and coaching to increase student achievement, develop cultures and processes for professional learning, strengthen authentic student engagement, and design and conduct program evaluation—all with an emphasis on appropriate use of multiple sources of data.

1

Asking the Right Questions

The tension was rising. I faced a roomful of staff developers from regional and state education agencies gathered somewhat against their will. I had been hired to do three things: (1) review the school effectiveness research as a shared knowledge base, (2) introduce and apply some concepts about school change, and (3) facilitate an integration of components from various improvement models into a common format for statewide workshops.

The planning session had deteriorated into a defense of each agency's preferred model for school change as the most current, most comprehensive, and most worthy of becoming a statewide model. Sincere, conscientious professionals who had spent the coffee break bemoaning the difficulties of breaking down departmental barriers in high schools were engaged in their own turf wars, talking at cross purposes about the same concepts, each armed with his or her particular guru's customized vocabulary. I asked myself, "Why is this happening, even in a group that *knows* better? What we need is to have a set of factors that are common to all these processes, use no educational jargon, and have *no* capital letters to turn into acronyms!"

The tension continued into lunchtime. The moderator of the meeting, an administrator with outstanding facilitation skills but limited history with the group, expressed a sense of failure due to the lack of progress, and a desire to go back to his office where he could accomplish something. The suspiciously convenient ringing of his cell phone granted that wish. By this time, doubting *anyone's* ability to meet the varied expectations of the group, I sincerely offered to withdraw and let the group clarify what it really wanted and determine whether another facilitator or approach would work better for them. One agency's representative actually asked everyone to give back her handouts, and went home. But one dedicated member of the group sat thoughtfully, apparently doodling on his napkin. We paused for a stretch break.

When the group reconvened, colleague Dennis Glaeser volunteered his napkin notes—five questions that reflected the themes evolving during the discussion of change models. The questions were as follows:

1. Where are we now?

2. Where do we want to go?

3. How will we get there?

4. How will we know we are there?

5. How can we keep it going?

This set of questions broke the gridlock, and the remaining participants began to link their desired topics and activities to the five key questions. As the content agenda developed, the original direction to ground the workshops in the knowledge base of school effectiveness research and change was restated. This focus on findings from school settings created a common ground with ideas that had originated in business and industry.

REFINEMENT OF THE FIVE CRITICAL QUESTIONS

As I continued to work with these five critical questions, the first three remained intact just as Dennis had written them. They were simple and straightforward: "Where are we now?" guides inquiry into the status quo. "Where do we want to go?" helps shape the vision of an ideal or preferred future and articulate goals to achieve it. "How will we get there?" generates the concrete action steps that must be taken.

The fourth question, "How will we know we are there?" bumped up against the realities of time involved in substantive change. Writers on school change had described a span of 3 to 5 years for a moderately complex change, and 5 to 7 years for major restructuring to move from being an innovation to becoming a routine part of how the organization conducts its primary functions. During one of his presentations, Michael Fullan (1999a) shared a general observation that he called the "3–6–8 rule." On the basis of his research and experience, he postulated that an elementary school could make significant change in 3 years, but it took 6 years to change a high school and 8 years to transform an entire school district.

With those time frames in mind, asking "How will we know we are there?" seemed inappropriate. Such a question implies that monitoring is exclusively summative, occurring at some distant point of completion in the future. In a society programmed for immediate gratification, motivation based on proof of successful results would be difficult with such a long lag time. The question "How will we know we are there?" thus became "How will we know we are (getting) there?" The added word in parentheses reminds us of the need for milestones or benchmarks that will verify gradual progress and reinforce continued effort.

Literature on stages of change also influenced the fifth question, which first read "How can we keep it going?" One of the most common problems faced by change agents in schools is the TYNT-NYNT syndrome: "this year's new thing" soon replaced by "next year's new thing." Michael Fullan, Matthew B. Miles, Michael Huberman, and others have pointed out the need to continue a change process from initiation to implementation and on to institutionalization. The "bandwagon" approach so common to school change efforts prevents this sustained momentum. At the same time, Richard Elmore and others have pointed out that the time and effort it takes to restructure schools are not warranted unless they directly affect the aspects of teaching that improve student learning. The importance of maintaining focus on student outcomes, as well as the momentum of energy and resources, is reflected in the current wording of the fifth question: "How will we sustain the focus and momentum?"

THE FIVE QUESTIONS AS A ROAD MAP

Change is a journey, not an event, so the five questions lend themselves to several travel metaphors throughout this book. "Where are we now?" is a starting point. "Where do we want to go?" is the destination. "How will we get there?" includes the route we will take, what we will pack, what we will need to buy new for the trip, and what we will leave behind. Hotel reservations, freeway interchanges, scenic outlooks, and excursions on the itinerary represent milestones that assure we are making progress—"getting there." Regular fuel, food, and rest stops are critical for "sustaining focus and momentum" on the trip.

Maps are visuals that make complex, written directions easier to understand. They also allow us to find our way back to the planned route if we lose our way or get detoured by events beyond our control. The school improvement framework is a visual map for our journey to higher learning for all students and closing achievement gaps.

With a few minor revisions, Figure 1.1 has served as a visual organizer that has been useful in my work with schools, districts, and state departments for over 20 years. I have reviewed district and school improvement plans developed under many models originating in educational or business settings, and all of them have included components of mission, data, goals, strategies, and action plans—although by a full thesaurus of various names. The concepts and interrelationships among the components are the essential understandings. The terminology can be changed, and I rarely argue semantics. In fact, the first step when I work with groups is to encourage them to change the labels to match their state, district, or school outline. Most recently, the Office of Field Relations in the Ohio State Department of Education adapted this figure to guide its statewide system of support for schools identified for improvement under No Child Left Behind.

The oval labeled **Mission** is the only oval on the page and has the first word of all five questions posed above it (Where? Where? How? How? How?). The unique shape and the reference to all five questions are visual reminders that the core values of the organization must be continuously and consciously introduced in all discussions of all decisions in a change process.

4

Figure 1.1 School Change as Inquiry

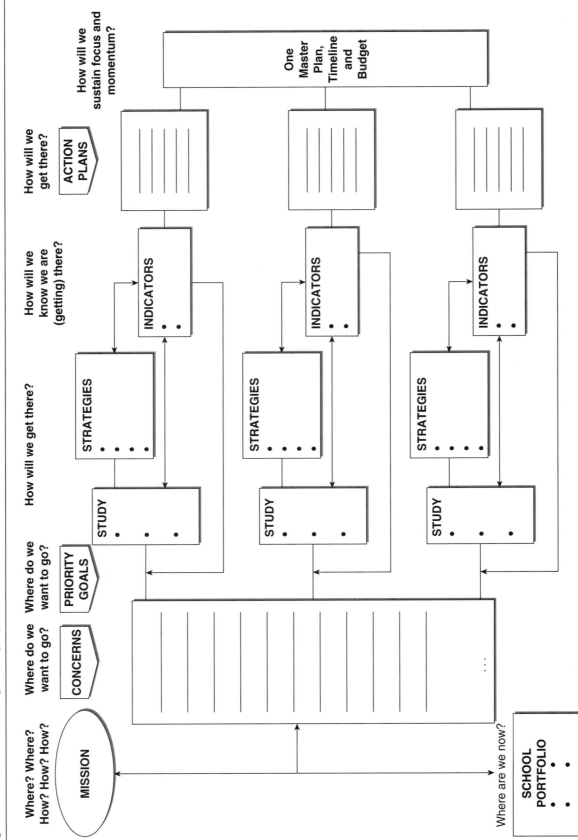

SOURCE: Adapted from *Getting Excited About Data* (p. 3), by E. L. Holcomb, 1999, Thousand Oaks, CA: Corwin Press. Copyright © 1999 by Corwin Press. Used with permission.

"Where are we now?" is the question posed above the **School Portfolio** component of the change organizer. The analysis of current status must include a variety and blend of objective data and perceptions of shareholders. The four bullet points in this component represent information on

- Student learning
- Student characteristics (e.g., demographics, behavior, attendance) and perceptions
- Staff characteristics, education, experience, and perceptions
- Parent and community characteristics and perceptions

The two-way arrow between **Mission** and **Portfolio** illustrates that the distance between what we *believe* and what we really *achieve* may be short or long. The courageous question "Are we walking our talk?" must be raised and confronted from the onset of a change process. The greater the discrepancy between our mission and our results, the longer will be our list of **Concerns.** From these, we must carefully select a limited number of **Priority Goals.** These goals further answer the "Where do we want to go?" question.

Once goals are set, collaborative groups undertake the **Study** process that will lead to decisions about the **Strategies** for "How will we get there?" and the **Indicators** that will be monitored to answer "How will we know we are (getting) there?" One reason that school improvement efforts fail is that too many schools leap into planning without devoting adequate time to analyzing their own issues internally and learning from others outside the school. The three bullets in the **Study** box represent different tasks:

- Dig deeper into the data available for more specific information about concerns, strengths, and challenges. Look for root causes. Confirm or contradict hypotheses and hunches to better understand the challenges and identify barriers that must be overcome.
- Review the research on effective practices that address the goal, and consult with other schools, districts, and education agencies that face similar challenges and identify their successes as best practice.
- Courageously compare the "best practice" findings with the practices and programs currently in place in the organization.

The multiple points in the **Strategies** box are less specific. There is no specific meaning for each one, as outlined for the three aspects of the **Study** phase. Instead, these multiple points remind us that there is no "one best way" that will guarantee success in reaching a goal. For example, increasing reading achievement may require a simultaneous combination of strategies, such as

- Changing or adding curriculum materials
- Learning new teaching strategies
- Revising the school schedule to allow for more flexible grouping and lower student–adult ratios
- Devising ways to attract and involve more parents/guardians in their children's education

The two points in the box labeled **Indicators** represent two types of evidence that will need to be collected to monitor progress and document success. In the above example, **indicators of implementation** would be criteria that are established to demonstrate that the agreed-upon strategies are actually being used. This evidence might include documents, such as the new school schedule and logs of parent activity, or observational comments made by the principal or peer coaches about new practices seen in classrooms. The **indicators of impact** would be measures of reading achievement that show that students are really learning more since the changes have been initiated.

Two-way arrows between **Strategies** and **Indicators** and back to **Study** illustrate that this is not a purely linear relationship. Sometimes groups have to think about how the desired situation would look and what evidence they would need to gather to have greater clarity about the changes in practice that are required. These arrows create a cycle within a cycle. If research-based strategies are faithfully implemented but the indicators do not yield evidence of improved results, further study and modified strategies will be needed.

Answering the "How will we get there?" question also requires development of **Action Plans** that clarify roles, responsibilities, timelines, and resources needed for implementation. The first answer to "How will we sustain focus and momentum?" is generated by assuring that these action plans are then coordinated as components of one **master plan.** Without this step, it is impossible to get a systemic picture of all the activity being attempted within a school or district. When the action plans are reviewed, competing demands for financial resources and professional development time become clear and can be adjusted so that the school's efforts are cohesive rather than fragmented and can be conducted in a coordinated manner and within the collective capacity of the organization.

THE WRONG QUESTIONS

Too often, I receive a question that echoes all the components of this road map, so it sounds good—at first. It goes like this:

> We've written a mission and analyzed our data. We brainstormed concerns and prioritized goals. We chose research-based strategies and decided what indicators to collect data on. Then we did action plans and tied them into a master plan. Now—how do we get buy-in?

Wrong question. First I have to ask about the "we" and "they" (their) who are referenced. Who did all the work described? In what setting and over what period of time? If, for example, the principal and a small group did it all over the summer and now want to "sell" it in September to a whole staff who were not involved or represented or even constantly informed, it's already "too little too late."

As I began to revise the book for this third edition, some readers asked for more content on "how we overcome resistance." Again, from my point of view, it's the wrong question. Authentic change in school culture and practices doesn't occur by "overcoming" bad practice. It occurs by building commitment to students that becomes so strong that people are willing to voluntarily let go of the old and move forward. As Linda Lambert (2003) points out,

> the benefits of participation—improved relationships, altered assumptions and beliefs, shared goals and purposes, increased maturity and cognitive complexity—emerge in a spiraling way: the greater the participation, the greater the development; the greater the development, the higher the quality of participation. (p. 12)

That is the intent of this book—to provide tools (skills and processes) that engage members of the school community throughout the process of facing the current facts, identifying shared goals, and mapping their journey of change.

It's not about "selling" or "overcoming" and it doesn't come "at the end." Every chapter is about building capacity and commitment, and Chapter 6 majors in sustaining and continuously expanding that effort.

PROFESSIONAL LEARNING COMMUNITIES

This kind of engagement that changes the culture of the school is similar to the transformation from teaching as isolated practice to teachers interacting as professional learning communities. The body of research on teacher collaboration goes back over 20 years to the foundational work of Susan Rosenholtz (1989); Jerry Bamburg (Isaacson & Bamburg, 1992); Milbrey McLaughlin (McLaughlin & Talbert, 1993); Gene Hall and Shirley Hord (2001); Linda Darling-Hammond (1994); Tom Sergiovanni (1994); Karen Seashore Louis (1995); and others.

More recent adaptations of teacher collaboration by Robert Eaker et al. (Eaker, DuFour, & DuFour, 2002) stress three themes underlying the PLC conceptual framework:

> (1) a solid foundation consisting of collaboratively developed and widely shared mission, vision, values and goals; (2) collaborative teams that work interdependently to achieve a common goal; and (3) a focus on results as evidenced by a commitment to continuous improvement. (p. 3)

Based on her extensive portfolio of research and work with practitioners, Shirley Hord (2003) reiterates five essential components for professional learning communities that are absolutely critical. They include

- Shared values and vision
- Shared and supportive leadership
- Collegial, intentional learning and its application
- Supportive conditions—structural and relational
- Peers supporting peers

Structural support is provided when time is allocated for collaborative work; appropriate technology and materials are available; external expertise can be accessed; and there are open communication systems connecting teachers, central office personnel, parents, and community members. Relational supports require a culture of sustained and unified efforts to change, norms of involvement and respect, a culture of trust, and visible recognition of outstanding achievement. When these are in place, peers can support peers by observing each other, providing feedback, and reviewing student work together.

Those components are a close match for the terms and tasks used in this book and outlined in Figure 1.2. The goal is the same—to bring professionals together with a focus on their own and students' learning, so the school becomes a true community of highly effective professionals.

THE FIVE QUESTIONS AND THREE MODELS OF CHANGE

Figure 1.1 links the five critical questions to the conceptual components or stages of an overall, ongoing inquiry process within an organization. But as Michael Fullan (2005) cautions, "terms travel well, but the underlying *conceptualization and thinking* do not" (p. 10, italics his). Participants need more specifics. This section draws on three widely used models of change to provide a more concrete breakdown of the specific tasks occurring within each stage. Figure 1.2 provides a matrix to help participants identify the work, and choose tools and activities that will engage participants successfully in each of those tasks. For now, just focus on the column on the left of Figure 1.2. You will see the five critical questions in bold. Directly under the five questions (in parentheses) are references to the stages of change expressed in the three models introduced here. Lowercase letters a, b, and c are keyed to these models at the bottom of the figure.

RPTIM: Readiness, Planning, Training, Implementation, Maintenance

The first of the three models of change is Fred Wood's RPTIM model, a classic from staff development literature. The acronym stands for stages of readiness, planning, training, implementation, and maintenance. The **readiness** stage includes identifying major problems of the school or district, working in collaboration with key groups to develop goals, and examining current practices. The **planning** stage includes identifying differences between goals, desired practices, and actual practices, and developing training activities based on that diagnosis. During the **training** stage, all affected groups, including central office administrators, principals, teachers, and others, receive training and develop, share, and critique action plans. **Implementation** requires that resources are allocated to support new practices and that additional coaching and training are provided on a continuing basis. The **maintenance** stage involves supervision and monitoring to continue new behaviors, and use of feedback to guide further improvement. Although Wood's work focused specifically on staff development and instructional changes, his framework has been

Figure 1.2 Matrix of Tools for *Asking the Right Questions*

Where Are We Now? (readiness, planning, and training;[a] initiation[b])	Histograms	Run Charts	Symbolic Displays	Surveys	Focus Groups	Think, Pair, Share	Flowcharting	Continuum	Affinity Process	Brainstorming	Nominal Group Process	Color Coding	Weighted Voting	Priority Grid	Pie Charts	Pareto Charts	Fishbone (Cause and Effect)	Force Field Analysis	Graphic Organizer	Decision Matrix	Action Planning	Innovation Configuration Map	CBAM-SoCQ	Venn Diagram	Quick-Write	Talk-Walk	Go for the Green	Action Research	Reflective Study Groups	Networking	Open Space Technology	Active Listening
Raise awareness of need for change			2		2	2	2	2	3	3		3					4	4				5		6	6	6			6		6	6
Clarify roles and responsibilities					2	2	2	2	3	3		3							4			5		6	6		6			6		6
Diagnose motivation for change (source, intensity)				2	2	2	2	2															6	6	6							6
Review existing philosophy, mission, belief statements				2	2	2			3			3	3				4	4						6	6				6			6
Diagnose governance and program factors				2	2	2	2		3			3			4	4		4	4			5	6	6	6			6				6
Diagnose student success	2	2	2	2	2								3	3	4	4		4	4			5						6				6
Diagnose shareholder perceptions	2	2	2	2	2				3			3			4	4		4						6	6			6				6
Diagnose organizational culture, climate				2	2	2		2		3		3				4		4	4			5	6	6	6		6	6				6

(Continued)

Figure 1.2 (Continued)

	Histograms	Run Charts	Symbolic Displays	Surveys	Focus Groups	Think, Pair, Share	Flowcharting	Continuum	Affinity Process	Brainstorming	Nominal Group Process	Color Coding	Weighted Voting	Priority Grid	Pie Charts	Pareto Charts	Fishbone (Cause and Effect)	Force Field Analysis	Graphic Organizer	Decision Matrix	Action Planning	Innovation Configuration Map	CBAM-SoCQ	Venn Diagram	Quick-Write	Talk-Walk	Go for the Green	Action Research	Reflective Study Groups	Networking	Open Space Technology	Active Listening
Where Do We Want to Go? (planning and training;[a] initiation;[b] plan[c])																																
Develop/affirm mission statement	2			2	2	2			3	3		3							4						6	6			6			6
Stimulate visioning			2		2	2			3	3		3													6	6		6	6		6	6
Prioritize concerns				2						3	3	3	3	3		2		4		4						6		6	6		6	6
Set goals/targets with focus on students			2			2					3																					6
Identify best practices																	4	4	4	4		5						6	6		6	
How Will We Get There? (planning, training, and implementation;[a] implementation;[b] plan[c])																																
Identify factors related to concerns	2			2	2	2			3	3		3			4	2	4	4	4						6	6	6	6				6
Identify barriers					2	2	2		3	3	3	3	3	3		2	4	4							6	6	6	6			6	6
Select strategies					2				3		3	3	3	3				4	4			5			6	6					6	6
Develop action plans							2													4							6			6	6	6
Identify indicators/data to monitor							2		3	3	3	3		3			4		4			5						6		6	6	6
Affirm mission and beliefs				2	2	2			3	3			3						4						6	6			6	6	6	6

Table: Tools matched to activities. Numbers in cells indicate the chapter in which the topic is covered.

Activity	Histograms	Run Charts	Symbolic Displays	Surveys	Focus Groups	Think, Pair, Share	Flowcharting	Continuum	Affinity Process	Brainstorming	Nominal Group Process	Color Coding	Weighted Voting	Priority Grid	Pie Charts	Pareto Charts	Fishbone (Cause and Effect)	Force Field Analysis	Graphic Organizer	Decision Matrix	Action Planning	Innovation Configuration Map	CBAM-SoCQ	Venn Diagram	Quick-Write	Talk-Walk	Go for the Green	Action Research	Reflective Study Groups	Networking	Open Space Technology	Active Listening
How Will We Know We Are (Getting) There? (implementation and maintenance;[a] implementation;[b] do and check[c])																																
Monitor progress on identified indicators/data	2	2		2		2									4	4	4					5			6	6	6	6	6	6		
Affirm mission and beliefs	2		2	2	2	2			3	3		3	3												6	6	6		6	6		6
Identify and respond to individuals concerns					2	2		2		3	3	3	3	3				4				5	6		6	6	6		6	6		6
How Will We Sustain the Focus and Momentum? (maintenance;[a] institutionalization;[b] check, act, and plan[c])																																
Cope with conflict																								6		6	6		6	6		6
Build culture of inquiry		2	2																			5		6	6			6	6	6	6	6
Monitor progress and adjust strategies	2	2		2	2	2	2		3	3		3	3	3	4	4	4	4		4	4	5	6		6	6	6		6	6		6
Affirm mission and beliefs	2			2	2	2																							6	6		6
Support leaders and followers				2	2					3		3	3						4				6			6	6		6	6	6	6

NOTES: Numbers in cells indicate the chapter in which the topic is covered.

a. From the RPTIM model (readiness, planning, training, implementation, and maintenance). See page 8.

b. From the Three I's model (initiation, implementation, and institutionalization). See page 12.

c. From the PDCA cycle (plan-do-check-act). See page 12.

generalized by school districts and regional labs to guide many school improvement efforts.

The Three I's: Initiation, Implementation, Institutionalization

A second well-known description of change is presented in writings by Miles, Huberman, and Fullan and is often referred to as the Three I's: initiation, implementation, and institutionalization. A key factor in the **initiation** of change is identification of a high-profile need that participants feel is relevant to them, for which a sense of readiness has been created and for which resources have been allocated to demonstrate the organization's commitment. The visibility of a few strong advocates who can present a clear model of implementation and actively move it forward is an essential aspect of successful initiation.

The **implementation** stage requires attention to unique local characteristics of the community, district, and its principals and teachers. Overall coordination is needed but must be balanced by shared control, which I refer to as shared leadership. The balancing of pressure and support through communication of clear expectations for progress and improvement, while providing technical assistance and rewards, is critical. Fullan's description of essentials for implementation includes vision building, initiative taking, staff training, monitoring, and evolutionary planning—with continual adjustment as data and feedback are received and analyzed.

Many change processes survive through initiation, and attempts are made to implement them, but they do not take root and do not become embedded in the culture. Among the reasons that this **institutionalization** does not occur are lack of close links to the teaching and learning process, and lack of continued training and support until new practices are in widespread use. Sustaining focus and momentum requires continued assistance with new practices and removal of competing priorities.

PDCA: Plan, Do, Check, Act

Other descriptions of organizational change and improvement have emerged from the business sector, especially the total quality management literature. A model that has been applied in schools is the plan-do-check-act (PDCA) cycle. The **plan** stage involves identifying a needed change, assembling available data and collecting new data to clarify what needs to occur, and identifying root causes of the problem. To **do** means to generate possible solutions, select and implement them on a pilot basis, and gather data on the results. A **check** verifies what has been accomplished, confirms what worked well and what did not, and analyzes results before implementing an attempted solution on a broader scale. Decisions are made to **act** on the results by either abandoning the new practice or standardizing it to ensure consistency throughout the organization. Processes are continually monitored, and the cycle is repeated.

These three models were included to engage readers from various past training and experiences. Looking again at the left-hand column of Figure 1.2, the breakdown of specific tasks that help answer each of the critical questions was synthesized from these common approaches.

TOOLS FOR INQUIRY AND COLLABORATION

In the Preface, I described how this book first emerged in response to calls for help. Individuals and groups were asking how to match up group processes they might have learned (or wanted to learn) with the tasks before them. In essence, they wanted to know what to use and when. So far, we have focused on the left-hand column of Figure 1.2, defining the tasks. The row of tools and techniques across the top has evolved from an initial brainstorming session with a small group of education agency staff. We listed the skills people already had in their collective repertoire (but didn't get much chance to use). Then we began to make connections to tasks that were part of their various roles with schools and districts in the region. They realized that *all* of them had enough background to have some tool to address each task, and that *among* them, they had a rich assortment of tools they could share and use to learn from each other. Every entry in a cell represents a combination of tool (from the top) and task (on the left) for which it can be useful. The numbers represent the chapter in this book where that tool or technique is described with its purpose, participants, materials, tips for facilitators, and "real-life" stories and examples.

USING THIS BOOK

Asking the Right Questions was conceived from a marriage of critical questions and group process techniques that teams can employ to answer them. Users of the book should include both internal and external change agents. The district's top academic leader may need to challenge traditional practices. The principal might be working to raise the expectations teachers hold for student success. A teacher leader may be voicing "the right questions" and need a way to expand the conversation with colleagues. As Linda Lambert (2003) points out, "everyone has the right, responsibility, and capability to be a leader. . . . [T]eachers need to understand and represent others, convene and lead conversations, identify and mobilize resources, and connect the thinking and planning of a given group with that of the whole staff" (p. 33).

Group processes have been organized here into a road map for inquiry (Figure 1.1) and a matrix (Figure 1.2) and offered as aids for team leaders, facilitators, and consultants. My goal is that they be helpful in some of the following ways.

As a Quick Index to Your Own Toolbox

In the Preface, I described an out-of-the-blue request for advice on how to handle a group process challenge. You may have those experiences, too, and you are probably familiar with most or all of these group process techniques. They are already "in your toolbox." But we often forget how much we know. I was recently watching my Green Bay Packers beat the rival Chicago Bears, when I noticed that Coach Mike McCarthy was standing on the sidelines with his own "cheat sheets," laminated pages of plays punched and held together by three snap-rings. On that day, quarterback Brett Favre tied Dan Marino's record of 60,000 career yards passing. If the coach who calls in the plays to record-breaking quarterback Brett Favre needs a quick reference guide to his playbook, we should not be embarrassed to use a quick reference guide to our repertoire of facilitation techniques.

Once I was asked to facilitate an activity but was cautioned, "no flip charts and no circles." I was happy to agree, but curious. It turned out that a consultant on a long-term contract with the district had only one tool in his toolbox—get in a circle, no writing instruments or surfaces allowed for participants, and reach consensus on everything, including the color of marker he should use to write on the flip chart. Sometimes we get into a pattern of using one technique over and over and forget some of the others we have enjoyed using and found to be effective in other settings. One use of this matrix is to help us quickly scan the tools we have so that we can select one that will match the task before us and provide a variety for our participants.

When asked to facilitate an activity, get enough information to know what question the participants are trying to answer. Are they figuring out where they are now? Are they trying to set a goal? Are they deciding how to get there? Or are they simply struggling with some natural conflicts that are part of change and growth? Find their question or task on the left and move across the matrix to choose one of the group process techniques that address their need.

You have also developed skills that I didn't include in this book. Print the matrix on a larger sheet of paper and add columns on the right for techniques you enjoy using. Think about the range of applications they have for answering the five critical questions. Place your own Xs in the cells of the matrix, and you have an even bigger toolbox.

As a Tool for Planning Personal Skill Development

As you read this book, you may recognize every group process technique described. If some of the activities are new to you, I'd suggest that you start like this. Get a highlighting pen and go across the top of the matrix. Highlight each technique you have used before and are confident you could facilitate with others. Go down each of those columns with the highlighter. Now you have a colored matrix to serve as a quick index to your own toolbox. You also have some "white spaces." These are the group process techniques you may wish to add to your toolbox. Read more about them here, find a workshop that includes them, and/or seek out a mentor who is willing to coach you as you practice them. This adds to your repertoire of skills and lets you color in more of the matrix as you develop new strategies.

As a Tool for Designing Team Training

Chapter 6 will emphasize the importance of continued training for sustaining the focus and momentum of change. One of the concepts mentioned is "just-in-time training." This concept is particularly relevant for group process techniques. The prevalent pattern of sending a group of people to a conference on teamwork leaves many feeling as though they accomplished little real work, and transfer of skills to their own setting is limited.

A more effective way to learn about teamwork is in the context of the immediate tasks that need to be accomplished. When you are asked to "give us some training in group techniques" or "teach us some strategies to use on our team," first get information on what the purpose of the team is and what tasks the participants are now trying to accomplish. Use Figure 1.2 to identify techniques team members can use for the task at hand, and design the content of their training to introduce techniques they can apply immediately. Provide time for them to plan how and when they will use the new technique and facilitate it with each other.

The Kentucky Leadership Academy used this book in a problem-based learning approach to team training. Figure 1.3 shares a handout from their materials. Participants were divided into groups and chose or were assigned one of the scenarios. They talked about how they could assist a group in this situation, chose one of the group process techniques, and talked each other through how they would facilitate it. Then they returned to their home teams and shared what they had learned and planned. This helped entire teams expand their repertoire. It also provided a comfortable way for them to share situations they were facing and ask for input and advice from others in the group.

As a Tool for Coaching New Facilitators

The matrix can also be helpful as you work with cadres of internal trainers or as you coach new facilitators. Have them highlight the columns of the matrix under skills with which they feel comfortable. This provides a starting point. You can observe your facilitators using those techniques to check their skill and provide feedback to help them refine their approaches. When you are also confident of their expertise in these areas, they can become coaches for others.

Also look at the white spaces your new facilitators have not highlighted. Go across the matrix horizontally. If there is a whole section—one of the five critical questions—that is mostly white, start their new learning with a group process technique that will begin to fill in that gap.

As a Tool for Diagnosing Your Organization's Status and Process

It's hard to believe that it's been 23 years since I began my own journey facilitating school improvement. Research on school effectiveness was fairly new, the roles of principals and teachers were quite well defined, and schools were conducted primarily according to decisions made at the district level. For several years, I worked with schools that were "blank slates." They had little prior history with decision making, and I could present the school improvement process as a relatively straightforward, step-by-step approach.

Then along came a proliferation of different approaches to school and district planning. It became much more difficult to work with a school. First, I would have to figure out their vocabulary and their model and adapt accordingly.

Figure 1.3 A Tool for Team Training

If . . . *the following scenario occurs*	*Then . . .* *which matrix strategy would you choose?*
1. As district leader, you have just received the action plan from the schools. You need a method of review. Identify a strategy that could be used to review all school plans.	
2. You are facilitating a districtwide committee, and 2 of the 8 elementary schools have identified significant science priority needs. Identify a strategy that could be utilized to facilitate decisions regarding use of district Title II funds.	
3. You have just received your budget allocation from the district office. Your task is to budget your consolidated plan. You don't know how to start this process. Identify a strategy that could be used for beginning this process.	
4. You have a committee that has identified key findings, and they are ready to prioritize needs. The committee begins to ignore the data gathered through the needs assessment and begins to establish priority needs based on beliefs not supported by data. Identify a strategy that could be used to complete the task.	
5. The language arts teachers are developing an action plan but have not completed the plan because they cannot agree upon specific activities to reach component objectives. Three teachers want to improve reading through implementation of whole-language strategies, and three teachers want to use district-instruction materials. Identify a strategy that could be implemented to resolve this conflict.	
6. Create your own scenario. . . .	

SOURCE: Used with permission of Debbie McDonald.

Since then, we've had chaos theory and complexity theory and "flow," and schools are not at the *beginning* of anything—they're right in the middle of a whole maelstrom of swirling processes and initiatives and new mandates. Intrinsic motivation is harder to stimulate in the context of the threats and punishments of No Child Left Behind. So Figure 1.1 can't be used in a linear "start here and follow the yellow brick road" manner. I had to write things down in some type of sequence, but we all know that real life is not that rational or linear. I do believe, and have discovered time and again, that a visual organizer such as Figure 1.1 can be useful to help people who are in the middle of the swirl to rise above it and look down and see the various parts of what's going on and make much better sense of the big picture.

As Linda Lambert (2003) reminds us, "approaches to participation . . . are most powerful when combined in a thoughtful and integrated school improvement process" (p. 18). It's not just about adults having meaningful collaboration and therefore greater commitment to the work at hand. The bottom line is a benefit to students. Lambert (p. 55) quotes Ann Lewis (2002), stating that "In Chicago, wherever teachers had created strong professional communities with frequent teacher collaboration, reflective dialogue, and shared norms, schools were four times more likely to be improving academically than schools with weaker professional communities." It's about providing greater opportunities for student success.

As a Starting Gun

So, where to start? Start *anywhere* that's a place where people are interested. If you already have strategies but no action plans, start there. If you have a lot of data but nobody's looked at them to see what they mean, sit down with the data and capture the list of concerns that arise in the conversation. If you're getting discouraged because people can't see that they've made a difference, revisit the indicators that need to be documented, displayed, and celebrated.

Start *somewhere.* School change may be "like pushing on a rope," but if you find someone who's willing to grab the other end and pull, just the two of you can begin to budge that issue together. One way to find that person is to start asking the right questions.

> **Answer Key**
>
> This book poses many questions for inquiry as individuals, small groups, and entire organizations. Tongue in cheek, after asking all those questions, it seems only fair to provide a space for an answer key. Sincerely, the key to your effectiveness is in your reflection and the answers you choose from the text, the applications you make to your own context, and the synthesis you create with your other experiences and learning. Here are some key points from Chapter 1.
>
> - Any change process can be grounded in five critical questions:
>   - Where are we now?
>   - Where do we want to go?
>   - How will we get there?
>   - How will we know we are (getting) there?
>   - How will we sustain focus and momentum?
> - Be sure that plans for change include all the components of mission, data, priority goals, thorough study before selection of strategies, and preplanning of evidence that will be monitored to demonstrate progress.
> - Realize that a change process includes many stages, phases, and steps. Accurately identifying the current task will lead to an appropriate tool for engagement.
> - Be sure that all those who are affected are engaged throughout, not "sold" at the end.
> - Draw upon all the skills you have, and continue to add to your toolbox.

2

Answering the "Where Are We Now?" Question

"The journey of a thousand miles begins with a single step." If school change is a journey, then colleagues and shareholders are the travelers.

In the first edition, I used the term *stakeholders* to describe individuals and groups who have a stake in the outcome of decisions about their school. I now prefer the term *shareholders*, believing that it more accurately conveys not only interest in the results but also a share in the planning and an acceptance of shared responsibility for accomplishment. Parents are certainly major shareholders, but other *external* shareholders must be considered as well, because parents represent a declining segment of the taxpayers who support the schools. The term *community* is used here in a broader way to include social service agencies, businesses, and taxpayers who do not have children attending school. There are also *internal* shareholders, because every employee of the district—administrator, teacher, social and health worker, clerical employee, custodian, food and transportation provider—is affected by how the organization functions. The interactions between and among these groups establish the culture of the organization and enhance or inhibit accomplishment of its mission and goals for students.

Unfortunately, some of these shareholders are serious explorers on the journey of change, while others are only ramblers, and some just stand on the side of the road and cheer or boo. Serious travelers follow their maps; ramblers follow their noses. Travelers have a destination in mind, and they lay out a route from here to there. Knowing the starting point is just as important as knowing the destination if the journey is to be safe, accurate, timely, and cost-effective. Travelers also check weather conditions, make lists, and assemble needed items. In short, ramblers say, "Let's go somewhere." Travelers say, "Let's gather some information, make a plan, and *then* go."

The journey of school change is never an easy one, and there are many hazards along the way, but the trip can get off to its smoothest start if we carefully analyze the present situation. This chapter includes tips and techniques for addressing the question "Where are we now?" (Refer back to Figures 1.1 and 1.2.) Three critical aspects of the school's or district's status must be analyzed: student performance, shareholder perceptions, and organizational culture and context.

When we think of data on **student performance,** our instinctive response is to visualize graphs of test scores and leave it at that. This initial limited scope implies that acquisition of discrete bits of knowledge is the sole and complete function of the school and gives the test makers more credit than they deserve. If a school or district justifies its large-scale (state test) results with claims that "these tests don't cover all the things we try to accomplish in school," then that organization must identify ways to assess a full range of learning and include results of short-term assessments and curriculum-based tests in the data they examine. The school that emphasizes its focus on the "whole child" must demonstrate that it does accomplish "all those other things" besides academic achievement. Desirable student results such as citizenship can be revealed in such data as attendance, participation in service activities, and occurrences of vandalism and disruptive behavior.

Schools and districts must acknowledge the reality that public education is a service industry that must be user friendly or lose its "market share" to vouchers, private schools, and for-profit enterprises. Surveys, telephone interviews, and focus groups are among the methods often used to gather **shareholder perceptions.** Gathering the information, however, is only the first step and can do more harm than good if not followed by analyzing, interpreting, and reporting the results back to the constituents and using the data in goal setting and planning for improvement.

The school **culture and context** include roles and relationships, the history of and motivation for prior change in the organization, and an awareness of governance and program factors that may inhibit or enhance new efforts. Only through sensitivity to the past can change agents link innovation with events remembered fondly and dissociate new practices from those that have left bitter legacies.

Site-based management is a significant aspect of the organizational context that must be addressed in this stage. Too little autonomy at the school level inhibits the leadership team's ability to build credibility and commitment for the change process through authentic decision making. Too much autonomy leaves the school in the position of navigating a river without knowing where the banks are. Immense amounts of energy can be expended "reinventing wheels" that could be provided at scale with district support. Lack of communication and clarification about the definition of site-based management in the local setting can create confusion, chaos, and frustration.

This chapter describes group processes that can be employed to help a school or district ask itself, "Where are we now?" Each description includes the purpose of the group technique, appropriate timing, recommended participants, materials needed, and tips to guide the facilitator.

STUDENT PERFORMANCE

Every school improvement effort I have encountered has espoused "increased student achievement" as its foundation. Given that commonality, I have been amazed at the number of school improvement plans that include no references to student performance or goals that relate to the process of teaching and learning. When most districts report on student performance, they use a mean (average) score based on aggregate (all scores mixed together) data. This type of reporting has contributed to myths such as the "Lake Wobegon effect" that "all the children are above average." Schools and districts with homogeneous populations and a strong cultural work ethic are lulled into complacency when their mean scores appear to rank favorably compared with schools and districts that face far greater challenges.

Histograms

Use of a histogram to depict the distribution of student performance can provide more accurate information than a comparison of means and lead to a better analysis of the current performance level of students and the school's success at teaching.

Purpose. A histogram is a type of bar chart or graph that shows a distribution of information. It allows educators to see the range and variation in student achievement rather than an overall average score. This provides a much better picture of how well the school is fulfilling its obligation to teach all children.

When to Use. An examination of current student performance should be one of the early steps in addressing the "Where are we now?" question. The same analysis should be conducted each time a general assessment is used, and each set of results should be added to the longitudinal trend data being accumulated.

Who to Involve. School psychologists and counselors are valuable members of a work group that is compiling data on student achievement and behavior. The group should also include teachers who work with the student population in the subject areas (of a cognitive assessment) or in the school environment (in case of behavior). Although test data may initially be compiled by specialists such as the testing companies or school district research and evaluation departments, interpretation of what the data mean should be done in concert with the teachers who work with the students on a daily basis. It is difficult to engage teachers in the use of data, especially if they are demeaned by having data returned to them with weak areas or low scores already highlighted as if they can't make those distinctions themselves. (Chapter 3 of *Getting Excited About Data* [Holcomb, 2004] is devoted to the reasons that teachers are reluctant to engage with data and suggests strategies for building comfort and confidence.)

Materials Needed. A histogram can be constructed to represent any type of data available and relevant for discussion; for example, test scores, grades, attendance, and discipline referrals. A laptop computer and appropriate software can make the job easier, but there is learning value in having groups do rough drafts of their histograms on paper.

Tips for Facilitators. The first step is to create a frequency distribution of the scores, number of absences, or other factors to be analyzed. The second step is to divide the full range of scores into a usable number of categories or classes. In the case of norm-referenced achievement scores, testing companies often array the scores in stanines (9-point standard scales). Another good set of categories for examining student performance is the use of quartiles. This divides scores into those that fall between the 1st and 25th percentiles, 26th and 50th percentiles, 51st and 75th, and 76th percentile and above. A histogram with one high bar in the third quartile may verify that a commendable mean at the 70th percentile really does represent success of all students. A histogram with a high bar in the third or fourth quartile but also in the lowest quartile can indicate that there are enough high-achieving students to influence the mean and mask the reality that the school is not meeting its obligation to another segment of its population. Many new state assessments report scores in levels of proficiency, so each bar on a histogram would represent the number of students in Level 1, Level 2, and so on.

For Example: Quartiles. Figure 2.1 is actually a combination of eight histograms. The math scores for each grade level are represented in quartiles. It takes only a glance to discover that the distribution of performance provides a lot more information than a mean score for the entire grade. Graphic displays such as the histogram provide information but are even more powerful in prompting further questions. Groups should be challenged to discuss the following questions: What else might this tell us? What do we do with this information? and What do we want these histograms to look like 3 years from now? The last question is particularly important if a school has not used data in the past and has only the "snapshot" data of the current year to use as a baseline.

Figure 2.1   Histogram of Student Achievement

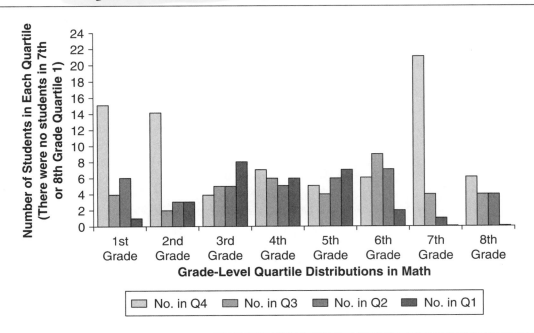

A Variation: Disaggregation. The histogram is introduced in this chapter as one example of how graphs can display data in ways that are understandable and that prompt further examination of student learning. Many schools with diverse populations made early commitments to equity and, long before No Child Left Behind, wanted to know whether the distribution of performance was the same for all groups within the total student population. Factors such as race/ethnicity and socioeconomic status (SES) were carefully considered. In Figure 2.2, the performance scores have been separated to compare the distribution of scores for students from low-SES homes with those from more affluent settings. This display is also called a *stacked bar graph* because the distribution is shown as boxes "stacked" within each bar.

The process of breaking up data to examine the performance of different subgroups is called *disaggregation*. Although this histogram shows that 63% of all students ranked in the top two quartiles, it also points out that only 37% and 39% of the students from minority groups achieved at this level.

Another Twist: Student Performance. The term *student performance* can encompass more than academic success. Schools often have other expectations that relate to goals such as good citizenship. These schools may use data such as attendance, punctuality, completion of assignments, participation in service projects, behavior, and level of vandalism to assess how well the school is helping students develop characteristics of good citizenship. Such data can also be displayed in histograms to help a school ask itself, "Where are we now in student performance?"

Run Charts

The histogram, pie chart (see Chapter 4), and most other graphs represent information at a certain point in time. In contrast, the run chart can illustrate trends in data over a span of time.

Figure 2.2   Histogram of Disaggregated Student Achievement

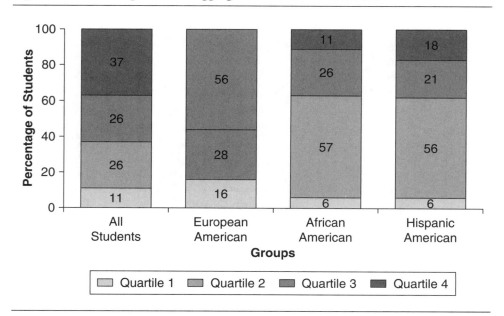

Figure 2.3   Run Chart of Reading Scores

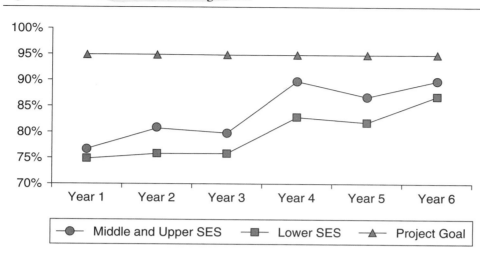

Purpose. The run chart monitors a situation or process through time to identify changes. Although the histograms in Figures 2.1 and 2.2 show distribution of student achievement on one year's scores, a run chart shows how students score from one year to the next and whether their achievement improves, declines, or stays the same.

When to Use. If a school or district has been collecting data over time, a run chart can be constructed in the early stages of addressing the "Where are we now?" question. Sometimes schools have not used test scores or other data in any systematic way, but they can go back and re-create a run chart to show a history of what has been occurring. In other cases, schools can gather data for the first time only now and use the data as a baseline. As the same data are analyzed every year, a run chart is gradually developed.

Who to Involve. As with all work using data, those who participate in the process under study must be involved in collection and analysis.

Materials Needed. Construction of the run chart itself can be done with pencil and paper or by using computer graphics.

Tips for Facilitators. The left-hand, vertical side of the run chart is called the y-axis and usually shows the criteria or factor being analyzed, such as percentage of dropouts or number of absences. The horizontal line across the bottom of the run chart is called the x-axis and represents the time being measured, such as class periods, days, or years. Be sure to clearly label both the vertical and horizontal axes.

One problem with a run chart is that observers tend to overreact to any fluctuation in the line. They may give themselves too much credit for any upturn or become overly dismayed by any downturn. A general rule is to look for at least 7 data points in a consistent direction before concluding that true change has occurred. It is interesting that this recommendation from statisticians corresponds so well with comments by educational change experts who say that it takes 5 to 7 years to institutionalize new practices.

For Example: Closing the Gap. The school that created Figure 2.2 had disaggregated its reading scores and discovered an achievement gap related to race. The district initiatives and the school's improvement plan focused on improvement of reading performance for all students and greater equity in achievement. Figure 2.3 reports the reading scores for each year of the same cohort of students, tested each spring from first through sixth grade. It shows a consistent direction of improved performance and narrowing of the gap between low-SES and middle-to-upper-SES students.

Whether creating or interpreting a run chart, the scores must be clearly labeled to identify whether these are the *school's* scores through time (e.g., every class of fourth graders) or *students'* scores through time (a cohort). Both are more fully illustrated in *Getting Excited About Data* (Holcomb, 2004).

Symbolic Displays

Histograms and run charts provide objective information and communicate accurately to the mind. But as Dennis Sparks (2006) points out, "Initiating and maintaining the momentum of significant change requires experiences that appeal to the heart as well as the head" (p. 1). Sparks then quotes Kotter and Cohen (2002), stating that emotion underlies lasting change and that emotion is generated more by vivid stories and images—even images that disturb rather than uplift. Symbolic displays can put names and faces to numbers that seem impersonal and therefore fail to challenge complacency.

For Example: D/F List. At the end of the first quarter, a high school principal reviewed the ninth-grade D/F list at a staff meeting and was surprised that there was so little expression of concern or interest in identifying the failing students and how to help them. For the next staff gathering, he printed an enlarged list of all the ninth graders and posted it in sections around the room. He provided silent time and asked staff members to start at various points on the list and scan as many as they could in the time available, using markers to place a check mark next to the name of every student whose face they could visualize. He then distributed the D/F list again, and asked them to find those students' names. He made no comment as the faces of staff began to register the relationship between students no one knew and students who were failing. He then challenged them to go back to the lists and use their markers to put a star next to the names of one or two students to whom they would deliberately commit time and attention. The symbolism of students who were known by many and those who were virtually invisible to staff created a more powerful message than any lecture he might have given.

A Variation: Who Do We Serve? How Are They Doing? The 23,000 students of the Kenosha, Wisconsin, school district attend schools that range from over 90% free and reduced lunch to less than 20%. The natural focus of each principal and staff member is on his or her own school, and connections to the big picture of the challenges of the whole system are not often made. On occasion, when challenges seem to outweigh capacity, disagreements may even occur about which schools have the toughest task or contribute the most to student growth. In an effort to illustrate the reality of our system as a whole and create a collective commitment to the "all students" of the district's mission statement,

Figure 2.4 Symbolic Display of Student Demographics: Race

Whom Do We Serve?

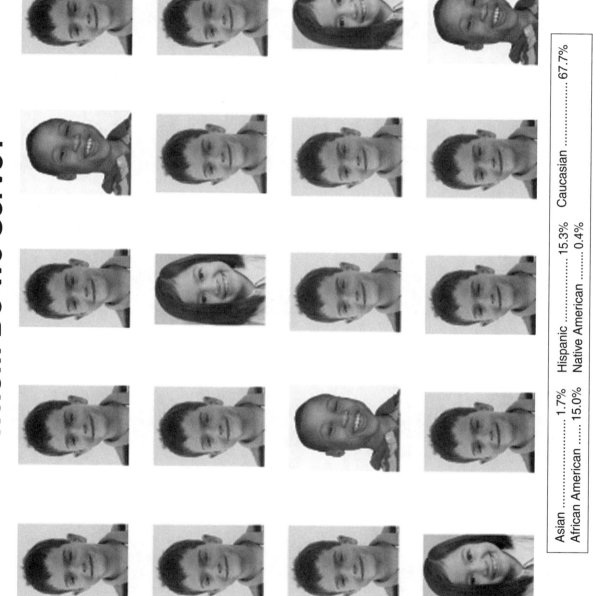

Asian 1.7%	Hispanic 15.3%	Caucasian 67.7%
African American 15.0%	Native American 0.4%	

Figure 2.5 Symbolic Display of Student Demographics: Socioeconomics

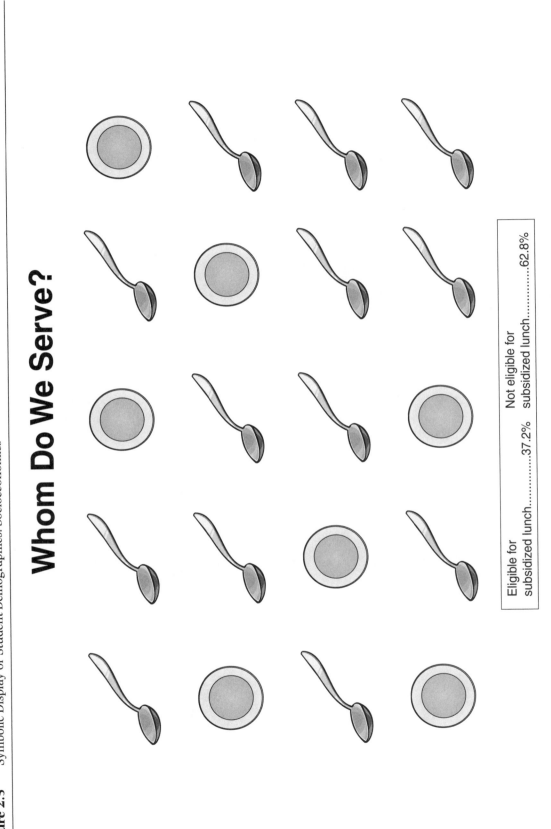

Whom Do We Serve?

Eligible for
subsidized lunch.............37.2%

Not eligible for
subsidized lunch.............62.8%

I created symbolic displays of a classroom of 20 that would represent the overall demographics of the district—the students we serve.

Figure 2.4 generalizes the specific data at the bottom into a symbolic picture of a class of 20 that would include three African American and three Hispanic students. There may not be a single classroom with this exact composition, but it conveys the reality of the overall demographics of the district that many do not "see" every day and therefore do not carry in conscious awareness.

Figure 2.5 uses the symbol of a plate to represent the students who qualify for free or reduced lunches. In a prototype classroom of 20, seven students would qualify. Some administrators were surprised to see the distribution, but *all* were silent when I presented the next two slides (Figures 2.6 and 2.7).

The concept behind these figures is this: If a school district is actually assuring the learning of all students, the group of successful students would have the same racial and socioeconomic distribution as the overall student population. The definition of "success" used here is that students should move through the system and, at minimum, be proficient in reading and mathematics. The data in Figures 2.6 and 2.7 reflect the demographics of all of our tenth graders who scored proficient or above ("passed") the tenth-grade state assessment.

Recalling that there were *six* students of color in Figure 2.4, the contrast with Figure 2.6 is startling. Our pool of successful tenth graders includes only *two*. In comparison with *seven* students eligible for subsidized lunch in the overall population (Figure 2.5), the district's successful group (Figure 2.7) includes only *three*.

There are obvious technical reservations about this display of the data. It's not the same cohort, there aren't as many minorities in the high schools, and so forth. Nevertheless, the power of symbolic displays is obvious in the murmured comments and questions: "So that's what disproportionality 'looks like.'" "Where did the poor and minority students 'go'?" "What are we doing about it?" "My school doesn't look like that—no wonder some schools need more support staff." "What do you mean there are fewer minority students in the high schools? Are you saying they all dropped out?" The purpose of a symbolic display is to raise awareness and articulate such questions and concerns. The awareness then creates readiness and identifies the need for a more indepth exploration from a more technical standpoint.

After I shared this example in a Foundations seminar for New Leaders for New Schools, a principal intern in Baltimore created similar images but used technology more skillfully. Cathy Miles showed faces actually fading into the background as students moved from grade to grade and fell behind. Writing to me about the experience, she noted that when "some of the faces nearly disappeared, there was an audible response in the room! Afterward several teachers told me that they really appreciated the direct relationship to children. They said that 'data is data,' but when they attached data to the faces of children, it hit a different nerve for them" (Miles, personal communication). Symbolic displays like this can provide a louder "wake-up call" than rows and columns of faceless numbers.

SHAREHOLDER PERCEPTIONS

The histogram and run chart were introduced to help answer the question "Where are we now?" in terms of student achievement. A school, district, or any

Figure 2.6   Symbolic Display of Student Success: Race

How Are They Doing?

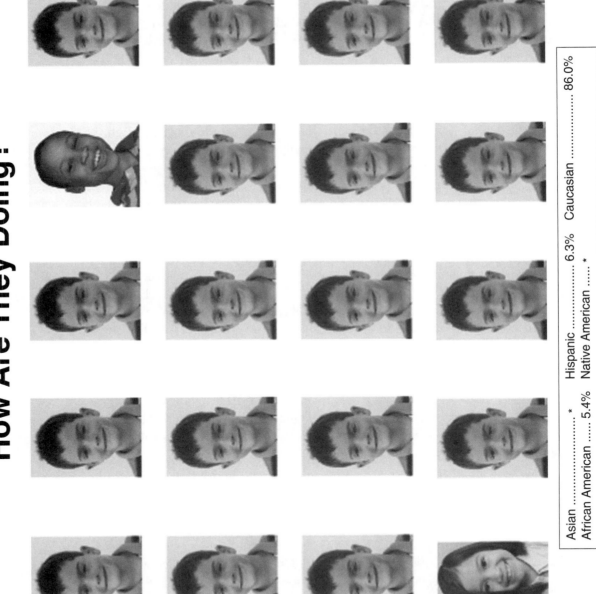

| Asian .... * | Hispanic .... 6.3% | Caucasian .... 86.0% |
| African American ..... 5.4% | Native American ...... * | |

Figure 2.7 Symbolic Display of Student Success: Socioeconomics

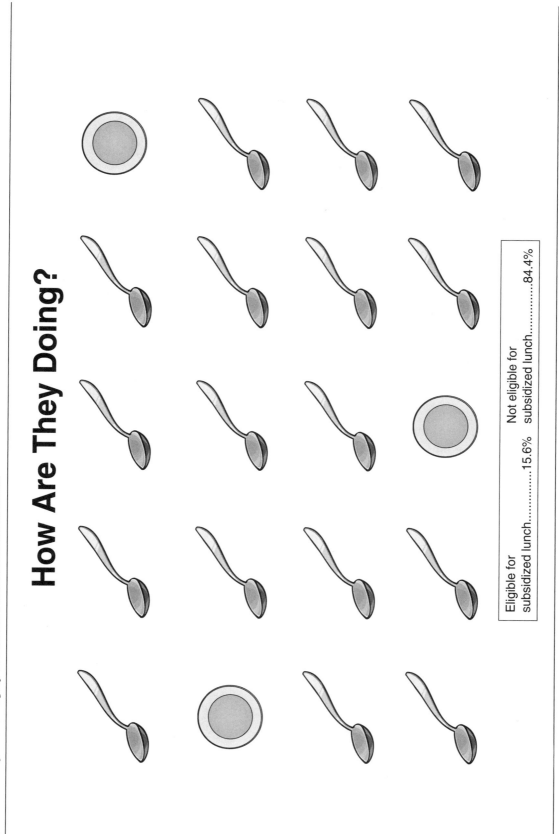

How Are They Doing?

Eligible for
subsidized lunch.............15.6%

Not eligible for
subsidized lunch.............84.4%

other organization also needs to know where it stands with its customers, clients, and community.

Surveys

Purpose. In the business environment, surveys are used to measure customer satisfaction. In much the same way, school leaders use surveys to learn what shareholders think about the school. Shareholders in an educational enterprise include *internal* groups, such as students, teachers, administrators, and support staff, and *external* groups, such as parents, taxpayers without students in the home, and businesses that employ the graduates of the system. The References and Further Reading at the end of this book can direct you to formal surveys that have been developed, with separate forms for students, staff, and parents, and these may include services for compiling and analyzing responses for an additional fee. The informal survey that is locally designed to get information on a specific aspect of the school, in a timely manner, is also valuable. Consultation with an expert in survey design greatly increases the usefulness of the instrument and the data it generates.

When to Use. Formal surveys, especially those packaged with forms for various shareholder groups, are most helpful when school leaders have limited experience collecting and using data. They can provide a level of comfort, a fair degree of reliability, and an aura of objectivity that is especially needed when the idea and experience of receiving outside feedback are unfamiliar. These instruments gather a wide range of overall perceptions on factors that research has linked to school effectiveness. This type of major survey should be conducted at the beginning of a school improvement process and replicated only after sufficient intervals to measure change. Many consultants suggest an interval of 3 years. Shorter, informal surveys can be used successfully at any point in a change process to gather recommendations on a specific problem or gauge reaction to a new innovation.

Who to Involve. For many years, schools were encouraged to survey every member of every shareholder group, and results were regarded as representative because of the widespread distribution of the survey. Unfortunately, many locally developed surveys fail to ask the right questions. Few school leaders have the statistical background to ask crucial questions about the results, such as the rate of return and whether returns came from all parts of the school's attendance area. In one city, a major program decision was made at the district level on the basis of "community input." Not until implementation of the decision encountered resistance of epic proportions did someone notice that the rate of return of the surveys was just over 1% of households and that the surveys were almost entirely from one board member's jurisdiction. The use of stratified sampling is now applied more often and is described in Tips for Facilitators, below.

As with every other type of data analysis, it is important that those who are part of the process being studied be involved in determining how the surveys will be administered and how the results will be analyzed and interpreted.

Materials Needed. Surveys have budget implications. The formal surveys from outside sources may be expensive. For locally developed surveys, printing costs may be a factor. Internal staff time must be provided for distribution and collection. If a survey consists primarily of multiple-choice items, bubble sheets and a scanner can shorten analysis time. If surveys are to be mailed to or from households, postage costs must also be considered.

Tips for Facilitators. If a school leadership group is developing its own survey, it is important to devote substantial discussion time to "exactly what it is that we want and need to know." Because shorter surveys get better return rates than do long ones, the focus of the items should be on the most essential information. Item responses should also be carefully constructed. For example, if response choices are *agree, disagree,* and *don't know,* surveyors will be amazed at the degree of "ignorance" indicated when many respondents take the easiest choice. Using a reference book on survey construction or including someone with a research background on the team is strongly recommended.

A resource person can also provide a more detailed explanation of stratified sampling. In simple language, stratified sampling means deciding who the major groups are within the total population to be surveyed. Within that group, a certain percentage of members are chosen at random. Survey forms may be coded by number or printed on different-colored sheets of paper. When they are returned, a tally can be kept of how many returns there are from each constituency. This will influence how the responses are interpreted and used.

For Example: All Voices Count. A school in a diverse area of the city wanted to gather parents' perceptions about the school and their role in it. The team had been using information from an earlier survey that indicated a high percentage of favorable responses such as "I feel welcome at my school," "I know how to get answers to my questions," and so forth. On the basis of their data, team members were puzzled by a recent letter to the editor accusing the school of being unfriendly to minority families, and they decided to repeat their survey. This time, they consulted with a parent who was also a realtor, and they determined how various neighborhoods within their attendance area were classified. Using the address field in their student database, they identified 10% of the families in each area and color coded the response sheets. Lots of pink ones came back, and the data verified their earlier survey. But almost no green or blue forms were returned. After several discussions, one member of the group initiated the idea of having the survey introduced by someone familiar to those parents, in their own territory. In one case, the association president of a subsidized housing project agreed to call people together and explain the survey. A local minister in another area agreed to invite a school representative to meet with a parent group at the church on a weeknight. The surveys were completed and returned, and they verified the sentiment expressed in the letter to the editor. These parents did not feel welcome and did not know how to approach the school. As a result of this extra effort, the tone of discussions about "parents who don't care" changed radically, and the school began to revise its methods of parent communication and conferencing.

Focus Groups

Many experts on survey construction will recommend at least one open-ended item to allow respondents to create their own answers. The difficulty is that few school leadership groups have the skill and time to do a thematic analysis of all these varied responses. Too often, they make for great lounge reading and speculation on who might have written which comments but provide little specific direction for planning.

Focus groups can meet this need for unstructured responses in a more efficient and useful way. The August/September 2005 issue of *Tools for Schools* was devoted to the topic of focus groups and is an excellent resource. As Joan Richardson comments, "If a district wants quantitative information—for example, how many people support a change in the school calendar—a survey will do a better job of producing that information. If a district wants information about why families favor one school calendar over another, focus groups would be a better research tool" (p. 2).

Focus groups are also useful in urban settings with multiple language communities of newcomers to America. Interpreters can be briefed on the focus group process and the questions, and sessions can be held at community centers in each neighborhood.

Purpose. The focus group builds face-to-face communication and gets more specific information than a survey can provide. Focus groups may be held to gather perceptions regarding the school's effectiveness on a particular factor, such as parent involvement. They can also be used after a survey has been given, to clarify survey responses and recommend changes that would be helpful.

When to Use. A focus group can be used when you need more specific information than a survey could provide or when a question is so complex that you have not been able to construct a survey item or design response options that seem appropriate. A focus group can also be used to help analyze and interpret data already gathered.

Who to Involve. A focus group generally includes 10 to 12 individuals who have personal experience with the question being discussed. If the issue is parent involvement, or if the purpose is to clarify parent responses to a survey or situation, the focus group should be made up of parents. In schools with racial or economic diversity, focus groups should be formed from each population so that individuals can express their views in a comfortable setting with peers. If an issue is student behavior, there may be a focus group of staff and one of parents, but the significant involvement of students themselves should not be overlooked. *Students Are Stakeholders Too!* (Holcomb, 2007) was written to focus on the lack of authentic engagement on the part of students. Linda Lambert (2003) also discusses use of focus groups with students. She proposes these questions:

- What does it mean to be a leader at school?
- Would you describe yourself as a leader? Why or why not?
- Has there been a time when you performed as a leader? Give us an example.
- What might we do to increase or improve student leadership in our school community? (p. 64)

Ideally, parents, teachers, and students would discuss school issues together, and some schools reach this point. However, most schools need time to build bridges of trust and respect before a mixed group can be as candid as a focus group should be.

Materials Needed. Inviting the right people to a focus group requires knowledge of who the opinion leaders are and skill in building rapport. Other materials needed are a comfortable setting and a tape recorder or process observer with a laptop computer.

Tips for Facilitators. When contacting persons to serve on a focus group, be clear about what will be discussed and how the group will be composed. Also let participants know that their comments will be recorded for future reference but in a way that is anonymous and confidential.

Assemble the group in a circle of comfortable chairs or around a table where the participants can face each other. The facilitator should not be seated in a place that implies leadership or authority. Refreshments and an opportunity for introductions and get-acquainted chatter are important.

If a tape recorder is being used, participants must know of its use, but it should be placed in an unobtrusive location. If a process observer is taking notes on a laptop computer, that person should sit outside the circle. The advantage of using a computer is that it saves the time and extra step of transcribing from a tape. Keyboards have become much quieter, and the noise is usually lost in the sounds of the discussion after just a few minutes.

Have a few key questions prepared, but don't be tied to them. Make an opening statement about why this group was formed and what type of information the school needs. Assure the group that specific examples are needed and will be held in confidence. Let the conversation flow, and resist the temptation to fill any moment of silence with another structured question. As in teaching, "wait time" produces more analytical thinking and more accurate answers.

For Example: What's Recognition? The leadership team had administered a formal survey, based on school effectiveness research, developed by a highly respected consultant group. Most of the responses made sense. There were no surprises except for negative parent responses regarding the format of parent-teacher conferences and "student recognition." The task force was cochaired by two members of the school improvement team and included volunteers who agreed to help analyze the survey data. They were not too concerned about the parent conference item. Teachers had talked for some time about how they needed to make different arrangements for these important communication opportunities. But they were quite distressed about the student recognition item, and they began to list all the ways in which students were recognized for good work, good behavior, helping others, and so forth. They wondered what more they could do and were about to propose a subcommittee to explore ways to get funding from local businesses to provide more student incentives, when one member said, "I wonder what parents thought student recognition means."

After a few moments of silent confusion, a first-year teacher timidly suggested, "Maybe we should ask them." It sounded like a pretty logical next move, and the principal helped identify members of a focus group, who were then invited to come and discuss the items on the parent survey and what they thought of as they read them. Through the focus group, school leaders discovered that the "student recognition" parents wanted was for the principal to know their children's names and for all teachers to get to know even the students who were not in their classes and to address them by name—or at least with more respect than "Hey, kid." The face-to-face communication of a focus group shifted the attention of staff to what really mattered for parents. They moved from initiating more extrinsic reward systems to looking at the culture of the school and improving the interactions between staff and students.

ORGANIZATIONAL CULTURE AND CONTEXT

When schools address the "Where are we now?" question, they need to consider their status in terms of student performance, perceptions of school effectiveness, and the organizational climate in which any change process must take place. Histograms, run charts, and symbolic displays were described as ways to portray student data. The use of surveys and focus groups to capture shareholder perceptions was discussed. Any of these can also be adapted for analysis of the school culture and context. Think, Pair, Share is a technique that helps assess the readiness of a school to examine itself and begin to improve.

Think, Pair, Share

Purpose. Unlike basic brainstorming, which relies for its value on quick generation of numerous responses without evaluation, Think, Pair, Share is designed to provide a structured opportunity to reflect on a subject before voicing participants' thoughts. Its purpose for the individual participant is to refine and clarify personal viewpoints, prepare rationale to support them, and mentally rehearse how to communicate them to others. The purpose for growth of a group is to share opinions honestly and openly but with greater sensitivity than in an "off-the-cuff" or "already-flown-off-the-handle" confrontation.

When to Use. Think, Pair, Share is a helpful technique to raise awareness of concerns or needs for change during the early stages of describing "Where are we now?" As Figure 1.2 indicates, it can also be used in many contexts during an improvement process to improve communication and manage conflicts.

Who to Involve. When Think, Pair, Share is used to look at needs for change, all parties involved in the change process should be represented. In the case of school improvement, participants might include members of the site leadership group. When Think, Pair, Share is used for conflict management, participants are those who are in conflict, or their representatives if large groups are involved.

Materials Needed. Think, Pair, Share can be used with no special materials. If common themes emerge during the activity, the facilitator may wish to record them with markers on easel paper or on overhead transparencies.

Tips for Facilitators. Give participants a prompt and a time limit of 2 to 3 minutes to think about the prompt in silence without interaction. Respond to individual learning styles by assuring participants that they may jot down notes or doodle if they so desire as they organize their thoughts. Let them know in advance that they will be asked to share their viewpoints verbally with one other person.

After the "think time" has been provided, have participants pair up and share their viewpoints. In most cases, pairs work best if they are self-selected. There may be times, however, when the topic lends itself to structured pairing, such as the Quick-Write example regarding site-based management described in Chapter 6. When Think, Pair, Share is used to address areas of conflict, the pairs should consist of a member from each side of the issue.

The sharing time may be informal or carefully structured, depending on the topic and composition of the group. In conflict management settings, it may be necessary to structure an uninterrupted time for each participant, as in the active listening exercise described in Chapter 6.

After pairs have shared, ask for voluntary comments on what they learned from each other. Exercise your own judgment about whether to record these comments for future reference. Asking "How many other pairs experienced this as well?" and "Shall we make note of it as a common response?" helps guide this decision.

For Example: Magical Metaphors. Metaphors, similes, and analogies make great prompts for Think, Pair, Share. They create strong visual images, encourage creativity, generate humor, and allow concepts to be expressed in a less threatening way than direct dialogue. Think, Pair, Share can provide a wealth of information for diagnosing organizational culture when participants are asked to complete this statement:

> If my school were a (choose your own category), it would be a (choose your own example) because _____.

During the sharing time, challenge participants to identify the positive and negative values embedded in the images. The following examples were written by school teams in the United States, Hong Kong, and St. Lucia. They imply strengths and weaknesses of the organizations that can be explored further in group discussions.

> If _____ School were an automobile, it would be American made because it has many options and is changing with the times.

> If _____ School were a form of entertainment, it would be the Late Night Show because we're No. 1, and we put in a lot of late hours.

If _____ School were literature, it would be an epic poem because of the magnitude, but only the first 12 lines are done, and the poets have a long way to go to complete it.

If _____ School were a government, it would be a democracy because everyone votes on everything, and now we're gridlocked.

If _____ School were a vacation spot, it would be Wacky Waters because you can choose to get in shallow or deep, there are slippery slides along the way, you get burned if you're not careful, it's popular and crowded, you can go home feeling that you've had a good time, and some folks are just "all wet."

If _____ School were a movie, it would be *The Wizard of Oz* because we never see the man behind the curtain, and we're always guessing about what things mean.

If _____ School were a group of animals, it would be horses because most are trainable, but some are wild.

A Variation: Recounting History. Answering the "Where are we now?" question can sometimes be made easier by asking the related subquestion "How did we get here?" The "think prompt" is to recall significant events in the school's history, including attempted innovations. Participants identify those that were successful or positive and distinguish the factors associated with them that differ from events and changes regarded negatively. The sharing time and reporting to the large group can help diagnose the legacy of change and guide change agents in their approach. Emphasis should be placed on how a new endeavor is similar to a positive change in the past and different from efforts perceived as failures. If, for example, introduction of "the new math" was an "absolute disaster" because "parents didn't have a clue what we were talking about," it is a strong message that communication with the public will be essential to any future innovation.

Another Twist: Focusing on Instruction. One approach to the development of a culture of professional learning has been advanced by Eaker, DuFour, and DuFour (2002). They advance four questions that could form the basis of a powerful Think, Pair, Share activity:

1. Does every teacher understand what each student should know and be able to do after completing the unit of instruction, course, and grade level?

2. What systems are in place to monitor each student's learning on a timely basis?

3. What happens when a student is not learning? How does the school respond?

4. What systems are in place to provide these students with additional time and support? (p. 39)

These questions provide a focus on effective teaching and student learning that was lacking in early iterations of school improvement that somewhat neglected the classroom level. (See the three levels of collaboration in Chapter 3.) I would propose an additional question inserted after #1 above: *In what ways do teachers plan initial instruction together so that more students will be successful?* Without this question, it becomes too easy to shift responsibility, which can happen when the classroom teacher falls into a pattern of "I taught it and tested it, and now 'the school' needs a place to send some of them for 'intervention.'"

Flowcharting

Think, Pair, Share provides opportunities to reflect and exchange individual perceptions of the school or district culture. Organizational diagnosis also includes a close look at governance and program factors that reveal how ready the system is to undertake change—whether its routine functions are likely to enhance or inhibit the effort. This is especially true for site-based efforts, which can be well conceived at the building level but crash against insurmountable barriers within the larger organization.

Purpose. Flowcharting is a graphic way to represent steps in a process and relationships between departments or other divisions in an organization. It can be used to illustrate how a process currently works or to design an ideal process. Sometimes groups try to diagram the current process first to see where it breaks down. Sometimes groups use flowcharting to visualize how the process should take place. On other occasions, the group may divide into two subgroups. One group may draw the current process, and the other may try to construct the ideal process to compare the two.

When to Use. Flowcharting can be used at the start of a change process to develop a visual plan of the steps that will be needed, critical decision points, and timelines. It can also be used for problem solving whenever an organization senses that its processes are inefficient or redundant.

Who to Involve. When flowcharting is used to create a new process, representatives of all shareholders should be involved. If flowcharting is used to describe existing processes or to troubleshoot problem areas, people who work with each step of the process should be involved. Trying to flowchart a process without the people who actually participate in it can create ill will that is difficult to overcome in a spirit of constructive criticism and continuous improvement.

Materials Needed. Flowcharting can be done using a computer but most often occurs first in small groups using easel paper and markers. Stick-on notes can also be helpful as an intermediate step.

Tips for Facilitators. Have the group begin by discussing what it takes to get a process completed, a product created, or a decision approved. The task is to draw each step of the process and connect it with arrows. Simple shapes should be used, such as circles, boxes, and ovals. In some cases, groups will choose a particular shape to represent a certain department, division, or group within the organization. One rule of thumb is that a diamond shape should be used to represent decision points, where arrows could go in more than one direction on the basis of the decision that is made. If there are more than seven participants, divide the group into smaller groups to complete this activity. Do not be concerned if their flowcharts do not turn out the same. Valuable learning occurs when participants realize that even within the organization and as part of the process, they do not have a common understanding of how it works.

For Example: Taking the Initiative. A middle school had begun to work with site-based management and school improvement. Initial excitement had prompted a number of innovative ideas, but most of them had foundered before implementation because their advocates did not know how to get them approved. The school site council wanted to be sure that any individual or group had the ability to bring forth a new idea and have it receive fair consideration. Members of the council spent several meetings struggling to describe such a process in words or numbered steps. Finally, a frustrated participant exclaimed, "It still doesn't seem clear. Maybe you'd better draw me a picture!" Figure 2.8 is the flowchart that was developed in response.

A Variation: Drawing From History. As school leadership groups begin to answer the "Where are we now?" question, they sometimes find themselves wondering, "How did we get to this state?" The past may need to be revisited, discussed, and laid to rest before the present can be assessed objectively to set new directions. Flowcharting can be useful in this situation as well. The shapes used can represent major events in the history of the school, such as changes of principals, new mandates from the state, shifts in student population, or internal conflicts. The diamond shape representing decision points is used to depict turning points, especially if the event caused members of the group to go in different directions. Drawing this type of flowchart can help a group understand the influence of past events and recognize what divisions or rifts may need to be healed during the readiness stage of a change process. When one school team completed flowcharting for this purpose, it discovered that many of the conflicts still being played out among the staff could be traced back 4 years to the district's attempt at implementing a merit pay plan. Once members realized how long they had been carrying old grudges, they made a commitment to bury them and move on.

Another Twist: Picturing Reality. As I worked with a steering committee in one district's boardroom, it became clear that there was a great deal of confusion about how the quality task force fit with the strategic planning process, how the district strategic planning group interacted with the facilities committee, how the school improvement teams fit with parent advocacy groups, and so on. The participants worked diligently to construct a flowchart and finally indicated that flowcharting was much too logical to fit the way things really happened in the district. The specific visual of a flowchart was abandoned, and participants were asked to use any type of drawing that would illustrate how they perceived the interaction of these various groups and who they would go to for approval of building-level initiatives. Two drawings were particularly intriguing. One showed a host of colorful balloons, strings dangling, floating haphazardly across a cloudy sky, with scorch marks on several. The creators of

Figure 2.8   Flowchart for an Initiative

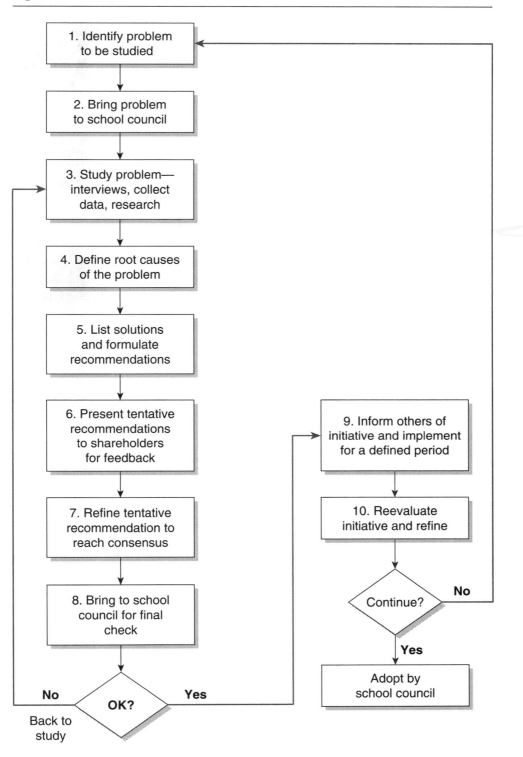

this visual image noted that the district seemed to have a lot of lovely ideas floating around but that they did not seem connected to anything, and they never knew whether a new idea would soar or be struck by lightning.

Another group created a complex marionette, with strings attached to ears, eyes, nose, mouth, and limbs. Each of the strings was connected to a different committee or group that it had earlier tried to depict in a flowchart. The artists stated that working on a site-based team in the midst of multiple district efforts felt like being "jerked around" by the conflicting expectations of each entity, none of which was aware of the others' work. When these two drawings were shared with the superintendent and board president, they clearly demonstrated why the schools could not move forward with site-based leadership until the district reached better consensus on and integration of its own projects. Needless to say, these artists remain anonymous.

Constructing a Continuum

Flowcharting is a visual way to guide a group through discussion of how a process occurs or should occur in an organization. As a school, district, or organization analyzes its culture and context, another need often emerges. Colleagues and shareholders who begin to engage in real dialogue about an issue discover that they are not all talking about the same thing. Every group has used a common term but has unconsciously defined or interpreted it in a different way. I was in Washington, D.C., for a policy conference on site-based management when a national expert referred to the old saying, "Let 'George' do it," and declared, "Site-based management is so ill defined, and the way everyone thinks it will solve everything . . . well, we might just as well call it 'George.'" Because so many districts now claim to have given their schools the freedom of site-based management, it is important to clearly define what that means.

Purpose. Constructing a continuum is a way to display the variation of perceptions and attitudes about an issue. It clarifies viewpoints by making them visual in relation to more objective factors and the opinions of others in a group. Once it is constructed, the continuum itself can be used as a communication tool to help others understand the situation.

When to Use. A continuum can be a helpful tool for moving discussion forward when members of a group seem to talk "past" each other or slip into arguments over semantics. (Chapter 6 includes an example of the Quick-Write activity that can serve a similar purpose.)

Who to Involve. If the issue needing definition or clarification is an internal problem of a small group, those individuals should participate in constructing the continuum. If those individuals represent larger groups, each participant could be a liaison and lead the continuum activity with his or her own group and bring back the results for further discussion in the small group. If the continuum activity has brought closure to an issue, the continuum itself can become a graphic element used by all representatives to create common explanations and messages to their constituents.

Materials Needed. Large paper and markers are the only things needed to construct a continuum. An alternative is to have individuals use stick-on notes for the items or factors they identify. This input can then be transferred to and clustered on a large version for discussion in a larger group. If the group members decide that the continuum they have constructed is useful for further discussion or as part of a document for future reference, it can be re-created on software and printed for distribution.

Tips for Facilitators. Prerequisite skills for this group process activity are active listening and analytical thinking. The facilitator must be able to sense when there is a need for this type of definition and must be able to identify the opposing or mixed messages and perceptions.

The simplest continuum is a two-way arrow with the two ends labeled with terms that are in opposition. An example of this is the "Motivation Continuum" provided in *Getting Excited About Data* (Holcomb, 2004). Its purpose is to build commitment to the use of data in decision-making processes and acknowledge that people accept the need to do so for a whole variety of reasons and to different degrees. The terms at the ends of the motivation continuum are *intrinsic* and *extrinsic.* More fully described in *Getting Excited About Data,* the essential outcome of the activity is to acknowledge that everyone needs to be more data oriented but that some will be motivated by a pragmatic realization that accountability is here to stay, whereas others are motivated by a deep intrinsic desire to know how to attain maximum effectiveness as an organization. Everyone's reasons are affirmed and celebrated, as long as they represent acceptance of the need and willingness to participate at some level and support the overall effort.

The ability of the facilitator to identify the outcome needed is critical. In the above case, the outcome was that all participants would be able and willing to express a way in which they could support the school's work with data.

The facilitator also needs to recognize the range of ways in which that outcome could be achieved. The "Motivation Continuum" was first created when I realized that a group was struggling unsuccessfully to get all members motivated *in the same way.* Those who had a real passion for the work were angry at others for not sharing the same intrinsic drive, rather than accepting and moving forward with those who could only go as far as "I know, we're stuck with it, so just get on with it." Recognizing the range of factors and feelings within the group helps the facilitator generate the terms for the ends of the continuum. As participants generate and record their perceptions, the construction of the continuum may be revised to provide a place for additional input.

Facilitator flexibility is also needed. As a group begins to place thoughts on the continuum, it may become clear that a more complex type of visual or process is needed. The facilitator needs to accept that as positive progress, not as a failure of this initial activity.

For Example: Site-Based Shared Decision Making. Figure 2.9 is an example of the need to move from a single continuum to something a little more elaborate. I was working with the school leadership teams from a large district. This district had recently developed a strategic plan and published a lovely three-color brochure assuring shareholders that all would be well with student achievement (and finance) because the district was embarking on a new approach called *site-based shared decision making* (SBSDM).

As we began to talk about the school change process and the leadership role that these groups would play, it was clear that every team had a different game plan in mind. Some thought that they would have complete autonomy to hire

Figure 2.9   Continuum of Site-Based Shared Decision Making

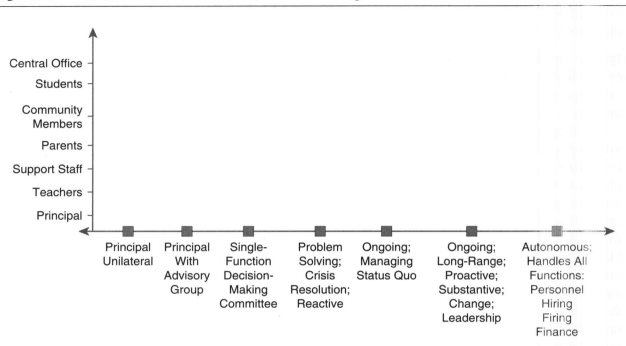

and fire everyone, including the principal—and this was before the first round of Chicago school reforms when a lot of principals *did* lose their jobs. Other teams actually *included* the principals, who thought the teams were going to function as advisory groups while the principals maintained their style of ultimate decision making. So there were disagreements about how the teams should operate and what issues they should address.

There was also disagreement about who should be the "sharers" in SBSDM. Some felt it was adequate to "allow" teachers to share decision making with the principal. Others had a broader reach in mind. They were thinking about the roles of support staff, parents, community members, and students—and one group even thought it would be helpful to have someone from the central office as a liaison.

Because there seemed to be two currents flowing in different directions, I created a double continuum, resulting in what can also be called a matrix or a grid. The left, vertical continuum represents the stretch from most limited participation to the most inclusive mentioned in the discussion. I was able to identify the factors on this axis just by looking at people's name tags as I moved about the room. At some tables, everyone was identified with a name and the role "Teacher," while other tables had a mixture of roles represented.

The horizontal continuum represents the various definitions of an SBSDM team that were held by the groups in the room. To generate the stations along this continuum, I had to ask each role group to take a piece of paper and use no more than seven words to describe the roles they anticipated in the SBSDM process. This took several minutes, after which we took a break, and I constructed the first version of Figure 2.9 on a transparency.

When we returned, I showed them the continuum and asked them to interpret the meaning of the terms or labels I had used. I then asked each team to send someone to the front to put an X somewhere on this continuum (or grid) to represent the team's position. After lengthy discussion, and consultation with the superintendent who fortunately and commendably was present, we came to the following agreements:

- The far right position was not a variation that the school board was going to find acceptable or had envisioned in its strategic planning process.
- The far left position of a principal with unilateral decision making was identified as no longer acceptable in the organizational culture being nurtured. (I knew this wouldn't fly, but here's another tip for facilitators: Sometimes it's useful to overstate the extremes at the ends of a continuum. This can relieve tension by generating humor or helping individual participants realize where they stand in relation to the rest of the group.)
- The ideal definition of an SBSDM team would be on the top line above the sixth position horizontally. This point represents an SBSDM team that includes the principal, teachers, support staff, parents, community members, students, and a central office liaison. The role of the team would be ongoing, with a long-range, proactive approach to such substantive issues as leadership for change.
- Not all schools would be "ready, willing, and able" to make one great leap from points on the lower left to this ideal. Each team was commissioned to take the continuum, with all the Xs on it, back to their schools. They could use it to stimulate discussion and determine "where they are now" and "where they want to go" as they move toward greater site-based shared decision making.

A Variation: CEO in Seattle. The Seattle School District has a long history of site-based management. The late Superintendent General John Stanford described the role of principal as "CEO of your building." Some principals already operated from a naturally participatory leadership style. Others learned and applied the skills of collaboration and shared decision making. But a few took the metaphor of CEO, coming from a superintendent trained in the military, as endorsement of an authoritative approach. This variation of interpretation, coupled with a lack of definition about what should be managed at the site level and with what degree of involvement, was partially resolved through negotiated language with the Seattle Education Association.

The master agreement between the district and the association called for collaboration on three primary functions: the school's academic achievement plan, budget, and professional development plan. As with any agreement, implementation was varied, which became a major issue in some schools. In collaboration with the Director of Labor Relations, Figure 2.10 was created to help increase understanding of the intent and reality of the contract language.

This graphic provides a visual explanation of several portions of contract language (notice the page number references) and places them in the context of other roles in the district, such as the board and central administration. Conflicts arising from two references to the hiring process are clarified by the high collaboration of a site subcommittee and the personnel role of the

Figure 2.10 Site-Based Decision Making

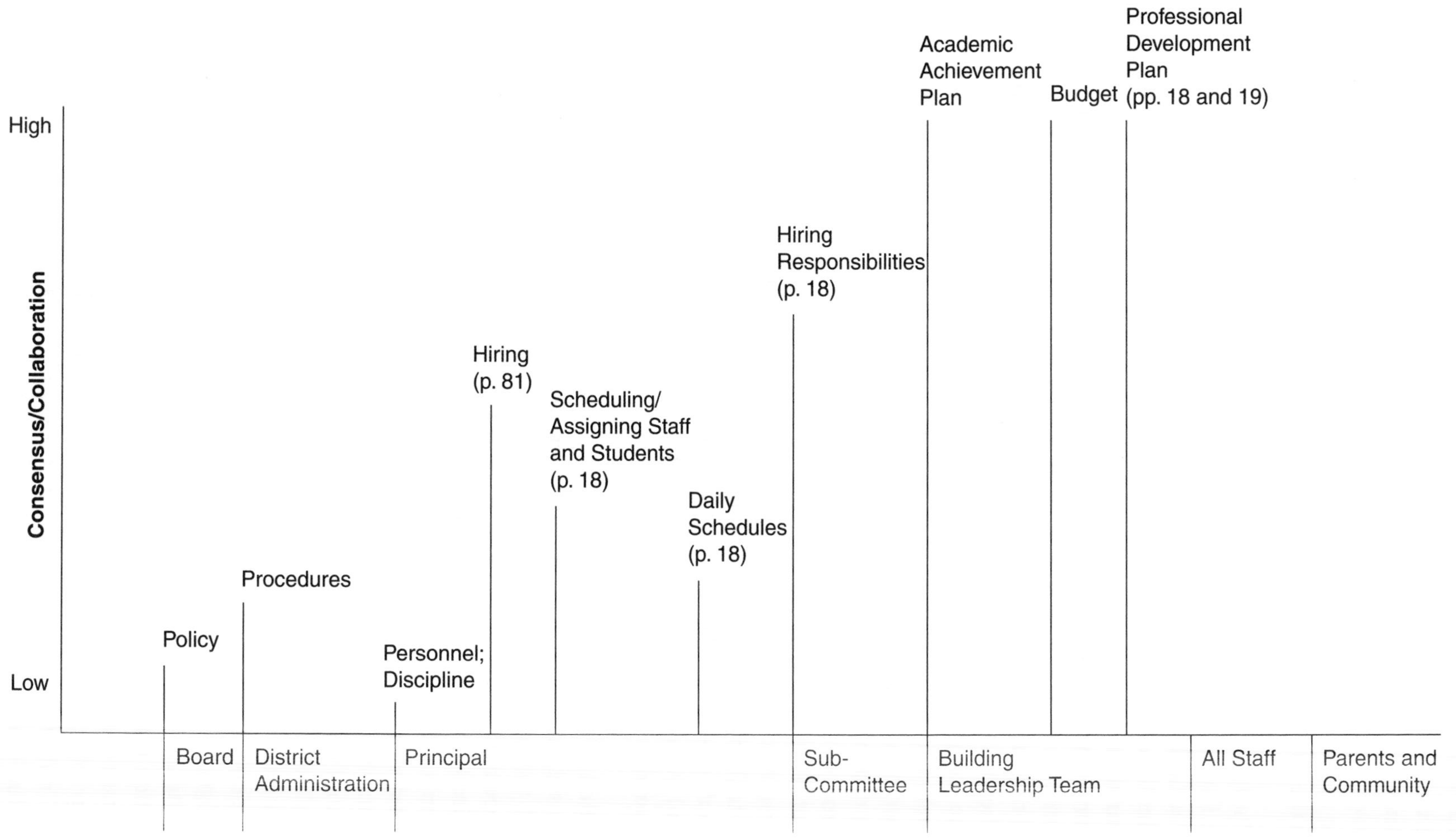

principal. This visual became a tool for training site teams and a reference for resolving individual issues and conflicts.

Meanwhile, the pendulum continues to swing. As I am about to wrap up this third edition, a *Seattle Times* article is headlined "Seattle Schools Changing Course" (Heffner, 2007). It begins with a reference to John Stanford and his "decentralization bandwagon" and states that "Under new Superintendent Maria Goodloe-Johnson and the possibility of a new majority on the School Board, the district is heading in the other direction: toward a centralized, more uniform way of managing public schools in Seattle." Examples of recentralization are listed, including aligning the curriculum and providing daily math lessons for use across the district.

So Seattle swings back toward centralization, while just across Lake Washington, a well-known superintendent is under the gun for carrying curriculum consistency too far (Tuinstra, 2007). Mike Riley brought national attention to the Bellevue School District for "making the honors track standard for all students and working to standardize what's taught from class to class and school to school." His resignation to take a position as senior vice president with the College Board (host organization for Advanced Placement courses and testing) brought mixed reactions, as some lauded the district's high levels of student performance, and others criticized the "big mistake of having mandated, daily lessons." These two paragraphs reference two articles that were in the same issue of the newspaper—one article by Heffner and one by Tuinstra.

An important aspect of describing "where we are now" is a careful analysis of the scope of decision making that is attributed to individual schools or retained at the district level. Once that is clarified, the school's own decision-making structure also needs to be clarified.

Rebuilding the Decision-Making Structure

Change takes time, and a case in point is the journey of school improvement at a Colorado high school. Ten years after the district first began its school improvement efforts, this high school was struggling to do the new work with the old leadership structure shown in Figure 2.11. In addition to the leadership council, the school had an instructional leadership team, an administrative team, a school improvement team, and a full range of ad hoc and standing committees. Not surprisingly, an additional clearinghouse was needed to facilitate shared decision making between and among these various groups.

Meanwhile, the district's school improvement efforts continued on—faster in some schools, slower in others—but overall, the results were disappointing. The school improvement process and teams were in place, but they weren't driving what happened in schools. District leaders were disappointed about a pattern of

- Schools not using the "tons of data" they received in decision making
- Malaise setting in as the excitement and energy wore down
- Vision statements being ignored or becoming obsolete
- Parents on teams not grasping the scope of school improvement as being about the whole school, not their individual child
- Principals doing multiple plans for multiple purposes

It was time to "revitalize school improvement."

Figure 2.11 High School Leadership Structure

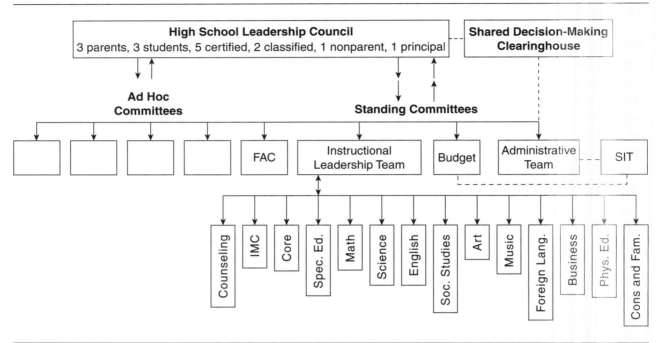

SOURCE: Used with permission by Kerry Moynihan, Principal; Thornton, Colorado.

Figure 2.12 Restructuring Options: Status Quo

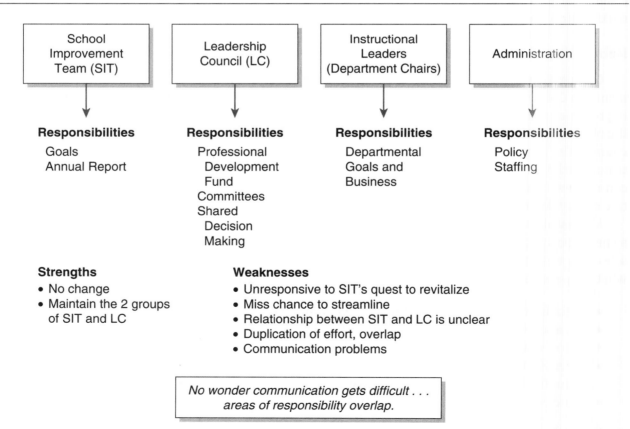

SOURCE: Used with permission by Kerry Moynihan, Principal; Thornton, Colorado.

Figure 2.13   Restructuring Options: Option A

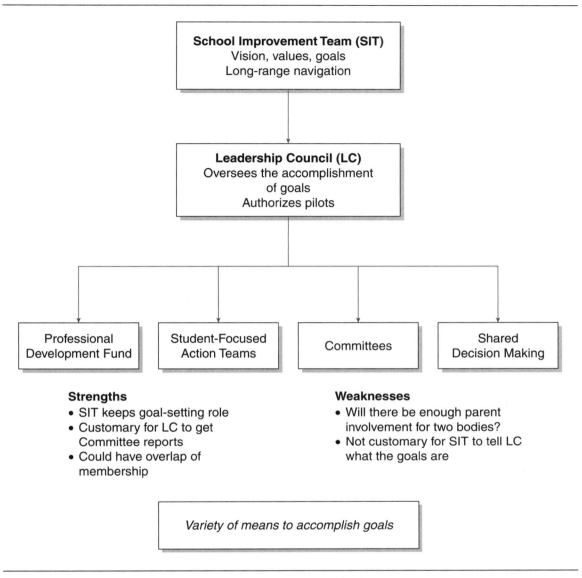

Variety of means to accomplish goals

SOURCE: Used with permission by Kerry Moynihan, Principal; Thornton, Colorado.

Figure 2.14   Restructuring Options: Option B

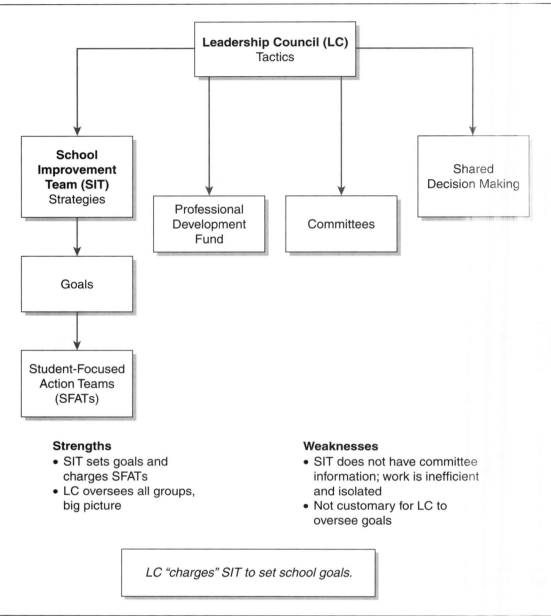

SOURCE: Used with permission by Kerry Moynihan, Principal; Thornton, Colorado.

Figure 2.15   Restructuring Options: Option C

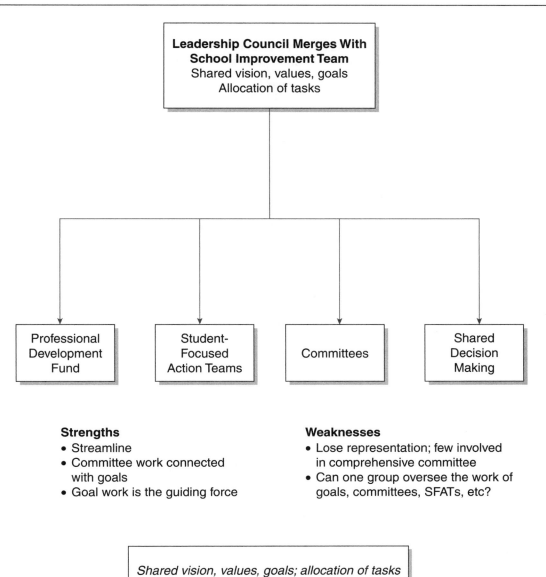

SOURCE: Used with permission by Kerry Moynihan, Principal; Thornton, Colorado.

Figure 2.16   New Organizational Structure

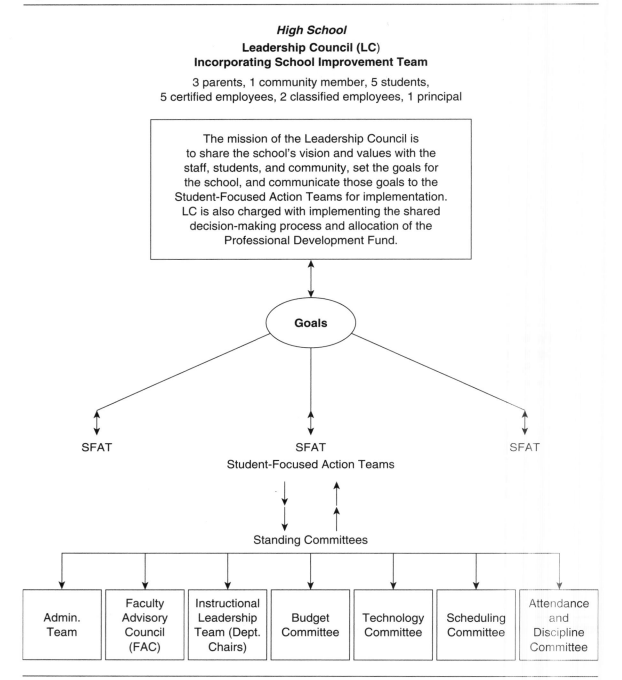

High School
Leadership Council (LC)
Incorporating School Improvement Team

3 parents, 1 community member, 5 students,
5 certified employees, 2 classified employees, 1 principal

The mission of the Leadership Council is
to share the school's vision and values with the
staff, students, and community, set the goals for
the school, and communicate those goals to the
Student-Focused Action Teams for implementation.
LC is also charged with implementing the shared
decision-making process and allocation of the
Professional Development Fund.

Goals

SFAT   SFAT   SFAT
Student-Focused Action Teams

Standing Committees

| Admin. Team | Faculty Advisory Council (FAC) | Instructional Leadership Team (Dept. Chairs) | Budget Committee | Technology Committee | Scheduling Committee | Attendance and Discipline Committee |

SOURCE: Used with permission by Kerry Moynihan, Principal; Thornton, Colorado.

The leadership at the Colorado high school also recognized the need to breathe new life into the collaborative work they were attempting. The first step was to review the 5-year-old decision-making structure and create options for restructuring. At the time, the term *restructuring* was new and evoked energy. "Restructuring was intended to create avenues for people to be together so that they could get to know each other and build relationships, hold genuine dialogue, explore ideas together, and generally interact in productive, beneficial ways" (Lambert, 2003, p. 11).

The existing decision-making structure was cumbersome, and some still didn't understand who was doing what and why. On the other hand, there were those who had a strong investment in it, so it couldn't be discarded lightly. The school improvement team and the leadership council went to work. First, they analyzed the status quo of the four main existing groups and their responsibilities (see Figure 2.12). They noted the weaknesses of the existing structure but presented it as a viable option and acknowledged that sometimes "no change" can be a good thing.

Although honoring the status quo, the team also went to work on alternative ways to define the roles and relationships within the school. Figures 2.13, 2.14, and 2.15 are three options that were presented to the school improvement team and leadership council.

Each one was discussed and analyzed in terms of the strengths and weaknesses seen in the visual models. The leadership council voted to approve a merged format.

Figure 2.16 shows the new streamlined organizational structure, focused on goals and with a renewed sense of mission. The merged model has been effective. All the team's efforts are truly focused on the school's goals. The team regularly revisits the data that monitor progress toward the goals.

This streamlined format has become a decision-making structure that will now be replicated in a new school. The Colorado school's determination to revisit, revise, and rededicate its efforts is also a model answer for the question in Chapter 6: "How will we sustain the focus and momentum?"

For a school, answering the question "Where Are We Now?' is more complex than pointing to a dot on a map. It means studying how our students are performing and how we are perceived by our shareholders. It also means analyzing our organizational context, both internal and external. These findings help pinpoint our current position. They also create a baseline for contrast as schools move into discussion of the desired reality that represents "where we want to go."

Answer Key

- To describe "where we are now," study data on student performance, gather shareholder perceptions, and analyze the organizational context at the district and school level.

- Do not rely on snapshot data. For significant, long-term decision making, utilize data from multiple years and multiple sources.

- Display data in ways that touch the heart as well as the mind.

- Seek clarity about the scope of decision making available to the school and the parameters set by the district.

3

Answering the "Where Do We Want to Go?" Question

Travelers and ramblers are certainly different. Unfortunately, too many school leadership teams look like the ramblers—"all packed up and no place to go." They've assembled trunkfuls of data and worked frantically to convince their peers that things are really not so good, that they need a change, but they can't get the show on the road because they don't know where they're headed. An old adage maintains that "if you don't know where you're going, any road will get you there." The problem is that it might be the wrong road, and you might end up in a spot even worse than where you are right now, and with time, energy, and motivation depleted.

Figure 1.1 links the question "Where do we want to go?" to the planning stage in the RPTIM model and the plan stage of quality management's PDCA cycle. Leadership teams must generate broad involvement in clarifying and affirming the values of the culture. The final semantics of vision or mission and belief statements matter little compared with the powerful dialogue that can build support for and commitment to a shared ideal.

AFFIRMING THE MISSION

The discussion and interaction that take place through the process of drafting a statement of commitment are essential. They open communication, increase interaction, and define a focus for the change process. But the rhetoric of belief statements is unavoidably general and idealistic. The written product is not the sole purpose. The process of developing it, and the even more critical decisions and action taken based on it, are the realities that make such activity essential. In or out of vogue, defining beliefs about why we exist is essential as an intrinsic motivator to help sustain a difficult and complex process.

Careful facilitation is needed to move a group toward acceptance of a common belief statement. It requires exceptional creativity to transform general, idealistic rhetoric into something specific and concrete. Identifying the tangible evidence that would be seen, heard, and observed if the ideal became real is an intermediate step that must take place before strategies can be chosen to achieve it.

When school leaders think about their values in concrete terms that would provide observable evidence, the most courageous will take time to compare those desired outcomes with the data that they have gathered about student performance, shareholder perceptions, and the organizational culture and context. This analysis is represented by the two-way arrow between "Mission" and "School Portfolio" in Figure 1.1. The group process tool "Monitoring Our Mission," provided in *Getting Excited About Data* (Holcomb, 2004), assists with this compare-and-contrast activity. Discrepancies between "what we say" we do and "what we see" as our results begin the list of concerns that might be addressed through planned school change. As groups review their data, the following questions identify issues that need further examination (see Chapter 4) and suggest possible goals:

- What do these data *seem* to tell us?
- What do they *not* tell us? What *else* would we need to know?
- What needs for school improvement *might* arise from these data?

Answering the question "Where do we want to go?" also requires careful selection of priorities from among the many concerns and possibilities. Just as the well-prepared traveler must make a choice from among a range of attractive destinations, school leaders must set priorities and focus their efforts where they have the greatest likelihood of creating change that lasts. Once these priorities have been established, goals can be set, study groups can identify best practices for meeting them, and progress can be monitored. Processes for building consensus, identifying observable indicators, and establishing priorities are needed to help schools and districts answer the question "Where do we want to go?"

Affinity Process

When I first learned about mission development, it was taught to me as an "affinity" process. Since then, I have seen the term *affinity process* used in quality management literature to describe a process similar to a force field analysis in which pluses and minuses are listed. I have not, however, found a different term to describe the process of combining ideas and topics that have a similarity with, or affinity for, one another. If you find my use of the term confusing in light of your prior knowledge, feel free to change it here and on Figure 1.2 for your personal use.

Purpose. The affinity process is designed to help persons with different values find those that they hold in common. These common ideals are then put into writing, and consensus is built so that they become the guiding criteria in decision making and planning.

When to Use. The most common use of this process is when a school or district is just beginning to examine itself and accept its responsibility for continuous improvement. To successfully answer the question "Where do we want to go?" an organization must identify a destination that's worth the trip. When a journey becomes difficult, it is harder to quit if the arrival is strongly desired by the travelers.

A process like this can also be helpful whenever an organization seems to be lacking focus. It should be repeated periodically to reaffirm that the same beliefs are still valued, to refine them as needed in response to changes in the environment, and to socialize new members of the organization.

Who to Involve. "The more the merrier"—or at least the more effective. Widespread involvement from all shareholder groups is needed if the statement of commitment is to drive decision making and change. Sometimes I hear statements such as "Yes, we have a mission statement, but it doesn't mean a thing, and no one knows what it is." A few probing questions usually reveal that the mission statement was written by an individual (the new principal?) or by a small group "on retreat" and delivered as a product. Although it is the responsibility of a leader to shape a culture and reinforce positive norms, I have never forgotten this advice from Bob Garmston: "My content is not as important as their process."

Materials Needed. The most expensive resources for this process are the human resources to facilitate it and the time required to allow adequate involvement (yet the process should also move along swiftly enough to avoid getting bogged down). The number of shareholder groups and the number of constituents from each group who wish to participate will influence the time element. Tangible materials needed are stick-on notes, construction paper, and chart paper. A room with a large, blank wall allows the activity to take the most concrete form.

Tips for Facilitators. This process has been successfully accomplished with groups of up to 100 when the participants are divided into small subgroups for appropriate steps. First, ask participants to reflect silently about one or more prompts that are visually displayed: What is the purpose of this school? What should it accomplish for its students? What characteristics should make this school stand out from other schools? What function is uniquely ours to accomplish?

Tell them to work **independently** and write each idea on a stick-on note. Urge them to use no more than five or six words to convey a thought. Caution them not to include more than one idea on each sheet. Guide them to use positive phrases to communicate the role of the school.

The next step is to have participants form **small groups.** These may be mixed groups of school staff, parents, students, and other shareholders, or they may be small groups based on similar roles. Composition of the groups is a judgment call by the facilitator, who should learn as much as possible about the history and culture of the school before accepting this responsibility. If there is great interest in participation, the initial steps of the process may be repeated at several meetings to give everyone a chance for input.

At each table, one person should introduce an idea that he or she has recorded and ask others if they have something similar. These stick-on notes should be attached to a sheet of paper. The next person around the table should introduce one of his or her ideas, ask for similar responses, and compile them on another sheet of paper. This affinity process should be repeated until participants have joined all their phrases with those of other group members.

For the next step, tell the groups to look at each sheet of stick-on notes and create a three- to five-word heading that expresses the main point or theme. Once the small groups have arrived at headings for their clusters, have them reassemble as a **whole group.** Ask one group to bring a heading sheet and post it on the wall. Repeat the process by asking other groups to add theirs with similar items. Continue combining sheets of notes until all work is posted.

Have participants return to **small groups** to discuss which concepts they feel are most important and what wording they see that best expresses the underlying thoughts. They may appreciate having a model such as a sample advocacy statement ("I like this phrase because it communicates that . . .") to help them describe their preferences in a positive manner.

Charge each small group with drafting a rough statement that uses the short headings it chose to most accurately convey its members' thoughts. If these rough drafts are completed in the same setting (such as a workshop), have them shared with the **whole group.** If the steps so far have been conducted in an afterschool or evening meeting, the small groups can finish their rough drafts and then submit them to the **leadership team.**

After receiving input from the groups at the workshop or from a series of meetings with shareholder groups, the leadership team begins to synthesize the main ideas from the various products and prepares a complete draft. This draft should be disseminated to **all individuals or groups** who participated in the first set of drafts. It is important to create opportunities for them to have discussion and provide direct feedback to the team, not just return the draft with written comments.

The **leadership team** uses the feedback to further revise the statement or document, but completion of the written product is not the end of the team's work. The mission or set of belief statements will guide the organization only if it is consciously and overtly introduced as a central focus for all future decision making. The team should plan a visible celebration and commitment event. Some schools have held signing ceremonies complete with special pens to commemorate the occasion. **All groups** who contributed to the process should participate in this public event. When the celebration is over, the **leadership team** has a continuing responsibility to plan ways of infusing the mission into all decision-making processes and into the culture of the school. The team may identify a subgroup or a small, separate committee and charge it to be "keepers of the vision."

Creating the statement of commitment is just the first small step in identifying what the school wants to create, the destination it seeks in response to "Where do we want to go?" Referencing and reaffirming the mission of the school throughout the change process will move it "off the wall" and "into the walk" of daily routines and practices. School leaders must challenge the organization on a regular basis with application questions such as "What are we doing to support our mission? Which of our current programs and practices are consistent with the values we espouse? Which are not? Are the things we measure and assess the things that we say are truly important?" One of the school leadership team's responsibilities is to plan activities that will consciously and intentionally inculcate the school's values into its cultural norms. Some ways to continually affirm the values of the organization are discussed in Chapter 6.

For Example: Mission Statements. The following mission statements were developed through the process described above. They are clear and concise, are strongly worded, and convey a sense of the organization's responsibility to accomplish them.

> The staff of _____ School believes that all students can learn and can achieve mastery of basic grade-level skills, regardless of their previous academic performance, family background, socioeconomic status, race, or gender. We believe that our school's purpose is to educate all students to high levels of academic performance while fostering positive growth in social and emotional behaviors and attitudes. We accept the responsibility to teach all students so that they can attain their maximum educational potential.

> The mission of _____ is to help students acquire the knowledge, skills, and attitudes necessary to become healthy, happy, productive adults; to help students become enthusiastic lifelong learners who are able to manage change; and to help students perpetuate and improve the democratic process and have an impact on their communities, their country, and the world.

> _____ Schools will create an accountable learning community that encourages all students to achieve, to their highest potential, the knowledge and skills needed to be fulfilled, productive members of a changing society.

An Accordion Note. In the group process described earlier, bold print was used to identify the roles of individuals, small groups, the whole group, and the leadership team. The expansion and contraction from individual work to small groups to large groups and back to small groups may be visualized with the metaphor of playing an accordion. The leadership team orchestrates the movements of the accordion. The more support it will need to accomplish a task, the more it will need to expand the accordion and bring in a greater volume of air and energy.

IDENTIFYING AND PRIORITIZING CONCERNS

Courageous examination of differences between beliefs stated in a mission statement and evidence of results gathered in a data portfolio will inevitably generate a set of concerns as illustrated in Figure 1.1. The list of concerns that may need attention will become even longer if participants address this question: What are *all* the things that *anyone* might say *could* improve our school? This query can be used to prompt the brainstorming process described below. It provides an additional opportunity for participants to check whether they have considered every voice and perspective and included all factors that may need attention. After an extensive list of concerns is generated, the tools of nominal group process, color coding, weighted voting, or priority grid help narrow the list to a manageable number of high-priority, high-impact goals on which to focus the time, energy, and money of the organization.

Brainstorming

Too often, the intense involvement of developing a commitment statement or set of beliefs has no impact because it does not direct the action of the organization. It's like a rambler saying, "I'd sure love to take the perfect vacation" without determining what criteria would make a vacation "perfect." Travelers, on the other hand, are more likely to say, "The perfect vacation spot would be quiet, isolated, with lots of sunshine, moderate temperatures, and hiking trails."

Purpose. Brainstorming generates as many ideas as possible related to a particular problem, issue, or goal. It is not tied to current reality, as are the processes described in Chapter 2. Brainstorming is designed to add new ideas to the status quo.

When to Use. You can tell from the number of cell entries in the brainstorming column on Figure 1.2 that this is a versatile group process. It can be used for many reasons at almost any point in a change process. It is described here as a follow-up phase after affirming the values of an organization. The specific purpose and timing are to make the mission more concrete by identifying observable indicators that would prove the mission was being accomplished.

Who to Involve. Active participation by a broad range of constituents from all shareholder groups was recommended for affirming the value system of the organization. Smaller groups with an understanding of the educational enterprise will be better able to contribute to this phase.

Materials Needed. Brainstorming requires open minds, markers, and poster paper.

Tips for Facilitators. Although brainstorming is versatile, it is not as simple as it looks or sounds. Facilitators must not assume that groups know how to use it effectively. Begin by reviewing the rules of brainstorming with participants:

- Quantity is more important than quality.
- Share every thought that occurs to you.
- Make no evaluative statements.
- Listen carefully to group members.

Focus the brainstorming on the problem or purpose. When addressing the "Where do we want to go?" question, the need is to focus on the tangible evidence that we could see and hear if an organization were living by its beliefs. A helpful phrase to use with groups is "observable indicators." This phrase acknowledges that some important aspects of school life are not measurable in the traditional sense of a quantified assessment but should be observed in the behavior of its members.

Record every idea that is expressed, in the words of the speaker. Do not edit comments or combine with others that you think are the same. Set a time limit of 10 to 15 minutes to create a sense of urgency. Within that time, be comfortable with moments of silence. The next contributions are usually even more creative and perceptive than those that came before a lull in the action.

For Example: Lifelong Learner. The mission statement was brand-new. It included phrases about basic skills, responsible citizenship, and respect. The school leadership team felt quite confident about writing goals and action plans consistent with those ideals. But the members were stumped by the phrase "lifelong learner." How would they incorporate that into their improvement plans and verify whether they had accomplished it? One member sardonically remarked, "Yeah, right! Now our postgraduation follow-up studies have to track them down at age 70!"

The pre-brainstorming challenge was for group members to first think individually of someone they considered to be a lifelong learner. The brainstorming task was to list what they had seen that person do, or heard that person say, that convinced them that he or she was a lifelong learner. The list included items such as "gets interested in something," "goes to the library to find out more about it," "is open to doing new things," "starts projects on her own," "tries to get other people interested," "keeps after it until he knows all there is to know and then is on to something else," and "likes to figure out her own way to do it." It was a fascinating list, but the group wondered how helpful it would be because they were describing adults.

The next challenge was a variation on the same theme. On the basis of the age of the students they parented or taught, smaller groups were formed and challenged to brainstorm about "What does each of those behaviors look like at age 17? at age 11? at age 7?" This second round of brainstorming yielded two results. One was the conclusion that most of those behaviors looked pretty much the same at any age and could be observed in the school setting. The other was a realization that many of the school's practices of grouping and scheduling limited a student's ability to demonstrate those behaviors.

Brainstorming is useful in the "Where do we want to go?" stage to set some criteria that distinguish the desired state from the status quo. These criteria also become factors to assess as the group monitors its progress.

Nominal Group Process

A mission statement helps describe where the organization wants to go, and brainstorming observable indicators generates criteria to make the statement more tangible. A third important part of answering this question is setting priorities for improvement.

Purpose. Despite general agreement about what the school should accomplish for its students, there is still a wide range of viewpoints about which aspects of the school should be improved to do so more effectively. Nominal group process gives everyone an opportunity to participate in selecting which areas to work on first.

When to Use. Because it is never possible to address everyone's concerns about the school, nominal group process is used in the planning stage to select priorities. It can also be used to reach consensus on other important decisions throughout a change process. The nominal group technique is particularly helpful in situations in which powerful individuals have a habit of dominating discussions and where "competing for air time" has been the prevailing way of gaining influence.

Who to Involve. All interested parties should be invited to participate. They must be made aware that nominal group technique will be used and that it is a structured process designed (and tested and proved effective) to allow an equal voice for all participants.

Materials Needed. The sequence of steps and rules for nominal group process should be posted. The facilitator will need markers, poster paper, an easel, and tape. Index cards or stick-on notes will help participants with their ranking.

Tips for Facilitators. Post and provide an overview of these steps before beginning:

- Individual brainstorming
- Round-robin listing

- Individual ranking of priorities
- Tabulation of ranks
- Discussion
- Individual ranking
- Tabulation of ranks

Call attention to the fact that, by design, "discussion" is far down the list. The sequence was developed to provide an opportunity for all ideas to be generated and included through brainstorming and to encourage individual reflection and decision making before group members begin to influence each other.

Stimulate the **individual brainstorming** step by posing a question such as "What are all the things that anyone might say could be improved about our school?" As the question is displayed, underline the word *all* and emphasize that this is their opportunity to create a comprehensive list for consideration and that they should be candid and list every concern they have. Call attention to the word *anyone* and remind them to present not only their viewpoints but also others of which they are aware. This is an opportune time to review results of survey data and be sure that the concerns of constituents are included, even if they are not present to participate. Stress that the word *could* expresses our commitment to continuous improvement and does not imply that the current situation is abysmal. Groups are often reassured and encouraged to be open by the statement that "when we talk about improvement, we're not thinking 'horrible-to-wonderful.' We're thinking 'good-better-best.'"

Observe the individual brainstorming and allow plenty of time until most participants seem to be done writing. Emphasize that every one of their concerns will be included but that it will be helpful if they look them over to be sure that they are specific and easily understood. Suggest that longer statements be reduced to a short, three- to five-word phrase. Mention that a concern such as "student test scores" will be more helpful if it is broken down into more specifics, such as "reading achievement" or "math problem solving." Even if that makes their list longer, it is good to subdivide such general items because reading scores and math scores would be approached differently if they became the school's goals.

If the group consists of 15 or fewer participants, serve as recorder and conduct the **round-robin listing** step of the process. If you are working with a large group, divide it into smaller units and have members select recorders. The recorders can give their lists to another participant who will be sure that items from both lists are included.

Round-robin listing means that each person states one concern from his or her list, and this is repeated around the circle. Emphasize that everyone must listen carefully and cross off the list any concerns that other persons mention to avoid duplication and keep the process moving quickly. The recorder should assign a letter to each item (see "For Example" below) to facilitate ranking and discussion later.

Once you have facilitated a small group, you will have one list of all concerns. If you divided a large group into smaller groups that represented different schools, each group has its own total list and will rank those items. If everyone in a large group was from the same school, however, you need to take a break and combine the separate group lists into a total master list. This can be done quickly during a break for the large group, either by repeating the round-robin exercise or by word processing all the responses and then printing the master list for each participant.

When the list of "all the things that could be improved" has been completed, give each person five index cards or slips of paper. Direct participants to choose the five items they are most concerned about and to put the letter of each one on a separate slip. If a group member is most concerned about the items labeled A, E, J, M, and P, there would now be a card or slip of paper with a letter A, another with E, a third with J, and so forth. Then tell the group it must further prioritize the items by shuffling them around until the most important concern is at the top, and the other four are lying on the table or held in the hand in descending order. The group should then put a number 5 on the top one, a 4 on the next, and so on down to 1. These directions must be clear, and you should check to see that they are being followed correctly. If you do not check them, some participants will **rank** their concerns in reverse order from the rest of the group. A value of 5 should represent their top priority, so that the highest total represents the greatest concern when all are compiled.

After ranking their items, members should rearrange their cards in alphabetical order. The recorder will call out a letter, and each person who ranked it will state the numerical value he or she gave it. The recorder should write down each ranking, rather than just add them mentally, and record a total. When discussion takes place, it will make a difference whether one concern has a total value of 20 because 10 persons ranked it a 2 or because 4 persons ranked it a 5.

Discussion begins after the rankings have been tabulated. By this time, almost every group can see agreement beginning to emerge around top-priority concerns. In some cases, a second round of **ranking** and **tabulating** is unnecessary because the priorities have become clear and the discussion does not indicate any strong disagreement. If there is disagreement or if questions are raised about a particular item, ask those who "gave it a 5" to share their reasons for being so concerned about it. Sometimes their responses will provide new information for other participants and cause them to shift their priorities. On other occasions, questions will raise the need for more accurate information before a final decision is reached. In this situation, help the group decide what information is needed, who can provide it, and how much time will be needed to get the information. Then schedule another meeting to look at the information before a second round of ranking determines the school's priorities.

For Example: The Top Three. The charts generated by one team at a workshop looked like the following:

A.	Classroom management	5, 5, 1, 3, 5, 4	23
B.	Teacher punctuality		
C.	Parental involvement	2, 5	7
D.	Time on task	5, 4, 2	11
E.	Teacher motivation	3	3
F.	Community participation		
G.	Student evaluation	4, 3, 5, 5, 1	18
H.	Physical environment		
I.	Quality of instruction	2, 4, 4, 5, 4, 5	24
J.	Teacher evaluation	4, 3	7
K.	Discipline		
L.	Student involvement		
M.	Pupil–teacher rapport	3	3
N.	Interpersonal relationships	2	2
O.	Staff development	3, 3, 2, 3, 2	13
P.	Cocurricular activities	1	1
Q.	Principal–teacher relations		
R.	Teacher involvement in curriculum development		
S.	Instructional leadership	5, 4, 5	14
T.	Staff supervision	2, 2, 1, 1	6
U.	Communication		
V.	School's curriculum		
W.	Student motivation		
X.	Staffing configuration		
Y.	Empowerment		
Z.	Homework policy		
AA.	Instructional materials		
BB.	Grant writing		

Completion of the nominal group process focused the school on the quality of instruction, classroom management, and student evaluation. Goals were written for each of these concerns. Although the interest in staff development did not surface as one of the top three priorities, its presence in the list encouraged the district to offer workshops related to the three goal areas that emerged.

A Variation: Goals Before and After Data. The nominal group process is a good way to give all participants an equal voice in setting priorities. There is a weakness inherent in starting with brainstorming, however. Too often, members of the group contribute concerns that arise only from their personal awareness. Sometimes the priorities that emerge have little connection with the beliefs that the school or district has created as its ideals. Of even greater concern is the omission of issues that were revealed by the data analysis done in response to the "Where are we now?" question.

A variation is to schedule a review of the statement of commitment and a short summary of the findings of the data shortly before the meeting at which the nominal group process will be conducted. Those who attend this review should be encouraged to think about the findings and participate in setting priorities for improvement. On a smaller scale, the facilitator may remind the group to think briefly about the organization's values and the data summaries that have been available for study and urge group members to include that information as they list areas of concern.

The influence of data on the priorities and direction of school improvement plans became obvious to me in a large district that I visited several times. On each trip, I provided school improvement training to a different group of school teams. Data from statewide assessments became available midway through this multi-phase training effort.

Priority concerns identified by nine schools before state test data were received are listed below. (The list totals more than nine because each school chose from two to five goals.)

Student attendance	3
Teacher attendance	3
Reading achievement	2
Student discipline	2
Home–school communication	2
Parent involvement	2
Math achievement	1
Quality of teaching	1
Minority achievement gap	1
Meaningful staff development	1
Student motivation	1
Parent commitment	1
Teacher commitment	1
Internal school communication	1

Priority concerns identified by nine similar schools after state test data were received by the district are as follows:

Reading achievement	8
Math achievement	5
Attendance	3
Student discipline	2
Parent involvement	1
Curriculum planning	1
Conflict resolution	1
Time to "do all this"	1
Home–school relations	1
Team functioning	1
Closing minority gap	1
Writing achievement	1
Staff buy-in	1
Student self-esteem	1

Eight of the nine teams who had test data before them and had reviewed the data prior to goal setting focused their priorities on student achievement, compared with two of nine that had not considered test data before the goal-setting activities.

Another Twist: Adding Mission and Reality. The previous example demonstrated how a review of the school's **data** helped focus the goal-setting process. Two other elements have turned out to be useful as shareholders deal with the critical step that will determine their route and destination as they continue the journey of school change. One of these elements is the **mission** of the organization. Priority should be placed on concerns that have a tight alignment with the mission and a direct impact on whether the school really lives by its stated values. The other element is the hard reality that some factors that desperately need attention may lie outside the immediate sphere of influence of the school. Energy should be invested in goals that are within the **power of the school** and are amenable to change.

Getting Excited About Data (Holcomb 2004) introduced a combination of the nominal group process from this chapter and a decision matrix, described in Chapter 4 of this book. That tool "forces" reflection by asking participants to rate each area of concern in three columns. The first column asks "**How**

severe?" to determine the severity of the situation, and directs participants to consider the data and rate each item from 1 to 5, with a 5 representing a concern that has actual data to demonstrate that it is a severe problem. The second column asks "**How crucial?**" and refers to the school's mission statement. Concerns are rated a 5 if they are absolutely essential and critical to the school's ability to live up to its promises. The third column asks "**How responsive?**" and acknowledges that some concerns are more amenable to change and are more within the power of a school than others. (My initial fear that this column would provide an escape route from the complex issues was unfounded. I have discovered a strange paradox. Allowing participants to voice the fear that "we can't do anything about that" seems to pique the creativity or stubbornness of others, who begin to think of ways they might.) An item rated 5 is one that members of the school community have a sense of efficacy about tackling.

Using this decision matrix, the "ideal" goal would be rated a 15. This describes a severe situation that is critical to the school's mission and that the school itself can change.

Color Coding

Color coding is not so much a group process as a way of identifying the sources of responses. In Chapter 2, printing surveys on different-colored sheets of paper was described as a way to be sure that results include representation from all groups or neighborhoods. If separate meetings are held for various shareholders to participate in the mission development process, different colors of stick-on notes can be used at each session. As responses are grouped, a visual scan can help ensure that contributions from all groups are included in the final product. Color coding can also be used when activities such as the nominal group process are conducted to establish priorities.

Purpose. Color coding shows which concerns or priorities are of most interest to which participants. This information may help school leaders find interested persons to help with change efforts. It can also highlight concerns that may need informal attention, although they do not emerge as the shared priorities of the overall group.

When to Use. Color coding may be used when there is more than one set of priorities or when more than one set of volunteers is needed to carry out a series of tasks.

Who to Involve. It is repetitious, but important, to note again that all who may be affected by a change or expected to help assist with its implementation should be included in determining the priorities.

Materials Needed. The facilitators will need chart paper, markers, and tape. Each participant will need a predetermined number of colored stickers or stars. The number of colors needed will depend on the range of constituent groups participating in the process.

Tips for Facilitators. Use brainstorming to generate the list of concerns or problems that participants feel should be addressed. This step is the same as the beginning of the nominal group technique, but the rest of the process is less formal. After the list of items has been recorded on large chart paper, be sure that each participant has five dots or stars of the appropriate color. Have participants go to the charts and place their five dots or stars by the five items that they consider to be top priorities for most immediate attention.

For Example: Curriculum Priorities. The district had been without a curriculum director for several months. Even before that, work on instructional programs and assessment had virtually ground to a halt because of budget cuts. An interim administrator was assigned to determine the areas that most needed attention and to set up a timeline for addressing them as funds became available. Because the district no longer had curriculum specialists, these assignments had been divided among the principals in addition to their building-level responsibilities. A method was needed for setting priorities and organizing work on them in the most efficient manner.

The first step was to brainstorm the list of issues and projects that had been neglected and needed attention. Once the list was complete, central office administrators were given five gold dots, secondary principals were given five purple dots, and elementary principals were given five green dots. A quick visual scan of their responses identified two issues that had multicolored responses and would be handled in a K–12 setting. Other issues that had only purple or green dots could be set aside to be addressed in specific subcommittees to address elementary or secondary needs. A few issues remained on the list for attention at some future date, but the delay would not cause any hurt feelings because the items had no preponderance of dots of any color.

Weighted Voting

Color coding helps show differences in the responses contributed by different individuals or groups. Through weighted voting, participants can show the relative value that they place on different issues. They can show that they feel more strongly about some concerns than about others.

Purpose. Weighted voting provides a measure of the relative importance placed on various items by individuals and groups.

When to Use. Weighted voting can be used when "not all items are created equal" in the eyes of the participants. If a participant in the color-coding activity had said, "Can I put all my five dots on just one thing?" it would have been a signal that weighted voting could be used.

Who to Involve. The same persons who would have been part of the other priority-setting activities would also be involved in weighted voting. This process is particularly appropriate when the participants will bear primary responsibility for the tasks that are identified. It gives them a greater opportunity to determine where they will invest their energies.

Materials Needed. The facilitator will need chart paper, markers, and tape. Each participant will need a predetermined number of dots, stickers, or labels, but they may all be the same color.

Tips for Facilitators. Start by having participants brainstorm the issues to be addressed or the tasks to be done, in the same way that the nominal group process began. As in color coding, the participants have five dots or stickers. The uniqueness of weighted voting is that participants may distribute their five dots (or votes) in any combination. If they feel that one item is crucial for immediate attention, they can use all five of their dots to indicate its importance. If they want to be sure that attention is given to two items, they may use two dots for one and three for the other. Depending on the number of participants and the length of the brainstormed list, the facilitator may allocate more or fewer than five votes per participant.

For Example: Making the Workshop Work. They had been teaching all day, it was hot, and the room had no windows. Because of budget cuts, the schools were not allowed to hire subs for professional development activities, so we were going to meet from 4:00 to 7:00 on three consecutive evenings. It was precious time, and the people donating it to learn how to function as a school leadership team were precious, too. Meeting their needs and making the content relevant were essential—but it was clear that they came with a range of expectations so varied that it could not possibly be addressed in 9 hours of less-than-prime learning time. The challenge was to focus the agenda in some way that would clearly show respect for their time and priorities. Knowing that we could not include them all, we listed the topics they had anticipated and gave five stars to each participant. As they left the first evening session, they placed their stars on the list to express their priorities. The results looked like this:

Selecting strategies related to curriculum	****************
Process used to develop implementation plan	*******************************
Timelines	*********
Moving from departmentalized to multidisciplinary	********
Team skills	*****************************
Strengthening our belief system	************
How to use data in decision making	******************
Ways to gather data	******************************
Motivating students with no role models or hope	**
	**
Difference between making easy and hard changes	**********
How to avoid bandwagons	******************
Difference between school improvement and strategic planning	***

It was clear that the strongest interest of the participants related to student motivation, which was no part of the planned training. Fortunately, the next set of priorities (development of action plans combined with timelines, teamwork skills, and gathering and using data) was part of the planned agenda. I was able to focus on those topics while having my materials on student motivation express mailed to me for the last session. Participation in the weighted voting activity created a high level of commitment that overcame the poor timing and conditions. Because participants could see the needs expressed by the whole group, those whose topics were omitted understood and accepted that result.

One comment on the evaluation sheet read, "This is the first time I've felt like I had some control over what we did in a workshop. I didn't mind the evenings, because I was getting what I came for." One way to turn ramblers into travelers is by using group process techniques to help them shape their own destination as you address the question "Where do we want to go?"

Priority Grid

Tools for prioritizing concerns presented in this section ranged from the complex nominal group process to fairly simple techniques of color coding and weighted voting. Another straightforward, objective way of establishing priorities is use of the priority grid.

Purpose. The priority grid captures a list of items in no particular order of significance and without any attempt to categorize. Each item is rated against every other individual item to provide a tally of preferences.

When to Use. The priority grid can be useful when time is limited, since it can proceed directly after a brainstorming exercise has generated a list of factors. Because it is simple and mathematical, it can also be valuable for a group in which participants have strong emotional connections to some of the items listed.

Who to Involve. At minimum, every individual who has generated any of the items being rated should be involved in completing the priority grid. This is automatic if the priority grid immediately follows brainstorming, as all the individuals are in the room. However, the priority grid may also be used after items have been contributed for consideration by several groups at different times. In this case, the priority grid should be made available to all of those original groups, and their results should be counted in the final numerical analysis.

Materials Needed. A copy of the priority grid (see Figure 3.1) is needed for each participant. If the priority grid is being used immediately after a brainstorming exercise, the items do not have to be listed on the form itself. They may be posted on chart paper and clearly numbered so that participants can refer to the chart to make their comparisons. In situations where items being prioritized were gathered from multiple sources and the priority grid will be used more than once before a final tally, the items should be listed right on the priority grid, as shown in Figure 3.2.

Figure 3.1 Priority Grid

Start Here

		1															
1	2	**2**															
1	2	3	**3**														
1	2	3	4	**4**													
1	2	3	4	5	**5**												
1	2	3	4	5	6	**6**											
1	2	3	4	5	6	7	**7**										
1	2	3	4	5	6	7	8	**8**									
1	2	3	4	5	6	7	8	9	**9**								
1	2	3	4	5	6	7	8	9	10	**10**							
1	2	3	4	5	6	7	8	9	10	11	**11**						
1	2	3	4	5	6	7	8	9	10	11	12	**12**					
1	2	3	4	5	6	7	8	9	10	11	12	13	**13**				
1	2	3	4	5	6	7	8	9	10	11	12	13	14	**14**			
1	2	3	4	5	6	7	8	9	10	11	12	13	14	15	**15**		
1	2	3	4	5	6	7	8	9	10	11	12	13	14	15	16	**16**	
1	2	3	4	5	6	7	8	9	10	11	12	13	14	15	16	17	**17**
1	2	3	4	5	6	7	8	9	10	11	12	13	14	15	16	17	18

TOTALS

1	2	3	4	5	6	7	8	9	10	11	12	13	14	15	16	17	18

Figure 3.2   Priority Grid: Design Features for New School

Start Here

1. Maximum of 500—big enough for two neighborhoods but no extra
2. Combine traits of both schools—arched windows, two colors of bricks
3. More small rooms for tutoring and small groups—four, not just two
4. Display of framed pictures of both schools and the original factory
5. Parent room near library, gym, and cafeteria
6. Gym to open out to hard surface and grass area
7. Self-contained Special Education rooms near office
8. Gym and cafeteria next to each other
9. Separate playgrounds for older and younger students
10. Space to create murals in the future
11. Storage area for laptops on carts
12. Built-in audio system in gym
13. Storage in art and music rooms
14. One computer lab on each floor
15. Area for afterschool program
16. Large open space in front
17. Lockers, not hooks
18. Natural light

Paired-comparison grid (each numbered feature at left is compared against each higher-numbered feature across the top):

Row 1: 1 paired with 2, 3, 4, 5, 6, 7, 8, 9, 10, 11, 12, 13, 14, 15, 16, 17, 18
Row 2: 2 paired with 3, 4, 5, 6, 7, 8, 9, 10, 11, 12, 13, 14, 15, 16, 17, 18
Row 3: 3 paired with 4, 5, 6, 7, 8, 9, 10, 11, 12, 13, 14, 15, 16, 17, 18
Row 4: 4 paired with 5, 6, 7, 8, 9, 10, 11, 12, 13, 14, 15, 16, 17, 18
Row 5: 5 paired with 6, 7, 8, 9, 10, 11, 12, 13, 14, 15, 16, 17, 18
Row 6: 6 paired with 7, 8, 9, 10, 11, 12, 13, 14, 15, 16, 17, 18
Row 7: 7 paired with 8, 9, 10, 11, 12, 13, 14, 15, 16, 17, 18
Row 8: 8 paired with 9, 10, 11, 12, 13, 14, 15, 16, 17, 18
Row 9: 9 paired with 10, 11, 12, 13, 14, 15, 16, 17, 18
Row 10: 10 paired with 11, 12, 13, 14, 15, 16, 17, 18
Row 11: 11 paired with 12, 13, 14, 15, 16, 17, 18
Row 12: 12 paired with 13, 14, 15, 16, 17, 18
Row 13: 13 paired with 14, 15, 16, 17, 18
Row 14: 14 paired with 15, 16, 17, 18
Row 15: 15 paired with 16, 17, 18
Row 16: 16 paired with 17, 18
Row 17: 17 paired with 18

TOTALS

1	2	3	4	5	6	7	8	9	10	11	12	13	14	15	16	17	18

70

Tips for Facilitators. Items or topics for consideration are assigned numbers. Participants consider each item against every other item as a one-to-one comparison and circle their preference. For example, moving down Column 1, the first item is compared to every other item on the list. If Item 1 is the preference, the number 1 is circled. If the other item is a higher priority, that number is circled. The total at the bottom is the number of times that Item 1 was preferred in comparison to any other item being considered.

For Example: Design Features for a New School. Two aging school buildings had passed the time when upgrades and renovations would be cost-effective. The two existing facilities would no longer be used, and the two staff and student populations would be merged into one and begin operation in a brand-new facility on a new site. An advisory committee had been asked for a prioritized list of features they would like to see in the new school. Their "wish list" was diverse, as shown by the items listed on Figure 3.2.

They needed to be prioritized, so the architect and contractor would know which were most critical to include in the design of the new building. Committee members had strong preferences and emotional ties to some features, so it was important to utilize a very objective, mathematical process.

ARTICULATING GOALS

The No Child Left Behind version of the Elementary and Secondary Education Act has resulted in mandated goals based on calculations of the amount of gain needed each year in order to reach the target of 100% of students scored as proficient by the year 2014. These needed gains are described as "adequate yearly progress" (AYP), and failure to achieve them results in various degrees of punishment, depending on the number of years the school or district has fallen short. Although states have found some ways to ameliorate the impact by pointing out the statistical reality of confidence intervals and creating "safe harbors" for schools making progress toward the AYP targets, more and more schools and districts are being labeled as unsuccessful.

In spite of these mandated goals—or perhaps even more because of the external punitive approach threatened for failure to meet them—it is essential to conduct goal setting as an internal, intrinsic activity. O'Neill and Conzemius (2006) stress the importance of SMART goals, recommending that they be Strategic and specific, Measurable, Attainable, Results-based, and Time bound. I continue to be concerned about local definitions of what is "attainable," because I have seen so many examples of weak goals that represent little challenge, indicate almost no commitment to equity, and simply reinforce low expectations for some groups of students in particular. Challenging goals must fall somewhere between what "feels OK" to keepers of the status quo and unrealistic mandates from a far-away federal government.

The three main points about goal setting that remain firm in my mind are these:

1. Goals must be challenging.

2. Goals must be limited in number.

3. Goals must include some that will focus *direct attention* on classroom practice.

There are two appropriate tests for whether goals are challenging but not totally out of reach. One would be a statistical test. Any goal that is set in terms of a small percentage of increase should be subjected to a test of whether that degree of change would even merit the description of statistically significant. Another test of challenge would be a comparison of the school's (or district's) performance against top-performing schools of similar demographics. If the desired level of achievement has already been met by others who face the same challenges, it must certainly fall within the definition of "do-able"—it's been done.

Goals must also be limited in number and include attention to teaching and learning. Some years ago, I observed that plans from schools that were making progress rarely included more than 5–6 goals, and at least two of those were directly linked to academic achievement. My more recent learning that the brain may readily retrieve a maximum of 5–7 bits of information, makes it clear that we must limit our focus to a number of efforts that the mind can recall.

Although it may seem obvious that goals should include a focus on teaching and learning, I have reviewed too many improvement plans to omit stating that obvious concept directly. Some school improvement plans have been totally based on goals related to factors like behavior and discipline, staff morale and communication, parent involvement, and increased use of technology, with no mention at all of student learning. When the plan creators later complain that "we worked so hard on our plan, and we checked off all of our action steps, but student achievement didn't change," I find it hard to sympathize. It has to be there in the first place.

Although I'm aware of the dangers of oversimplifying complex concepts and processes, and avoid it whenever possible, I've seen groups get stuck on how to write their goals. When pressed, I have shared the following:

By _____ (time), _____ (quantity) of students will _____ as measured by
_____.

Using the word *students* right in the goal statement greatly increases the focus on student learning as the measurable outcome (end) for which all other goals and strategies are the means.

VISUALIZING THE
CULTURE OF COLLABORATION

In *Leadership and Sustainability*, Michael Fullan (2005) emphasizes the need to focus on the "moral purpose" underlying the work of educators at all levels. He defines moral purpose as having three dimensions:

1. Commitment to raising the bar and closing the gap of student achievement for all individuals and schools;

2. Commitment to treat people ethically—adults and students alike (which does not mean being soft . . .), and

3. Commitment to improving the whole district, not just one's own school. (p. 68)

When schools are deciding "where we want to go," they need to include discussion of the ways they want to interact on the journey. In Chapter 2, readers were challenged to analyze the current culture and context in which they work. The Colorado high school's struggle to restructure its internal design for decision making was provided as an example of a school that realized right away that the current structure was a barrier in and of itself. In this section, the challenge is to look ahead to a preferred or desired future of collaboration. External shareholders (parents and community) are omitted from this section because the focus is on educators working together at the classroom, school, and district level. The chapter ends with a "picture" (Figure 3.4) of collaboration at all three levels.

Teaming Structures

The affinity process was introduced at the beginning of this chapter. Bold print identified roles for a leadership team, small groups of staff, and the whole group of all staff. This is one way of structuring the work to complete a specific task—developing the mission statement—or structuring the roles and responsibilities for the complete school improvement process. The opening and closing of an accordion was presented as a metaphor for making sure that opportunities for input and involvement are available to all within the school, especially at key decision points. Linda Lambert (2003) emphasizes the importance of teachers as the heart of the "high leadership capacity school." She eloquently points out that

> Teachers who exhibit vitality are energized by their own curiosities, their colleagues, and their students; they find joy and stimulation in the daily dilemmas of teaching and are intrigued by the challenge of improving adult learning communities. Teachers become fully alive when their schools and districts provide them with opportunities for skillful participation, inquiry, dialogue, and reflection. . . . Because teachers represent the largest and most constant group of professionals in schools and districts, their full participation in the work of leadership is necessary for high leadership capacity. (p. 32)

Lambert (2003) goes on to describe participation patterns that range from the general faculty meeting to a variety of team structures (pp. 13–16). These include the leadership team, also referred to as the site-management team, plus study groups, action research teams, vertical learning communities, the vision team, and curriculum teams, Some of these structures are described more fully in Chapter 6 of this volume. The important focus of discussion at this time is "where do we want to go" with our school's culture and structure so they facilitate and model the kinds of interaction and learning that we want to see with students.

Norm Setting

Fullan's (2003) description of moral purpose (stated above) included a commitment to treating people ethically. In other writing about moral purpose, he used the words "treating people with demanding respect." Such a phrase is an example of words we often take at face value, without exploring the specific ways individuals may interpret them. Some readers will hear the "demanding" resonate loudly, while others will focus on the softer "respect," and the combination may not mean the same to all members of the same group. Assumptions about common understanding can be disastrous later on, so it's important to establish specific norms for any group that will work together regularly over a period of time.

Purpose. Norm setting creates common expectations for how group members will treat each other as individuals and work together as a group.

When to Use. Conducting a norm-setting activity or discussion may become meaningless if regarded as a "hoop to jump through" every time a group is assembled. It should primarily be used with groups or teams who will meet regularly over a period of time and have a charge to accomplish. Since these are the kinds of groups that may encounter stress and frustration, they are the ones who will most need a previously agreed upon set of norms for reference and resolution.

Who to Involve. All members of the group, but *only* members of the group, should establish the norms by which they will conduct themselves. A facilitator may be very helpful but must maintain a neutral role.

Materials Needed. The simple approach of public recording with markers on chart paper is adequate. In some cases, the process of norm setting may need to be guided or informed through use of examples, as described below. In this situation, a handout of material for reading and reference would be useful.

Tips for Facilitators. In most settings, norms can easily be identified from the knowledge and understandings of the group. If the group is large, it can be divided into smaller groups and a Think, Pair, Share format can enable participants to reflect on their previous experiences in groups and generate characteristics of successful teams that they would emulate. If the group is less than

10 people, this can be done as a whole group. All of the contributions from individuals or subgroups are considered, and a small number (approximately 6–8) are selected. If the initial list of suggestions is lengthy, similar items could be clustered as in an affinity process, and then common wording could be selected. General wording of norms, such as "be respectful to each other," may need more specific wording to make the expectation more clear. "No interrupting" is an example of such a specific, concrete example of respect. Norm-setting discussions are often simple and straightforward, resulting in a list of items written on chart paper. Although meeting notes may later be recorded electronically, saving the original charts and posting them at each meeting until they become tattered and torn provides valuable evidence of group members' commitments to each other and increases continuity and consistency.

In some situations, past negative history or mistrust may make it difficult to generate authentic responses when participants are asked to suggest norms for the group. An alternative is to create a shared base of knowledge and experience by introducing content about norms and examples for discussion. I recommend and use the following seven norms of an adaptive school from Bob Garmston's (Garmston & Wellman, 1999) work:

1. Pausing

2. Paraphrasing

3. Probing for specificity

4. Putting ideas on the table

5. Paying attention to self and others

6. Presuming positive intentions

7. Pursuing a balance between advocacy and inquiry (p. 37)

In some cases, discussion about "someone else's" set of norms is safer for individuals than volunteering their own desires. The discussion may even provide an opportunity to surface and heal pain from previous interactions. With some rewording, these norms can be accepted by all members of the group. However, the terms may mislead by their simple wording, because the concepts are complex, and skillful use takes practice. Training or reading Garmston's material will be needed to assure that these norms are really understood by all and that skill in their use will continue to develop.

Once norms are accepted, the group must also deal with the issue of what ought to happen when one of the norms is violated. In a healthy environment, the answer is usually, "we'll just say the number [of the norm on the chart], and people will get the point." Sometimes a good-natured penalty may be assigned. A recent United Way drive in one school district was supplemented with additional revenue thanks to a penalty of $5 per cell phone ring heard in administrative meetings. Sometimes an uneasy group will ask the facilitator to "remind us when we're not sticking to it." Eventually, group members become comfortable enough to pick up that role on their own.

For Example: The Honors Criteria Committee. It seemed that it would be a short-term ad hoc group. Nine high school administrators and central office staff were gathered "just" to resolve three questions that had been identified the previous spring and held over for "immediate" action the following school year. The first step I proposed was to gather the information that would be needed from each school. When "past Board reports on Honors courses" was added to the list of needed information, it became quickly apparent that the group was not going to be content with the limited scope of answering the three questions. And when some voices started rising above and cutting off others, I realized that this was going to be more complex than I had anticipated. The next day, I received an e-mail from one member of the group that verified my thinking: "I appreciate that you noticed I was getting cut off and you kept coming back to me so I could say what I wanted, but I think we are going to need some norms for future meetings."

I certainly agreed, and our first activity at the next meeting was brainstorming norms. The expanded scope of work that was identified provided an easy explanation as to why we had not done this at the first meeting, but were taking time to do it now. And so far the following meetings have been polite and productive. I'm not making any hard and fast predictions about how soon the new and expanded scope of work will be accomplished, but we are staying friends and having more fun because we took time to set some norms.

Team Accountability

Probably the most frequently asked question in any of my workshops is "How do you find time?" Based on that observation, I would venture that time for teamwork is the scarcest resource in the educational setting—and that leads to the need for assurance that the time is spent well and leads to results that benefit staff and students. As Lambert (2003) points out, "Discussion during unskilled collaborative time tends to focus on two main topics: individual problem students and instructional materials and activities" (p. 21). She goes on to describe an elementary school where

> teachers take turns leading teams and all-staff professional development sessions in discussions of teaching practices and student work. Every time the teams meet, they complete a communiqué that informs the school of their activities, needs, and accomplishments. Teachers learn to facilitate different teams and capture the key ideas of each session for the school community. (p. 21)

Figure 3.3 (from Holcomb, 2004) provides a template for similar communication of results from the group as information for the entire school. A school in western Washington used five clipboards hung on nails in the teachers' lounge to provide transparency for the ongoing work of teams in their school. After each meeting, the team put their quickly summarized notes on their clipboard, and any staff member or visitor could readily observe the topics being discussed and the progress of the teamwork that was occurring.

Figure 3.3   Team Report Form

Team Meeting Date: _____

Your Representative: _____

Members Present:

_____   _____   _____

_____   _____   _____

_____   _____   _____

Goals for This Meeting

-
-
-
-

I. Issues Discussed

   (For each issue, use bullets for main points and asterisk the input you provided from your grade/department.)

II. Decisions Made

   (List each decision, who will be affected, when it will take effect.)

III. Tasks Accomplished

   (List project, process, or product completed and how it will be distributed and used.)

IV. Next Steps and Meeting Date
   -
   -
   -
   -

V. Input Needed

   (For each topic, include method for input and deadline.)

SOURCE: Adapted from *Getting Excited About Data* (p. 45), by E. L. Holcomb, 1999, Thousand Oaks, CA: Corwin Press. Copyright © 1999 by Corwin Press. Used with permission.

A View of the District

A respected colleague challenged me at the break during a workshop on using data to maximize student learning. Her words were crisp and biting.

> The *state* has been hitting us with standards and assessments and test data and accountability goals. So we've been spending hours and hours and all our staff development money at the *district* getting our curriculum aligned and checking our course outlines and writing performance assessments to be sure our students are ready. Now you're just talking about *school* improvement and how real change has to happen at the *school* level. Are you saying we've spent the last 2 years doing the wrong things? What about all our hard work already?

Her sincere question cut right through me as I recognized my teaching error. By what I had left unsaid, I had conveyed the impression of an either/or relationship between school and district leadership in change. The truth is that both are essential. Too much emphasis on either the school or district is problematic, and lack of clarity about "who does what" is one of the biggest barriers to forward movement and systemic thinking.

Creating the proper balance is elusive. The most recent issue of *Education Week* (vol. 27, no. 13) carried two back-to-back articles—one with an update on New York City returning "more power to schools" (Olson, 2007), and the other explaining "why we need district-based reform" (Supovitz, 2007). The first article described the intent of the move, but also reported on some down sides. Jacquelyn Ancess of Teachers College pointed out that "one would have difficulty finding fault with the ideas behind this," and "for principals who are strong instructional leaders, this is a good thing" (p. 25), but cautioned that there are no safeguards preventing poor decisions. For example, one school went through five math programs in 3 years trying to find the best one.

The president of the Council of School Supervisors and Administrators sees some principals taking advantage of the autonomy: "Some people who have been very good at getting what they wanted anyway are still getting it, and more. Those who were not as astute at making the system work for them are still having some of the same problems" (p. 24). And the threat of progress reports in the form of letter grades for schools has deflected the focus. As the chairwoman of the New York Performance Standards Consortium states, "There's not a lot of emphasis on instruction. Everybody is waiting for the ax to fall" (p. 26).

I strongly believe that there are systemwide strategies that should be activated to provide economies of scale and thereby accelerate the school-level work and improve its positive impact on student learning. Supovitz (2007) lists six of these:

- Develop a clear vision of instructional quality in the major content areas.
- Balance persuasive and coercive methods of influence to build systemwide commitment to the instructional vision.

- Build capacity through employee development at all levels of the organization.
- Marshal external resources.
- Use data formatively to inform both individual decisions about students and programmatic decisions.
- Develop strategies to sustain reform efforts over longer periods of time. (pp. 27–28)

The easiest way I can explain what should be done at which level is through this commonsense summary:

> If an individual teacher can not make the change in isolation, it must be addressed by the grade level or department. If a small group of teachers cannot make a needed change because of factors beyond their control (e.g., master schedule, schoolwide discipline procedures), then the issue must be resolved through a schoolwide process and plan. If an individual school cannot make a change (e.g., it would violate school board policy), then the conversation must occur at the district level.

That summary is based solely on adults. Another way to discuss "what should be done at which level" is to think about students and their families. If a change in any classroom-level or school-level action or practice represents the potential for negative impact on continuous learning and smooth transitions for students, it needs to be discussed at a higher level.

THE PICTURE OF COLLABORATION AT ALL THREE LEVELS

These issues of "what should be done at what level" relate directly to the concept of organizational reciprocity. Lambert (2003) describes "a dynamic of mutual responsibility characterized by shared vision, leadership, learning, expectations, and resources" (p. 84). She maintains that this is distinctly different from the typical either/or implied in the term "loose/tight" where "loose" refers to decentralization and "tight" refers to decisions held at the district level. I agree. After struggling with language like "loose/tight," and "bottom-up" versus "top-down," I now feel most comfortable talking about "in-out" and have tried to illustrate my thinking in Figure 3.4.

By "in," I mean the most intimate relationship in our educational environment, which is that between teacher and student. The body of evidence on teacher quality is now so strong that it cannot be ignored. Nothing matters as much as the relationship between teacher and student and the effectiveness of the teacher's instructional and assessment practices. The inner group of characters in Figure 3.4 represents a classroom of smaller figures (students) and more than one adult. The classroom level of collaboration includes how students work together and how adults interact. Marzano's (2001) meta-analysis of the nine most powerful teaching strategies includes cooperative

Figure 3.4 Three Levels of Collaboration

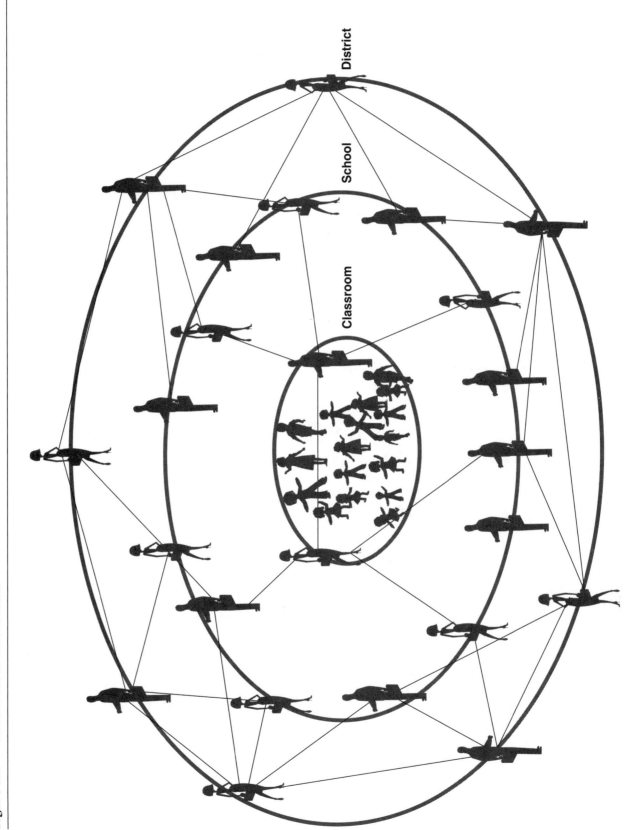

District

School

Classroom

learning, implying that collaboration between and among students is a powerful contributor to learning. Philosophies of inclusion and the introduction of "response to interventions" (RtI) as a feature of the most recent special education law, coupled with the increasing numbers of English Language Learners, increase the obvious need for collaboration between the classroom teacher and other educators with various areas of expertise. In Figure 3.4, the line between the adults in the classroom represents that important collaboration.

Moving "out" from the teachers and students, another set of adult figures surrounds the classroom. They represent the school as a whole. Lines in the figure represent their collaboration at the grade, department, and school level.

Farther "out," surrounding the school, there is a set of fewer figures that represents the district. Lines connect the figures to each other. Other lines from district-level staff to school-level educators represent the reality that teacher leaders in the same building have contact with a variety of district-level personnel and that district-level leaders have contact with multiple schools. School-based staff know their own school best. District-based professionals may have a better grasp of the systemwide impact and issues involved in school recommendations and priorities. District administrators must also work collaboratively so that school staff hear the same messages, regardless of which district leader is working with them.

When Michael Fullan discusses *Leadership and Sustainability* (2005), he reminds us that

> capacity building throughout the system at all levels must be developed in concert. . . . Finally, for the system as a whole to change . . . you must have school and district leaders who are committed to interacting laterally with other schools and districts in order to learn from each other. (p. 11)

Answer Key

- Answering the "Where do we want to go?" question requires three major tasks: affirming the mission, articulating goals, and visualizing the culture and structure for collaboration.

- Don't get hung up on the term "mission statement" if it prompts less-than-enthusiastic reactions. Other terms may be used. What's critical is the discussion and process that lead to written statements that become the parameters for what's acceptable, what's not acceptable, and what the overarching purpose is for all processes and decisions.

- The affinity process is useful for writing, revising, or affirming mission statements. Remember to take both a horizontal and vertical look at Figure 1.2. You will see other techniques that can be used for identifying and focusing on organizational values, as well as other times when you can utilize the affinity process.

- Don't leap to goals too soon. First gather and honor the concerns of all shareholders. Then, use one of the group process tools to prioritize them.

- If an individual or group of shareholders expresses strong sentiment about concern(s) that do not wind up as priority goals, be sure to follow up with them and assure that they see how the school or district will respond.

- Goals must be challenging, limited in number, and must include a direct focus on classroom practice.

- Studying and planning for each of the priority goals will require collaborative work. Pay specific attention to structures and norms that are embedded in the culture. They may need explicit attention.

- Leadership roles and relationships may need clarification. Be sure to include teacher leadership as one of the levels in those discussions.

4

Answering the "How Will We Get There?" Question

You may have heard the old saw about how to identify the "big wheels" in an organization. They're the ones who are always going in circles.

Too many school change efforts go nowhere because the leaders confuse choosing the destination or goal with having a plan. Although change processes must be flexible enough and adjusted often enough to be evolutionary, the initial implementation plan must be specific enough to let everyone know what's expected—and be revolutionary.

Development of a plan or map for the journey blends planning, training, and implementation aspects of the RPTIM model, shown in Figure 1.2. Training is needed in *how* to plan, and the plan itself will identify needs for *more* training about best practices and how to implement appropriate strategies. In the Three I's model, this phase includes implementation of the school change process itself, within which specific strategies are identified and initiated. In the PDCA cycle of quality management, answering the "How will we get there?" question is the planning stage.

Addressing the "How will we get there?" question requires organizations to be honest about why they are not there yet. The "Study" box before "Strategies" in Figure 1.1 emphasizes the need for thoughtful analysis and new learning before leaping straight into action. The three points in the "Study" stage represent three types of inquiry:

- Deeper analysis of data related to the priority concerns that were articulated as goals

- Study of relevant research and best practices in other schools and districts
- Further study of the school's practices and local factors related to the goal

The tools in this chapter include a cause-and-effect diagram and force field analysis for exploration of these local factors. Advance organizers are introduced that help a school analyze its programs, and a flowchart guides discussion of school and district roles in improving student achievement.

For any problem, there are multiple solutions, and organizations such as schools that have limited resources and high visibility need to choose those most likely to produce the intended results. Use of a decision matrix improves choices of strategies. Development of the action plan for each new strategy is relatively simple in concept but requires discipline and perseverance to work out the specific steps needed, decide who will be involved and who will take primary responsibility, align the resources that will be needed, and project a timeline that keeps things within the scope of "humanly possible."

In the classroom, we know that we must make thorough lesson plans yet be willing to surrender them to the teachable moment. In the same way, we must make careful and complete plans for school change, pursue them with power and passion, yet hold them lightly enough so we can monitor and adjust as we go.

DIG INTO THE DATA

Deeper analysis of data is represented by the first bullet point in the "Study" box related to each priority goal in Figure 1.1. This step includes a more detailed analysis of the student achievement data, as well as a careful review of other sources of data for clues about related factors and possible strategies. The next section provides questions with which to query the student performance data. Then, three examples describe what school teams learned when they took a second look at data on instructional time, discipline problems, and the needs of homeless students. Pie charts and Pareto charts are introduced here but can obviously be used in the initial School Portfolio. They are described in detail in this chapter because they provide such relevant examples of further study to guide the choice of strategies for change. The "fishbone" story later in this chapter provides an example of how a more in-depth analysis of individual data can change the direction of a planning process.

Query the Student Performance Data

Chapter 2 provided tools and examples for displaying student performance data so discussion can raise awareness of concerns and lead to priorities in goal setting. But data become powerful information only when analyzed through the right lenses and over time. Important decisions should be made on the basis of multiple measures over multiple years, not based on a single snapshot of performance on a single instrument. When individual teachers, professional learning groups, school improvement teams, or entire school faculties examine data, they should be looking for answers to questions about specific skills and specific students:

- In which strands (standards or skills) are students making the most progress? Some progress?
- In which strands do many students have ongoing challenges?
- Which strands (standards or skills) do we consider most critical for long-term success in school and beyond?
- Do all of our student groups show evidence of the progress we're making? If not, describe the differences.
- Do all of our student groups experience the same challenges? If not, describe the differences.

In areas where the vast majority of students of all kinds have made progress, celebration should be rowdy and raucous. In the areas where all or many students have struggled, instructional programs and curriculum should be examined. In the areas where individual students and subgroups have had varied success, strategies that provide additional support will be needed.

Pie Charts

A pie chart is a way to display data that is easy to understand and interpret. Like the histogram, it can be used in the initial School Portfolio to answer the "Where are we now?" question. It can also be used in a further study of local factors and added to the School Portfolio at that time.

Purpose. The pie chart is particularly useful for demonstrating how a resource is used. Time, money, materials, and personnel are resources that must be used efficiently to help schools be as effective as possible in serving students and their communities.

When to Use. Pie charts can be useful to describe how a resource is apportioned for various uses. It can also show how students are divided into various groups, courses, or activities.

Who to Involve. The important aspect of involvement with any use of data is that those who are part of the situation being analyzed must be included in both gathering the information initially and then analyzing and interpreting it. When people are directly involved in collecting the data, they are much more likely to accept the results as an accurate representation of their situation.

Materials Needed. Developing the pie chart can easily be done by any individual using paper and pencil or software graphics.

Tips for Facilitators. Pie charts work best when there are a limited number of slices in the pie. If a resource is divided into so many uses that the pie has numerous slivers, the pie chart will not be as effective in delivering the information at a glance, and another type of graph or table should be used.

For Example: Instructional Time. The pie chart in Figure 4.1 illustrates the use of an important resource—instructional time. Students were observed in classrooms, and their behavior was tallied as interactive, noninteractive, or off-task. With few words of explanation, it is easy to see that students were actively engaged more than half the time but were passive receivers almost one third of the time and off task 13% of their time in class.

Pareto Charts

Pareto charts (named for Italian economist Vilfredo Pareto) can be constructed to break down a major problem into more specific causes. School leaders then have a range of options to consider as they identify "where to start" to improve the situation.

Purpose. A Pareto chart can be used when many factors are involved in a situation and you need to know which to address first. A Pareto chart is a form of vertical bar graph. Its unique feature is that it presents items in order of frequency so that a group can deal with "first things first."

When to Use. A Pareto chart may be helpful after a survey or focus group has been conducted and a wide range of problems have been generated or recommendations have been proposed. A Pareto chart can also display data on aspects of student behavior, such as various causes of student absences.

Who to Involve. A Pareto chart can be constructed by one person. Discussion of what the data mean and what to do about them should involve representatives

Figure 4.1   Pie Chart of Student Instructional Time Audit

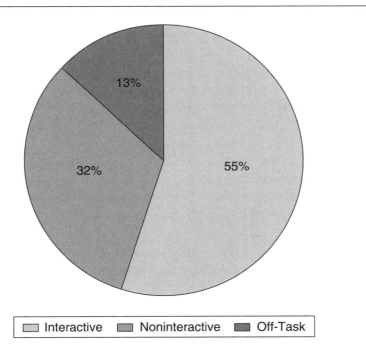

Interactive   Noninteractive   Off-Task

of those who provided the data (such as survey respondents) and those who have responsibility for the factors described in the data.

Materials Needed. A Pareto chart can be constructed using the data with paper and pencil or computer software.

80/20

Tips for Facilitators. Like any graph, a Pareto chart has horizontal and vertical axes that must be clearly labeled. Sometimes data have identified a problem but provide no information on probable causes or related factors. It may be necessary to brainstorm what these causes or factors are and gather another set of data. On the Pareto chart, the results are displayed like a bar graph or histogram but with the factors placed in descending order of frequency.

In most cases, efforts toward improvement should begin with the factors that have the tallest bars. The "Pareto Principle" or "80/20 Principle" (Koch, 1998) expresses the hypothesis that "a minority of causes, inputs, or effort usually leads to a majority of the results, outputs or rewards" (p. 25). Based on this principle, energy would be misspent dealing with low-frequency causes, since removing two or three of the high-frequency causes would eliminate most of the problem. Common sense must prevail, however. If even a small percentage of cases is caused by some factor that is dangerous or may have legal ramifications, those situations must be addressed immediately.

For Example: Student Discipline. Staff members at one school were concerned about the number of students sent to the office for disciplinary reasons. They wondered whether student behavior was getting worse, whether the offenses actually merited the principal's attention, and what relationship there might be to the new discipline policy that had been developed the summer before. They analyzed the reasons stated on the "pink slips" that students carried with them to the office and constructed the Pareto chart in Figure 4.2.

First, they noticed that the greatest number of discipline referrals was related to violating school rules outlined in their new policy. This discovery led them to reconsider the consequences in the policy and build in more responsibility at the classroom level before sending students out of the room. They also acknowledged that they could have been more conscientious about teaching the new rules to students and communicating them to parents.

The second bar on the Pareto chart prompted a decision to provide classroom management training for teachers, to help them be more proactive in preventing classroom disruptions in the first place. By the time they got to the third bar, they discovered that the cause they were most worried about (physical violence) was not the most frequent problem, and when they compared it with previous years, fighting had not increased at all.

Note that 880 discipline occurrences were analyzed altogether. Addressing just the first two causes would affect about half (441) of the incidents analyzed, validating the premise of the Pareto principle. Without the Pareto chart, school staff might have worked hard to reduce fighting—certainly a valid effort—but with far less success at reducing the sheer number of students standing in line at the office.

Figure 4.2   Pareto Chart of Student Discipline

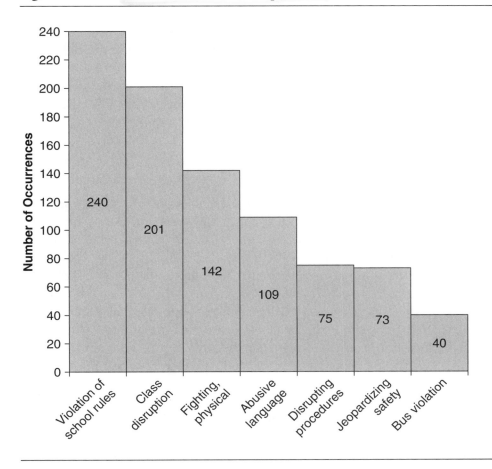

A Variation: Homeless Students. Teachers from a middle school in a deteriorating section of the city were attending a graduate course on total quality improvement. Their assignment was to work as a quality improvement team on a problem within their school. They had become concerned about the number of transient students who were housed in homeless shelters within their attendance area, and they decided to make that issue a focus of their study. Caring members of the staff had begun trying to find clothing for the students and made other efforts to help them but felt frustrated and overwhelmed. They didn't think that the school could function as a social service agency, but they were aware of the economic realities of these children.

To gather data for their project, the graduate students decided to conduct private interviews with the homeless students who were now attending the school, to find out what they most wanted. They particularly anticipated responses such as clothing and social acceptance and feared that they would get requests they would not be able to do anything about. When they came to the next class, they were carrying a Pareto chart and wearing expressions of amazement and chagrin. The tallest bar on their Pareto chart identified a perceived need for security guards. These students had moved away from a major inner-city area where crime was rampant, and they felt insecure in an environment that did not have guards as a visible presence. The second-tallest bar amazed them. These homeless students indicated that they needed the school to provide "help with our class work" much more than any of the things the adults thought they would want. Teachers who had been saying, "We're a school, we're here to teach, we can't be a social service agency" discovered that kids felt the same way. They wanted to be taught. The quality improvement project shifted focus from "We're not social workers" to "How can we quickly diagnose their skill levels and provide basic instruction that will move them forward, even if they are with us only a short time?"

STUDY RELEVANT RESEARCH

Chapter 3 emphasized the importance of shareholder involvement that builds commitment around goals that are supported by data and closely reflect the core values of the organization. How demoralizing it is, then, when strategies are selected by brainstorming on the basis of existing knowledge, are implemented without learning from other sites, and end up failing to produce the intended results.

Once the goals have been established, study groups (also called subcommittees, task forces, etc.) should be formed to investigate the situation thoroughly and bring forward recommendations for the strategies or interventions to be implemented. Three important areas of study are research, best practice, and deeper analysis of the current situation.

Others may have a different set of definitions, but I distinguish research from best practices in this way: *Research* is the body of literature that represents current theory and findings from studies conducted by people who are full-time scholars, not practitioners. For example, neurolinguistic science and brain research include theory and investigations that we should be following closely. New discoveries about language acquisition are important if we're concerned about development of reading skills or the arrival of students learning English as a second language. *Best practices* are those identified through formal studies, informal action research, or networking among colleagues. When a school improvement team identifies the highest-performing schools with similar demographics and visits or consults with them to determine what has made them successful, it is zeroing in on best practices.

If we have goals related to students' behavior and social development or character development, we should become knowledgeable about the literature on resiliency and the studies about youth assets. But in this particular context, what I classify as research provides only information. It may define the "what" and may suggest some "shoulds," but this type of research doesn't—and wasn't designed to—answer the educators' all-important question of "how." To move from information to application, we have to connect with those who have begun to put the research into practice.

EXPLORE BEST PRACTICES

Where do collaborative teams of teachers look for best practices? The answer is anywhere and everywhere! They read and discuss books and professional journals. They search the Internet. They attend conferences and workshops. They belong to professional associations. And they visit other schools that are having outstanding success. (Eaker et al., 2002, p. 20)

Exploring best practices sounds simple—but it comes with a price tag. It means that teachers reach out to other teachers, schools reach out to other schools, and districts reach out to other districts. It requires us to admit to other people that we don't have all the answers and that—although we're doing a good job—we want to do even better than we are presently.

School leaders and shareholders will have more and more creative ideas, but here are three basic avenues to explore to learn about best practices: literature, site visits, and Web sites. Literature about implementation includes practical research, such as the reports conducted on Chicago school reform. Journal articles that report on "lessons learned" fall into this category. In his book *Accountability in Action,* Doug Reeves (2000) described "90/90/90 schools." These are schools that serve a student population with 90% or more from minority groups, 90% or more considered economically disadvantaged, *and* 90% or more reading above standard. The leadership team of any school with the first two factors should pursue more information about these schools to see how they accomplished the third.

Visits to other schools and districts have a powerful impact on both the visitors and the visited. Word of mouth and consultation with staff members in the state department of education and regional agencies will help identify potential partners. Be specific when you ask around about schools or districts that model "best practices." Mention the goal you are trying to achieve, the barriers you perceive, and the characteristics of a school or district you want to visit.

Test out the recommendations you're given by verifying whether these sites are getting the type of results you want from their innovative practices. Take into consideration their location and characteristics. For example, in Washington State, a principal can query the state database to find schools with similar demographics that had superior performance on the state assessment. These would be the schools to contact or visit. Some of the locations you want to visit may be a prohibitive distance for a road trip. Fortunately, the increasing prevalence and effectiveness of school and district Web sites make it possible to do a virtual visit.

CONSIDER LOCAL FACTORS

Decisions in the school change process should involve new learning from both outside and inside the school. The previous two sections in this chapter provide the external focus of learning from research and best practices in other schools and districts. The emphasis in the next two sections is on learning more about your own setting through analyzing each area of concern that gave rise to a priority goal. The cause-and-effect diagram and force field analysis are tools that help sharpen perceptions and highlight assumptions that must be tested. The last part of the chapter provides graphic organizers and a flowchart to examine instructional programs and coordinate district and school work on behalf of student achievement.

Cause-and-Effect Diagram (Fishbone)

A cause-and-effect diagram is a visual representation of the relationships between contributing factors and an issue or problem. Because the picture usually branches out like the skeleton of a fish, it has become known as a "fishbone."

Purpose. A cause-and-effect diagram is helpful when groups need to better understand why a problem situation exists and how it developed. This information can help teams identify the factors with the most impact and choose the most promising entry points for interventions.

When to Use. The cause-and-effect diagramming process is helpful when groups have agreed that a specific issue or problem should be the focus of planning and change. It can also be a useful tool in conflict management by providing greater understanding of elements that have contributed to the conflict situation.

Who to Involve. Any of the shareholders who have been identified earlier may be involved in small groups to develop cause-and-effect diagrams and share their product and insights with others. In my experience, this group process is one uniquely suited to groups that include skeptics. The example that follows demonstrates how it can defuse some of their resistance by acknowledging that many of the causal factors are beyond the control of the school, and can help shift their perspective from negatives to possibilities.

Materials Needed. Completing a cause-and-effect diagram is a simple, paper-and-pencil process. If small groups will be reporting to a larger group, easel paper and markers should be used.

Tips for Facilitators. Explain to the group that before making snap decisions about how to solve a problem, participants need to be sure they understand it thoroughly. This activity will encourage looking back for causes before looking forward with plans. Have groups state the problem they are addressing in a simple phrase such as "student absenteeism" or "lack of problem-solving skills." The phrase should be written in a box (or the artistic may draw a fish head instead) halfway down the right-hand side of a large, horizontal sheet of paper. A line should then be drawn across the middle of the paper, like a spine leading to the head of the fish. As the group members brainstorm the factors that contribute to their concern, they write each one on a diagonal "bone" attached to the spine, or on a "barb" connected to a bone if it relates to a cause already mentioned.

Some formal group process handbooks emphasize that causal factors tend to fall into categories and that the categories should be identified first and bones attached to the appropriate category. For example, quality management fishbones often include the four categories of procedures, people, policies, and plant. Having seen too many groups get bogged down deciding what the categories should be or arguing about which category a factor belongs with, I have left the process unstructured. It seems to be just as effective without the predetermined categories. Some groups recognize their own categories after working for a while and revise their fishbone accordingly.

A version of the quality improvement technique of "Ask why five times" can strengthen the fishbone exercise. When a contributing factor is identified, the repeated question "And where did that one come from?" or "And why is that?" can add more specificity to the analysis.

After the cause-and-effect diagram is drawn and discussed, guide the group to identify any follow-up steps. Factors over which the organization has no control may be acknowledged. There may be a need to gather more data on some of the factors, to see how much influence they actually have. Most important, the group should star or circle causes that it feels have great impact and that it is willing to address.

For Example: Absenteeism. Ten school leadership teams had been selected to participate in a 3-day workshop that would guide them through the process of developing a school improvement plan. They had been asked to bring student data and draft versions of any work they had already done on mission statements, goals, or action plans. It was fascinating to observe their approach to the day.

At one table sat a group of newspapers—at least, that's what it looked like. All I could see were the open sports sections of *USA Today* and local and state publications.

At another table, a group of early arrivals were poring over a stack of computer printouts, heedless even of the caterer's late delivery of the pastries. Heads together, the participants were engrossed in a discussion of which subtests matched their curriculum and mission closely enough to merit major attention as they set their improvement targets.

Another group entered carrying the lid of a copy-paper box with waves of green-and-white-striped computer printouts spilling haphazardly over the edge. Locating the table with the school's name on it, the carrier dropped the box on the floor and used the side of his foot to slide it—none too gently—under the table out of sight. Having dispatched the data, this group attacked the coffee and doughnut table with much greater zeal. I overheard one say, "So what's with this woman we have to listen to about effective schools? Did someone report us defective?"

It was already shaping up to be one of those marvelous "opportunity days," like the tough games that some coaches refer to as character builders, when one of the speaker's companions approached me and said, "In all fairness, I really ought to let you know that there's no reason for us to be wasting 3 days at this workshop. We already have our school improvement plan done." Swallowing hard, I asked him to tell me what they had planned for the coming year. "Well, we got our biggest problem figured out. It's kids not coming to school. And we got two plans for working on it. First of all, we got a business partner that's going to donate us some equipment so we can program it to call those kids and get them going in the morning. Second of all, we got a committee all lined up to work on our attendance policy so these kids can't get by with skipping. Anything wrong with that?" By now I was *gulping* hard, but I managed to thank him for his honesty and suggested that they stick it out for at least this first day, listen carefully, and think about their plan, and we'd talk at the end of the day about whether their attendance at the next two would be worthwhile. "Well, I guess we might as well," he answered, "we're already here."

During the first part of the morning, I shared some background on effective schools research with the group. When we did carousel brainstorming to record their impressions of the correlates identified by Ron Edmonds and other researchers, I praised this group for addressing attendance and linking it with orderly environment, high expectations for students, and opportunity to learn. I assured my new friend that his group was exactly right—kids aren't going to learn if they're not even there.

Later, I asked them to talk about whatever data they had available and what concerns emerged from this discussion or others that had already taken place at their school. This group repeated that their attendance data showed a need for improvement.

Lunch was provided in the room right next door, so I figured that this group would stick around for the afternoon. That's when we got to discuss how important it is to understand the problem we're addressing and know just what is causing it so we know where to begin changing it. The group in question began its fishbone of student absenteeism with "parents don't care" and went right on to list items such as "no transportation," "babysitting younger kids," "pretty low socioeconomics," and "stay up too late at their night jobs." The other groups were getting along well, so I tried to coach this group a little. I commented, "You seem to have a pretty good handle on their family situation. Got any thoughts about the kids themselves?" The group started the next phase of analysis with "kids don't care either" and "unmotivated" (when they have night jobs?) and went on to "discipline problems," "low achievers," and "a couple of them are pregnant." About this time, I noticed one member of the group sort of digging around under the table, but it had a skirt around it, and I didn't want to get too nosy, so I ignored him.

The work on the fishbone was bogging down, so I tried again. "It's really too bad some kids are like that, but I'm glad to see you're aware of them. Could there be any other source of factors that relate to whether kids come to school or not?" A soft voice from the other end of the table said, "Well, they don't like school when they do come." Several people just stared at her, so I reached over and wrote "don't like school" on a new fishbone. A few others added things such as "don't participate in anything," "can't see the point of learning," and "don't seem connected to anyone."

Just then, a head popped up with the copy-paper box lid in his hand and an expression of amazement on his face. "Wait a minute. I've just been digging through here, and it looks to me like there are about 20 kids or so in the whole school that are causing our absence rate to look so bad." My friend responded immediately: "Oh, yeah? So *who?*" As the analyst mentioned a name or two, other members of the group began to comment on the individuals. "Well, if _____ can just make it from the bus to the door without a fight, he does pretty well in class." "_____ doesn't have any trouble getting here, but he's so interested in messing around in the art room, he doesn't follow his schedule." "If _____ wasn't so worried about her weight, she might have time to think about her work."

Because of a little data, the participants suddenly began to talk about students. And as they did, one brave soul said, "You know, if they are such low socioeconomic status, do you think they'll have phones to call?" Another drew courage from that colleague and said, "If they really don't care about school, what good will a tougher attendance policy do?" My friend shrugged and said, "Well, maybe our plan isn't quite right, but look at the stuff on that fish thing. We can't do anything about that stuff."

I was delighted and plunged right in. "You're right, you know. I have to agree with you that a lot of these things we can't control. Let's put a check mark by them. And then let's see what we *can* tackle."

Figure 4.3 shows the results. Not too many items got checked off because some members of the group began to argue that *maybe* the system could make some type of provision for transportation and in-school child care. What they circled became the basis of a new action plan.

The next morning, this group arrived first. By the end of the day, they had developed a plan to provide each of the chronic absentees with an adult in the school (teacher, custodian, or volunteer) who would check in with the student every morning before school and follow up to see if that student was taking work home afterward.

The next fall, I asked my contact in that district how the teams were getting along and what progress the members had made on their plans. "Well," he said, "they're all making progress, but only one school is really implementing what they talked about in June." It was the school whose leadership team originally didn't even want to be at the workshop.

A Variation: Barriers to Student Achievement. As part of the New Leaders for New Schools program, Cathy Miles serves as Resident Principal at Waverly Elementary/Middle School in Baltimore. When she engaged the staff in a cause-and-effect analysis, the result was a long list of barriers to student achievement. Many of them, such as poverty, fell outside the scope of the school's influence. Even when those were deleted from the list, the long list in Figure 4.4 remained.

To move their focus beyond the barriers, Cathy challenged staff to turn them into ideas for strategies that would move students from Basic to Proficient performance (see Figure 4.5).

Helping students reach proficiency still wasn't enough for this determined administrator-in-training. She was not content until barriers were also converted into possible strategies that could move students from Proficient to Advanced (see Figure 4.6).

As I relished the excitement and absorbed new energy from this promising future principal, we discussed her next steps, using more tools to evaluate and

Figure 4.3   Cause-and-Effect (Fishbone) Diagram of Student Absenteeism

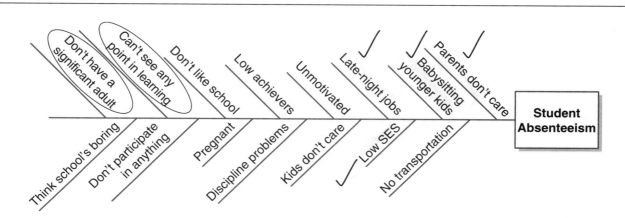

Figure 4.4   Barriers to Student Achievement (Generated by Fishbone)

Poor classroom management	Poor quality interventions	Special education with IEPs not current
No breakfast	Lack of motivation	Need differentiated instruction training
Poor attendance	Student not doing homework	Student labeled as "bad"
Personality conflict with teacher	Low parent involvement with studies	Class distractions
Lacks mastery of basic skills	Need improved instruction	Curriculum not aligned
Lack of teacher resources	Need teacher mentoring	Need for remediation
Lack of communication between teachers	No access to technology	No positive rewards
Poor nutrition	Workshops for parents not attended	Low paper supplies
Need anger management	Need conflict resolution	Lack of community resources
Not scaffolding	Lack prerequisite skills	No pretesting
No workshops for parents	Low interpersonal skills	Poor discipline
Distractibility	Out-of-zone students are behind	Low self-esteem
Lack of research-based interventions		Lack of materials
Low teacher morale		Large class size
		Restricted curriculum

SOURCE: Used with permission of Cathy Miles.

Figure 4.5   Strategies for Moving Students From Basic to Proficient

Skill repetition	Differentiate instruction
Peer teaching	Summer enrichment
Tutoring/peer tutoring	Creative instruction
Coach class	Small-group instruction
Afterschool tutoring	Reading class (reading and comprehension)
Small-group instruction	Creating more assignments in difficulty areas
Learning games	Peer coaching
Infusing literacy and basic math in all classes	Saturday school
Flexible grouping to address personal needs	MSA tutorials
Intervention with skills support	Make students aware of their test scores and how close they are to the next level
Add rigor	

SOURCE: Used with permission of Cathy Miles.

Figure 4.6   Strategies for Moving Students From Proficient to Advanced

Afterschool tutoring	Projects/critical thinking activities
Begin a GATE program	Make students aware of their test scores and how close they are to the next level
Teach/assign skills based on the next grade level	
Afterschool math club	Afterschool enrichment/tutoring
Gifted/talented afterschool program	Project-based learning
Integrate core subjects in all classes	Online interaction/intervention with peers
Differentiate with enrichment activities	Real-world applications
	Coach class
Summer enrichment	Creative instruction
Independent learning	Infusing literacy and basic math in all classes
More challenging/advanced work	Tutoring peer-to-peer
Independent study	Add rigor
More practice with skills	More exposure to advanced skills
Challenging activities	Small-group instruction

SOURCE: Used with permission of Cathy Miles.

prioritize these possibilities and shape them into definite action plans to improve student learning in her host school.

Force Field Analysis

The cause-and-effect diagram helps groups identify the factors contributing to their problem or concern. Force field analysis goes a step further, looking at factors that work both for and against the desired result.

Purpose. Force field analysis is used to identify barriers that must be overcome and to focus on positive forces that can be mobilized for progress.

When to Use. A group may use force field analysis when it is considering a change effort. The results can help the members be more aware of barriers they didn't recognize. It can also increase a group's sense of efficacy by identifying advantages and possible allies that could help it succeed. Occasionally, time spent doing a force field analysis saves a group from investing time and effort when restraining forces so outweigh driving forces that it's clearly a lost cause from the outset.

Who to Involve. All shareholders should feel welcome to participate directly or through their representatives on the leadership team or task force. It is particularly important to include those who were strong voices in identifying the issue or problem under consideration.

Materials Needed. Force field analysis is a paper-and-pencil exercise. Using easel paper and markers makes it easier to share the completed analysis with others.

Tips for Facilitators. Force field analysis is simply a structured version of brainstorming, with a format provided for responses. The rules of brainstorming should be reviewed. Like the cause-and-effect diagram, it is important to push the participants beyond "filling in the blanks." They need to discuss and select which restraining forces they can minimize and which driving forces they will use to their advantage. From this discussion will emerge strategies that can be further developed as part of the action plan.

For Example: Year-Round School. An inner-city school team was concerned about the gap created in children's lives between May and September and had spent considerable time discussing and debating the value of year-round school. Most members agreed that it was a good concept but wondered if it was feasible to focus their school improvement efforts around restructuring the school calendar. They decided to complete a force field analysis and "calculate the odds" before going any further. Figure 4.7 shows their analysis.

After looking over their analysis, they decided to work on summer provisions in collaboration with social service agencies and focus their grant funding toward those efforts. They concluded that their resources would get to children much more quickly this way than by trying to influence the district, state, county, and parents in favor of year-round school.

ANALYZE CURRENT PRACTICE

Earlier in this chapter, I listed the study of best practices as an essential step in preparation for making decisions for school change. Unfortunately, too many school leaders and shareholders learn about best practice, nod, and say, "Oh, we do that," pat each other on the back, and carry on the status quo—without actually knowing what instructional programs and practice really look like within their schools. Specialized models, such as curriculum mapping, can capture the written curriculum. Less formal, more personal approaches are needed to understand the taught curriculum and the instructional methods in common use. Many of the tools already introduced can be adapted for this purpose. For example, the focus group strategy can be used in grade-level, department, and interdisciplinary groups to compare current practice with best practice. One way of synthesizing research and best practice, and using it as a tool to analyze current practice, is to develop a graphic organizer.

Graphic Organizers

A graphic organizer is simply a drawing or diagram that helps the viewer organize his or her thoughts or see the components and relationships within a complex problem or situation. Figure 1.1, which illustrates the relationship of the five guiding questions to the stages of school change, is an example of a graphic organizer. It provides a common focus to tie together the parts of this book, so that the reader can turn to it when wondering, "Now where does *this* fit?"

Figure 4.7   Force Field Analysis for Year-Round School

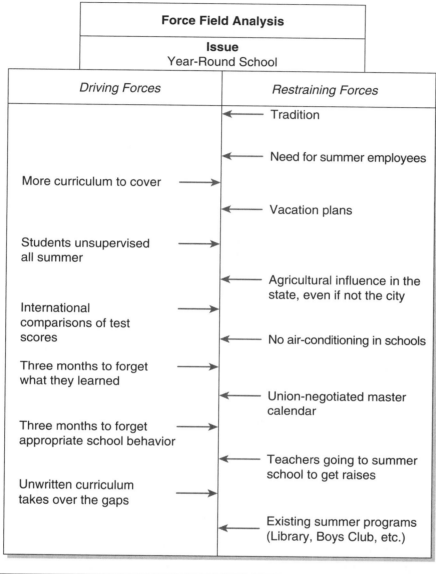

Purpose. A graphic organizer is designed to illustrate complex relationships. It is also a powerful way to synthesize pages of text into a one-page reference guide.

When to Use. Teachers often develop *advance organizers* to introduce a new topic of study and help students anticipate what they will be learning. In a similar way, a school study group may develop a graphic organizer to share what they have learned with the rest of the staff. It's a visual tool that does not require a lot of reading to highlight the main points. A wise senior management team might stop in the middle of a school year and say, "Whoa, how many new initiatives have we already begun, and how are they related?" Team members might need to draw a picture to explain it to themselves and then be able to improve communication with shareholders.

Who to Involve. With most group process activities, we know who should be included by asking who is affected by the outcome. Developing a graphic organizer may be unique in the need for participation by individuals who have expert knowledge and are in a position to be able to see the big picture. For example, the graphic organizers in Figures 4.8, 4.9, and 4.10 were developed in groups led by curriculum consultants who were experts in their disciplines.

Materials Needed. The sky's the limit of how elaborate graphic organizers can become through the use of technology. But all that's needed initially is paper, pencil, and analytical thinking.

Tips for Facilitators. Develop the graphic organizer with a group if you have one that includes the expert knowledge and systems thinking that you need. This isn't always possible. Sometimes you need to do your own sketching and then have it reviewed by a group or several individuals before you introduce it as a group process tool.

If you are leading a study group, the components of the graphic organizer may come from various sources. Persons or subgroups report what they learned and contribute where they think it belongs in the big picture. One way to synthesize a jigsaw cooperative learning activity is for the home group to develop a graphic organizer of what it learned.

For Example: The Three R's. What do you do when you have had several years of successive cuts in curriculum and instruction staff, coinciding with emphasis on site-based planning and budgeting, and now a state accountability system prompts the school board to ask how reading is taught in the schools? What do you do when aggregated test scores show the public that overall improvement in student achievement is occurring across the district, but you also know that some schools are struggling and some are even declining? The challenge is to find out what's being done—and not being done—and assist schools, without violating the culture of site-based autonomy and without starting a war over the "one best way" (such as the example later in this chapter).

When Joan Dore was the lead reading specialist in Seattle, Washington, she faced this challenge: She needed a way to condense all the research she knew about balanced reading programs into something visual, nonthreatening, and easy to talk about with individuals and groups of teachers. She knew that every school was doing at least part of the puzzle well, but many were missing important pieces. She wanted to value what every school and teacher was doing but stretch their awareness and build the rest of a comprehensive reading program in every school. So she drew a picture of the essential components of a reading program (Figure 4.8). As the district began a major literacy initiative, this graphic organizer guided the diagnosis of each school's practices and served as a reference point for professional development. As new instructional strategies were introduced, external trainers, internal consultants, administrators, and teachers referenced this organizer, explaining that "We're learning this because it fits *here* and will strengthen *this* part of our reading program."

The graphic organizer for reading was so well received that teachers asked for similar examples for writing and mathematics. Charlotte Carr and Allison Harris developed Figures 4.9 and 4.10 to stimulate professional dialogue and

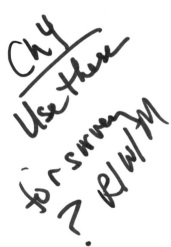

Figure 4.8   Graphic Organizer: Essential Components of a Reading Program

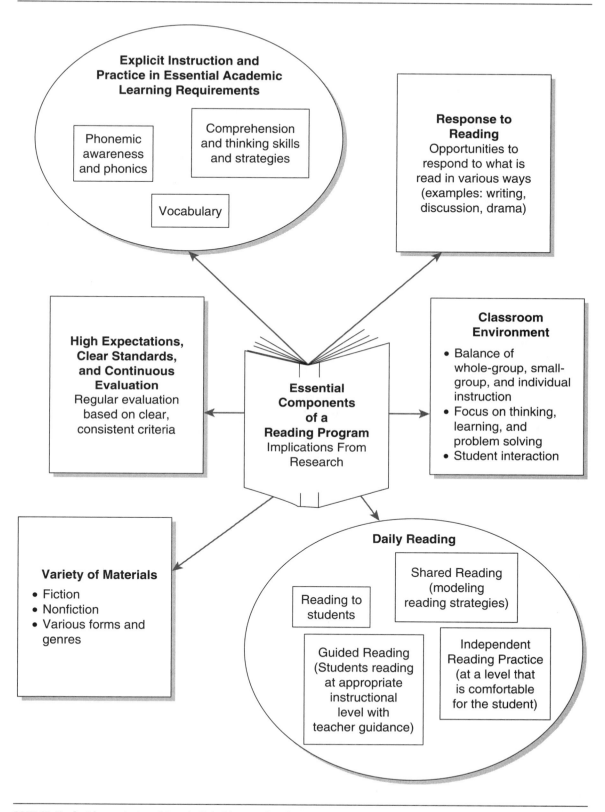

Figure 4.9 Graphic Organizer: Essential Components of a Writing Program

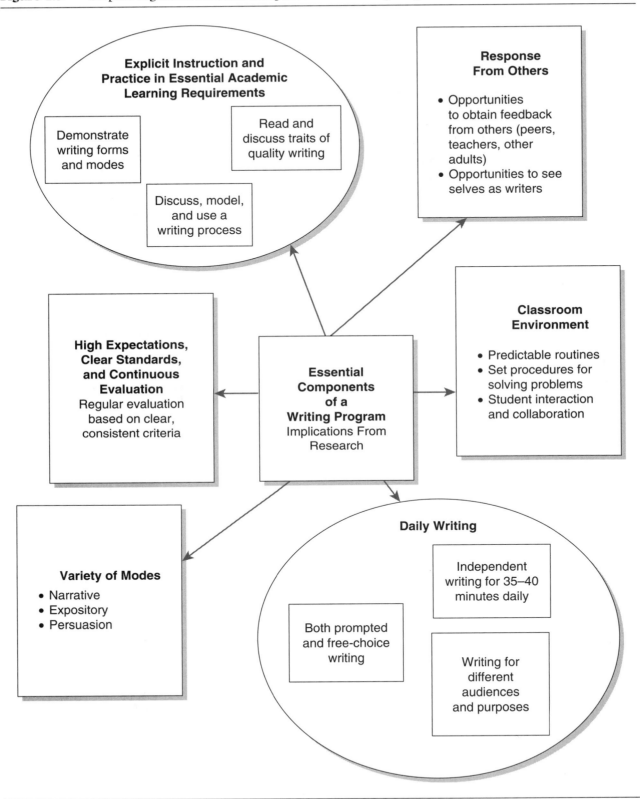

SOURCE: Used with permission of Joseph Olchefske, Seattle School District, Seattle, Washington.

Figure 4.10   Graphic Organizer: Essential Components of a Mathematics Program

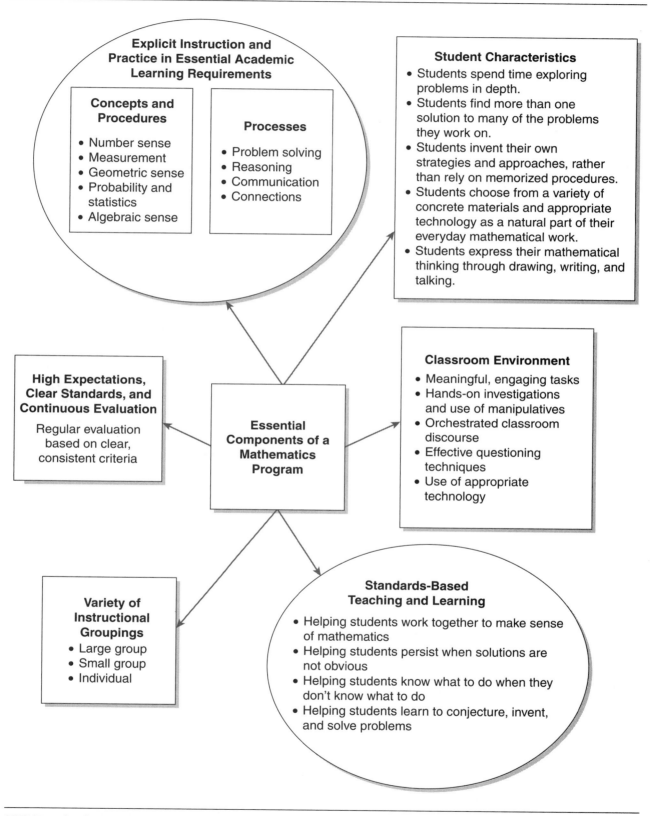

SOURCE: Used with permission of Joseph Olchefske, Seattle School District, Seattle, Washington.

analyze current practice in their disciplines as well. Does that mean that every school in Seattle now has the same instructional programs and methods? No. It does mean that—whatever they call it, however they schedule and staff for it—the district expects each school to demonstrate that every component of the curriculum is being provided to the students in their school.

PARTNER WITH YOUR DISTRICT

This heading may seem self-evident, but it's tragic how many schools see the district as an enemy rather than as a partner. School districts need to frame their work as support services to the schools, and schools need to know how to access the services that are available. I concur with Lambert's (2003) statement that "I used to believe that the school was the primary unit of educational change, and the literature repeatedly insists that it is. However, I'm now persuaded that we can't save education one school at a time" (p. 80). The children are moving on through the system, continuing to struggle, and any role the district can play to stimulate improvement is critical.

For example, Marzano's meta-analysis of *What Works in Schools* (2003) identified a "guaranteed and viable curriculum" as one of the factors that has major impact on student achievement. And Uri Treisman (2007) described the shift to "a managed district curriculum" as one of the changes that improved student performance in Charlotte, North Carolina, under the leadership of Eric Smith. The students who benefited most from an increase in curriculum consistency were the poorest students because they are the most mobile from school to school within a large urban setting.

Michael Fullan (2005) also points out that

decentralized schools will have variable capacities to engage in continuous improvement, and therefore some agency has to be responsible for helping develop capacity and for intervening (with a goal of developing capacity) when performance is low. The second reason is even more fundamental for sustainability: We can't change the system without lateral (cross-school and cross-district) sharing and capacity development. It is very much the district's role to help make the latter happen. (p. 66)

The concept of organizational reciprocity and collaboration at and among the three levels of classroom, school, and district was introduced in Chapter 3 and applies here also. In a large district (which I define simply as "more than one high school," since that greatly elevates the complexity), the central office can coordinate teacher collaboration in ways that create economies of scale and can generate models that guide and expedite individual school efforts.

The flowchart in Figure 4.11 was developed from my perspective as both an outside consultant and a practitioner, having worked in multiple roles at both the school and central office levels. When an area of need is identified through analysis of student performance data, a series of questions guides both the district and school response.

Figure 4.11 Flowchart: Integrating District and School Roles to Improve Learning

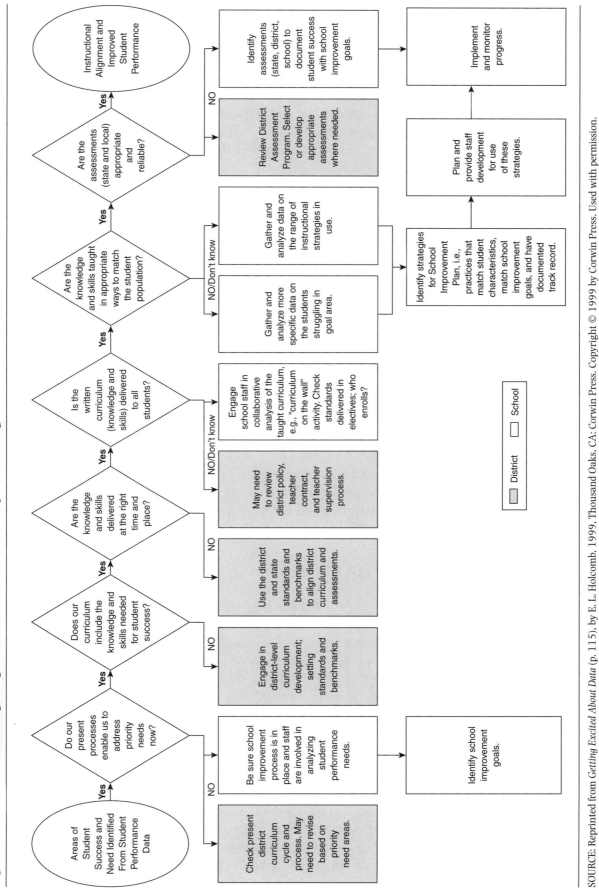

SOURCE: Reprinted from *Getting Excited About Data* (p. 115), by E. L. Holcomb, 1999, Thousand Oaks, CA: Corwin Press. Copyright © 1999 by Corwin Press. Used with permission.

For example, Washington State's standards include five strands of math concepts and procedures: number sense, measurement, geometric sense, algebraic sense, and statistics and probability. Let's say that state assessment results indicated that students performed quite well in number sense and measurement but poorly in the other three strands.

The first question on the flowchart prompts discussion at both levels, so that both district curriculum work and the school improvement plan will focus on the need. The second and third questions ask whether geometric sense, algebraic sense, and statistics and probability are included in the curriculum—and at what level—and must be answered for the district as a whole. Teacher representatives would participate in necessary revision, but this task should not have to occur simultaneously and independently at every school. If the curriculum doesn't include adequate attention to probability and statistics, that needs to be remedied immediately for every mathematics student and teacher.

The district, however, can provide only the aligned curriculum and materials. It's the school that must determine whether all strands of the math curriculum are being or will be delivered to students and whether teachers are skilled in the methods that will reach their students. If additional teaching strategies are needed, the school's improvement plan would include professional development provisions to meet the need. The district may, in turn, support coordination of that training.

The assessment question resides at both levels. State and district decisions govern the large-scale assessments that are administered to all students. Schools use data from those assessments in their decision making and also make decisions about the types of classroom evidence that they will collect and the indicators of progress that they will monitor as they work toward their goals. The reciprocal role of the school and district in assessment is explored further in Chapter 5.

SELECT STRATEGIES

As I wrote this section for the first edition, I could look up from my work table and gaze at the Horsetooth, a rock formation in the front range of the Colorado Rockies. To get from there to Estes Park and over the top to Granby, there is really only one route, the Trail Ridge Road. But the view from the deck on the other side of that house was different. The high plains stretched as far as the eye could see. To get from there to Minneapolis, I could choose several routes. Having a clear destination does not complete the planning. If there are many possible routes, choices must be made that will get the most people onboard and headed in the same direction.

Decision Matrix

Purpose. A decision matrix is used to help groups reach consensus on the best solution to a complex issue or problem. Choosing criteria that would define an appropriate strategy helps participants focus on common values. Brainstorming all possible solutions brings out greater creativity and can counteract the "only one right or best way" thinking that is so prevalent.

When to Use. A decision matrix is helpful when multiple strategies have been suggested, especially if there are intense feelings about several of them. It should definitely be used when organizations have a history of simply adopting the latest innovation and assuming that it will match their needs or when they show little evidence of connecting their data and their value system to decision making. Use of the decision matrix should have been preceded by study of the organization's own data ("Where are we now?") and study of best practices for achieving the results desired ("Where do we want to go?").

Who to Involve. Group processes should be open for participation. When a decision matrix is used, it is particularly important to include those who are most affected by the current situation and those who will be most responsible for implementing the chosen strategies.

Materials Needed. Chart paper and markers will be needed for the first two steps. Each participant will need a copy of the decision matrix. There are two ways of providing this. Blank copies of the matrix form can be distributed, and as the possible solutions and criteria are generated, each participant can fill them in. Another method is to complete the lists of solutions and criteria, enter them on a laptop computer, and print the matrix during a break. The three steps of listing solutions, setting criteria, and ranking the possibilities may even occur on different occasions.

Tips for Facilitators. Engage the group in a review of what was learned in answer to the "Where are we now?" and "Where do we want to go?" questions. Summarize what has been learned by study groups who have researched best practice to achieve the desired results.

Divide the large group into smaller groups or table teams and have them list all the possible strategies that might be employed to accomplish the goal or address the concern they have identified. As with brainstorming, encourage participants to generate as many variations and solutions as they can. Allow brief periods of wait time to stimulate more divergent thinking. Save the lists from all groups.

After a break or at another session within a few days, have the groups shift into a more reflective mode. Review the mission or belief statements that identify their core values. Ask them to consider what criteria would describe an ideal solution. List these criteria.

The decision matrix is constructed by listing the suggested changes or strategies along the left side of a grid. The criteria for a good decision become headings across the top.

To use the matrix, have participants go down each column and give each suggested solution a rating from 1 to 5, with 5 representing those suggestions that most closely fit the criterion heading for that column. Repeat this with each column. Participants can add the ratings across each row to get a total value for each of the suggested strategies. Their individual ratings can then be used in a whole-group exercise, such as nominal group process or weighted voting.

For Example: The Reading Debate. The elementary school team had reviewed test data and determined that one area of focus should be improvement of reading achievement. Deciding how to accomplish this goal awoke a history of conflict between the "phonicians" and the "whole languagers." The progress that had been made to heal wounds and strengthen the school culture was at risk because staff members were approaching the goal of improved reading achievement as an either/or proposition. The facilitator had difficulty getting more than those two possible solutions generated in the first attempt at this process and had to temporarily abandon it.

Instead, the group put solutions on hold and began to generate criteria that would characterize a good solution. The members agreed that an acceptable solution

- Would be consistent with their mission and beliefs
- Would help staff work together, not be divided
- Would include a component of parent participation
- Could be implemented with existing resources

As members focused on these criteria, they began to realize that neither phonics nor whole language, in and of itself, contained all these elements. More ideas

Figure 4.12   Decision Matrix

Possible Solutions	Criterion #1	Criterion #2	Criterion #3	Criterion #4	Individual Total
List all items under consideration	Rate each item 1–5, with 5 being ideal. Example: Consistent with mission and beliefs	Rate each item 1–5, with 5 being ideal. Example: Increases staff unity and collaboration	Rate each item 1–5, with 5 being ideal. Example: Includes component for parent involvement	Rate each item 1–5, with 5 being ideal. Example: Needs no new resources	

emerged for the "possible solutions" list, and they were able to construct their decision matrix. They realized that they had rejected a third program (Success for All) because they lacked the resources for full implementation of this labor-intensive approach. At the same time, they discovered that there were aspects of the model that they could adapt to their situation. What resulted was a unique approach that alternated days between whole-language activities and cross-grade, flexible-skill grouping similar to the Joplin plan (which was one of the foundations of the Success for All design). They also discovered that parent volunteers could be readily engaged in whole-language activities, freeing teachers for more intense skill work with students. By focusing on their criteria, they invented their own creative solutions that in turn created a stronger sense of commitment.

A Variation: Perplexed About Portables. Another school was challenged by increasing enrollment and the district's decision to remedy overcrowding through the use of portable classrooms. Initial discussions about who or what should be housed in the portable classrooms were rapidly becoming characterized by discussions of seniority and comments such as "I've taught in this room for 22 years, and I have only 3 more to go, and you'd have to carry me out in a coffin before I'd give up my room." As each grade level was listed for potential location in the portables, the objections changed from "The children are too small to be wandering from one building to another; they might get lost" to "They're too big to be wandering from one building to another; they'll disrupt everything." The list of possible solutions then shifted to "special" programs. They were all written down, despite objections such as "How can you have art without a sink?" and "Why have the traffic of all 500+ kids going back and forth when there's only a need for three or four classrooms?" and "You can't put the computer lab there because it would be too easy to break into."

Although the facilitator ignored the comments and objections when recording all the possible solutions, he reintroduced them during the discussion of criteria for a good decision: "I understand that security from break-ins is important. Do you want that as a criterion?" It was included, along with others such as "least number of students moving" and "should fit program needs." As the criteria were identified, a whole new solution was introduced. Two teachers had wanted to try team teaching, but their rooms were too far apart, and they had been afraid of the noise and hall traffic of exchanging students. This suggestion started a whole new line of thought, and two primary teachers mentioned that they had been interested in multiage classrooms but hadn't thought too much about it because they were so crowded. The resulting decision was to use one portable for team teaching and one as a multiage primary unit. Not only did the school solve its "who gets the portables?" problem, but it also had an opportunity to introduce two new instructional settings that had never been tried before because the interested teachers had been "locked into" their existing spaces.

DOUBLE-CHECK: GOAL OR STRATEGY?

Two of my prized experiences were whitewater adventures—8 days on the Colorado River in the Grand Canyon and 10 days on the Talkeetna River flowing from the base of Denali in Alaska. Both were whitewater adventures, and both occurred in the summer, but they required much different planning. For one destination, the equipment included long underwear, wetsuits, and knee-high mud boots. For the other, swimsuits, shorts, and walking shoes were sufficient. On the Colorado River, there were several days when choices had to be made about taking the direct route, shooting right through a Class IV rapid that was acting like a Class V due to high water levels, or hauling equipment on foot and hiking around. The goal was to experience high adventure, but also to arrive alive—so sometimes the strategies had to be reevaluated.

In the journey of school improvement, travelers sometimes lose their way because they confuse goals with strategies. There are two topics I have encountered frequently and will use to illustrate this potential confusion—parent involvement and use of technology.

Increased parent involvement is often stated as a goal. I do not mean that it never should be the goal but that teams must raise the question of whether it is the "end" or the "means." For example, perhaps the school wants parents more involved in order to increase their knowledge and satisfaction with the school. Then satisfaction with the school is the "end" in mind, and the evidence of progress would be higher survey results. More often, the school wants parents more involved because they believe that parent involvement will result in better student learning. In this case, the goal is student learning, and parent involvement is assumed to be a means to that end.

However, research by Joyce Epstein and others (2002) discriminates certain types of parent involvement that have direct kinds of impact—and only one type of parent involvement is associated with increased student achievement. In this case, parent involvement is not a goal in and of itself. Parent involvement in curriculum-related activities with students would be the strategy related to the goal of improving student proficiency in reading or math. Examples of such activities include student work folders sent home with specific feedback from the teacher on the students' progress and suggestions for ways to help, grade-level newsletters including a learning activity to match the essential skills being taught that week, and parent workshops as a "mini-refresher course" on math concepts being learned by upper-grade children.

While this book focuses on the work of educators within the classroom, school, and district and not on the role of parents per se, this admonition from Michael Fullan (2005) is important to remember:

> [U]nder conditions of power asymmetry with poor parents, vulnerable and unconfident in their relationships to schools, it is incumbent on principals and teachers to reach out, be empathetic, and create possibilities for parent involvement. When they do, as Bryk and Schneider found (in Chicago) . . . greater connection is made with parents and students, and achievement goes up. (p. 61)

The case of technology as a school improvement goal or strategy is somewhat similar. Most regard technology as a tool, not an "end" in itself. Yet the mandate to develop a long-range technology plan every 3 to 5 years causes it to take on the appearance of a goal. Instructional uses of technology (distance learning, online learning, computerized independent practice programs, etc.) should be identified as strategies aligned with the appropriate goals for increasing student achievement, not as stand-alone initiatives.

PLAN THE JOURNEY

A common characteristic of school improvement plans that never happen is that they identify strategies they will use (cooperative learning, a self-esteem program, multiple intelligences) without analyzing what implementation of those strategies will entail. Any one of the strategies just mentioned represents many substeps needed to provide training and support for implementation. When schools identify popular topics such as multiple intelligences and learning styles, their plans often involve training in the content knowledge without sufficient consideration of changes that would need to be made in the school itself to reflect those concepts. Although plans will surely be adjusted during implementation, they must be sufficiently developed to clearly describe the magnitude of change they require and the demands they will place on people, time, and budgets.

Action Planning

Purpose. An action plan is developed to lay out the specific steps that will be required to put a new strategy or program into place. Answering the question "How will we get there?" identified some "whats" (the strategies). Answering the "Where do we want to go?" question included focus on the belief system of the organization as the "why." Action planning helps a group work out the "who, when, where, and how."

When to Use. An action plan should be developed after the organization has set priorities for improvement, studied practices and programs that have been effective, and chosen the approaches best suited to their goals and school context.

Who to Involve. Because an action plan needs to identify specific steps, timelines, and resources, it is important to involve people who have information about and access to the school calendar and budget and who have a big-picture perspective of all that is occurring in the organization. School teams often find it helpful to include a central office support person in the action-planning stage. If a major innovation, such as multiage classrooms, is being implemented, it is advisable to invite a consultant or a team member from another school that is already using the approach. These resource persons can provide advice on how they approached the change and even more valuable insights about problems they didn't anticipate and what they might have done to avoid them.

Materials Needed. Chart paper, markers, and large stick-on notes are commonly used for drafting an action plan as a group. The plan can then be typed on a laptop computer and printed for everyone to review. Once it is in the computer, it can readily be revised as it is adjusted throughout implementation.

Tips for Facilitators. Formats for school improvement plans can be found in many of the resources listed in the bibliography. Some action plans are developed in chart form, and others are written in narrative. The common elements are steps to be taken, who will be involved, who will be responsible, resources needed, time required and schedule, and indicators of completion or progress. A simple way to begin is by using these elements as column headings on a large bulletin board or wall. The sequence of development is "work all the way down, and then across." In other words, first list all the steps that need to be taken. As facilitator, repeatedly ask, "And what else does that involve?" This helps the group break down major tasks into their component parts. Another common question to ask is, "What would need to happen before that?" This question guides the group to identify missing steps and create a sequence.

The group will continually recognize missing steps and rearrange the sequence of tasks, which can make messy recording for the facilitator. Writing each task on a large stick-on note makes moving tasks around and inserting new ones neat and easy.

When the sequence of steps or tasks seems complete, the group works across the chart horizontally for each step. Have the group identify the person responsible for each step and the people who will participate. Discuss whether there is a budgetary consideration. As the group members move to the timeline column, remind them that "time is money." If released time is going to be provided, there will be substitute costs. If compensation for time must be provided, that cost needs to be estimated. Timelines should consider the school calendar and capitalize on any staff development days or inservice time to fit with the school's action plan for improvement.

A most neglected but essential column is the last column, often given the heading of "Monitoring" or "Evaluation." Too often, this column is simply used to check off completion of the activity; for example, "All staff attended a workshop on cooperative learning." This is inadequate because it does not assess whether anyone actually went back to the classroom and applied the knowledge and skills that were learned in the workshop. The example of brainstorming used in Chapter 3 generated observable indicators that distinguish the behavior of lifelong learners. In similar fashion, the criteria that will be observed or measured must be identified at the time the action plan is developed to ensure that progress can be reported as results achieved, not just steps taken (see Chapter 5).

For Example: Mentors for Chronic Absentees. Earlier in the chapter, the group process technique of cause-and-effect (fishbone) diagramming was introduced with the example of a school leadership team that changed from revising an attendance policy to creating one-to-one mentoring relationships between chronic absentees and caring adults in the school environment. Figure 4.13 shows the action plan developed by the team to implement that new approach.

Figure 4.13 Action Plan for Mentor Program

School: Any Town Middle School

Improvement Objective: To improve student attendance

Members of Team or Task Force:	
M. Black	M. Green
J. White	J. Jackson
B. Brown	

Strategy: Develop 1:1 student-adult mentor relationships for chronic absentees

Rationale: Research findings Indicate that student engagement and personal bonding with adults in the school are related to attendance and achievement.

Activities: Steps to Be Taken	Persons Responsible	Persons Involved	Resources Needed	Timeline	Monitoring, Evaluation
Develop criteria to identify the chronic absentees	Counselors	SIT subcommittee	Part of June workshop time	During June workshop	Criteria approved by SIT at August meeting
List the students who need to be involved	Counselor on SIT	Homeroom teachers	—	During June workshop	Presented and approved by SIT at August meeting
Set expectations for students who participate	Counselor on SIT	Homeroom teachers	—	During June workshop	Presented and approved by SIT at August meeting
Notify parents and get permission to contact students	Counselor	Counseling secretary	—	Before registration in August	Parent permissions returned
Set expectations for adult mentors	SIT subcommittee chair	SIT subcommittee	—	During June workshop	Approval by SIT at August meeting

NOTE: SIT = School Improvement Team

(Continued)

111

(Continued)

Activities: Steps to Be Taken	Persons Responsible	Persons Involved	Resources Needed	Timeline	Monitoring, Evaluation
Develop training for mentors	Assistant principal/staff development coordinator	SIT subcommittee/homeroom teachers	Food for picnic	July	Approval by SIT at August meeting
Recruit and select mentors	Assistant principal	Homeroom teachers	—	July and August	List of mentors
Match students to mentors	Assistant principal	Counselors	—	July and August	List of possible matches
Hold mentor training and gain commitment	Assistant principal/staff development coordinator	Mentors/homeroom teachers	Stipends for 2-hour training sessions ($1,250) (25 mentors at $50)	August	Mentors sign commitment forms
Hold meeting of students and mentors or make individual contact with students	Counselors/assistant principal	Students/mentors/homeroom teachers	—	August	Students return commitment form
Determine times and places that mentors will contact students	Mentors	Students	—	First week of school	Schedules turned in to assistant principal
Schedule and hold mentor meetings	Assistant principal	Counselors/mentors/homeroom teachers	Early release time once per month	Monthly, October–May	Minutes of meetings; summary of student attendance and grades
Reexamine attendance data	Counselors	—	—	Weekly by student; monthly for all	Graph attendance and grades each month as run charts
Plan celebration for mentors and students	Assistant principal	Students/mentors/families/homeroom teachers	Budget for food, certificates, etc.	May	Progress certificates to students with targeted percent improvement

NOTE: SIT = School Improvement Team

IS OUR PLAN POWERFUL?

At this point, goals have been set and strategies selected to achieve them. The route for the journey is laid out through action plans. The next question will be to identify the milestones that will verify that "we are (getting) there." Before tackling that next question, some tests need to be applied to the work done so far.

The Test of Alignment

Earlier in the chapter, readers were cautioned about the danger of confusing goals with strategies. Which are the "ends" to be accomplished? Which are the "means" to those ends? Goals must be held tightly. Strategies may need to be revised, abandoned, or substituted to sustain the effort toward the goals (see Chapter 6).

If Figure 1.1 has been in use as an organizer for the school improvement journey, it now contains key words of the mission, critical bullet points about findings in the data, reference to the long list of concerns first generated, identification of priority goals, and a set of strategies selected for each goal. At this point, readers are urged to look at the strategies that have been selected so far, and confront two questions:

- Would the *combination* of this set of strategies raise achievement for all students?
- Would the *combined set* of strategies also directly address disparate learning needs—narrow achievement gaps?

An essential strategy is aligning the curriculum (Figure 4.11), and it is a strategy that will raise achievement for all. If that consistent curriculum is not *delivered* to all, it can actually exacerbate gaps. Will the strategies accomplish the true intent of the priority goals?

The Test of Scope

It's a delicate balance—"enough" strategies to effectively accomplish the mission and goals while not overtaxing the implementers with "too much." This chapter concludes with three lessons learned and a rule of thumb from my own experience.

A recent column in *Changing Schools* (Goodwin & Dean, 2007) outlined three school improvement mistakes, one of which is the test of scope. Mistake #1 was listed as "treating the symptoms, not the underlying problem." A tool like the cause-and-effect diagram can help push thinking toward the underlying, or root, causes. The second mistake identified by Goodwin and Dean was "focusing only on tangibles and ignoring intangibles." This book has urged readers to look at beliefs and the culture of both the school and district as part of analysis and planning. The test of scope is stated as "Mistake #3: Biting off more than you can chew."

I'm always honored to work with a district or regional agency and help principals and their leadership teams focus on ways to increase student achievement.

Answer Key

- Answering the "How will we get there?" question includes further analysis of the status quo: digging into the data, studying relevant research, exploring best practices, examining local factors, and analyzing current practice.

- Visual displays of data from other sources can stimulate thinking about strategies that will improve student learning.

- Schools need to be partners with staff at the district level as they select strategies and develop implementation plans.

- Figure 1.1 can be filled in to serve as the "big picture" of the components of the school improvement plan, while action plans provide specifics for implementation.

- Before investing time, energy, and human spirit in implementation, be sure that the combined set of strategies in the school improvement plan will raise achievement for all students and narrow learning gaps among groups of students.

This always involves doing some diagnostic work to see how they have developed improvement plans and what those improvement plans include. I provide each team with two copies of Figure 1.1, expanded onto large poster paper. They are allowed only two copies, which forces them to work together and limits them to no more than six priority goals. I ask them to set aside whatever lengthy improvement plan they have been required to produce and submit, and just capture "the big stuff going on in your school right now." They usually "begin in the middle," writing down all the initiatives that are under way as strategies, and then figuring out what goals they connect to. After 20–30 minutes of guided work, they usually realize that there are "a lot of things going on that aren't/weren't in the plan" and that there are alignment issues. For example, a particular strategy is consuming immense amounts of time and energy, and there are no data to suggest it was even needed. Multiple experiences with similar results have led me to this rule of thumb: (1) Have no more than five priority goals, at least two of which must be directly related to student achievement; and (2) if you can't capture the essence of your plan on two pages, it is too complex for anyone to remember. How can something be the driving force of the school if people can't even remember it?

5

Answering the "How Will We Know We Are (Getting) There?" Question

It seemed as if all my friends were going to exotic places that year. One group went to the Caribbean on spring break. Others were taking summer vacations in Europe. A couple were going through the selection process for overseas teaching with the Department of Defense. All of them had invited me to come along, but I couldn't seem to muster much enthusiasm. Some recalcitrant part of me kept saying, "There are so many wonderful things to see in our own country. When I've done all the states, I'll start in on the world."

That made me curious about how many states I had already visited and which ones I still needed to see. On impulse, I bought a child's cardboard puzzle with each state outline forming a piece, and I glued on all the ones I'd been to as a child on family vacations or as an adult. I was amazed to discover that there were only 17 left, and most of them were in the Northeast. So while my friends planned for Europe, I planned for New England. I didn't want to be locked in with too tight a schedule to explore, but I did want my route laid out, so I had AAA prepare a TripTik for me. A TripTik is a set of maps about the size of a shopping list pad that's bound at the top with a coil. It's easy to hold and glance at while driving. Each page represents somewhere between 100 and 200 miles. For 3½ weeks, I marked my progress by the number of pages flipped in my TripTik. When I got home, I celebrated my accomplishments by gluing 13 more state pieces onto my puzzle.

The journey of school improvement is much like that, although an organization rarely reaches a state of completion as visible as a completed puzzle map of the United States. There will always be more destinations to pursue. That's why motivation for school improvement has to come from proof of *progress*, because *perfection* will never be attained.

In previous chapters, we explored three of the critical questions of school improvement. The first was "Where are we now?" which required us to look carefully at the culture of our organization and at the performance of our students. Use of data was important in that answer. The second question was "Where do we want to go?" To set a clear goal, it was important to define the characteristics or observable indicators of the desired state in contrast to the status quo. The third question was "How will we get there?" Development of action plans required us to identify behaviors and results that can be observed or measured to demonstrate our progress (see "Indicators" on Figure 1.1).

If those first three phases were completed carefully, answering the question "How will we know we are getting there?" should be fairly straightforward. Knowing whether we are getting there simply means doing what we said we would do in our plan and checking what we said we would check. That's like the *D* (do) and the *C* (check) of the PDCA quality improvement cycle (see Figure 1.2). In the RPTIM model, it is the *I* and the *M*. Fred Wood used the *I* for implementation and the *M* to stand for maintenance. I believe *M* must also stand for monitoring as it does in the Three I's model. Unless the progress of implementation is monitored, institutionalization may never occur. There is substantive truth in the aphorism that "what gets measured gets done." There is also truth in the flip side—that what *doesn't* get measured or monitored often *doesn't* get done. It's just so easy to let things slide if they have no deadlines or checkpoints.

On Figure 1.1, the question "How will we know we are (getting) there?" is posed above the box labeled "Indicators." The two bullets in the "Indicators" box represent two types of monitoring that must occur. The first is **indicators of implementation.** Most of us have seen posters with the slogan "Plan Your Work—Work Your Plan." This chapter raises the question "Are you working your plan?" and discusses the importance of making sure the strategies that were chosen are actually being used. No new practice can become part of "how we do things around here" (institutionalization) until it has moved from planning and training into consistent, skilled implementation.

The other bullet in the "Indicators" box represents evidence of progress toward the desired results. These are called **indicators of impact.** Once you have a plan, and know you are working the plan, it's time to ask the toughest question: "Is your plan working?" The overarching purpose of school improvement is to improve student performance. The time, energy, and commitment for change will be misplaced if the change is not clearly linked to greater effectiveness with students.

The "How will we know we are getting there?" question is also represented by the second "How?" above the oval labeled "Mission." It reminds us that a mission statement isn't something that we write, print, and file. It's a living document that captures organizational values. These values should surface and ground every substantive discussion on every major decision.

I recently attended a seminar on high school reform. A panel of principals and teachers took turns describing their schools' demographics and settings and reasons for starting down their path of change. In a second round of comments, each speaker outlined the particular changes each school had made and how the staff went about the decision-making process. Knowing how complex high school change is, the audience took copious notes and applauded every presenter. But during the break, the main question in the halls and restroom (the women's, anyway) was this: "So-and-so went on and on about the *Breaking Ranks* [1996, 2004] recommendations and how their main goal was to personalize education, but then she said they voted to increase their schedule to an eight-period day. How can they think that more, shorter class periods will personalize education?" The point of this example is that those who watch and listen to our work in schools are checking whether the actions we take match the rhetoric we speak. Later in this chapter, you'll read about a high school that applied the principle of personalization in quite a different way.

ARE WE WORKING OUR PLAN? EVIDENCE OF IMPLEMENTATION

In Chapter 4, we met a team of middle school teachers who were concerned about attendance. They began with a "crack down on absentees" attitude and planned to communicate electronically with their homes and to develop a more stringent attendance policy. But a more precise look at their data prompted discussion of individual students, and they refocused their energy on a plan to match each chronic absentee with an adult mentor. Their analysis was illustrated in Figure 4.3, and their action plan was featured as Figure 4.13. This action plan includes a column called "Monitoring, Evaluation," which identifies the evidence that will show goals being met. This evidence should contain indicators of implementation and indicators of impact. Figure 4.13 shows that the initial steps involve planning, training, and implementation, so the implementation indicators are items such as criteria approved, parent permissions returned, lists of mentors and students, commitment forms, and schedules. These documents are kept on file. If this project were grant funded, they would be part of the grant evaluation. They demonstrate that the adults are "working their plan." They represent evidence of implementation but do not yet indicate whether there was an impact on the rate of absenteeism.

Indicators of Standards-Based Teaching and Learning

Washington State is one of 49 states with education reform legislation that identifies state standards (essential academic learning requirements) and mandates a statewide performance assessment system. Because the tests in reading, writing, communication, and math were initially given at the fourth, seventh, and tenth grades, the state standards were benchmarked at those three levels to provide the test specifications. Beyond that, an understanding of what should be taught and when was left up to districts and schools.

In my work with the Seattle schools, it was clear that the district already had a long history of curriculum work, so it was imperative to implement the state standards by building on and integrating them with the existing curriculum frameworks and other previous projects. More than 300 teachers were then engaged in a Standards Network to backward-map from the state benchmark levels and clarify the benchmarks for the intervening grades. (Note: Several years *after* individual districts created their grade-level benchmarks, the state provided the "GLE's"—grade-level expectations.)

Seattle took two steps beyond the grade-level benchmarking so there would be indicators of implementation and impact. One step was identification of the characteristics of standards-based teaching and learning that should emerge in schools and classrooms. The other step was to develop classroom-based assessments that would reflect the format and level of challenge of the state tests, pilot them, and develop anchor papers and scoring guides directly from the work of our own students in Seattle schools. We believed that the best way to understand what a standard really demands is to see how it looks from the assessment end of the instructional cycle.

The 15 Indicators of Standards-Based Teaching and Learning are presented in Figure 5.1. They seemed pretty clear, until we ran into the reality previously quoted from Fullan (2005), that "*terms* travel well, but the underlying *conceptualization and thinking* do not." (p. 10). This list of characteristics had to be discussed multiple times for clear understanding. Then it was used in many ways, each of which led to deeper understanding. For example, the Indicators of Standards-Based Teaching and Learning were introduced to principals in breakout sessions at a principals' retreat 4 months before the standards and benchmarks were even taken to the school board for adoption. Principals were asked to discuss each indicator and informally rate their schools on a loosely defined scale:

4—Fully implemented by all teachers

3—Mostly in place

2—Off to a good start

1—Still catching on

Through a simple show of hands, we tallied their ratings, and participants observed which indicators were already in evidence and could be used as a foundation for next steps. We also noticed which indicators were least in evidence across all schools. This helped us focus our staff development plans for the coming year.

In addition to the use of the 15 Indicators in training workshops and videos, principals used this set of characteristics to develop implementation plans for their individual schools. They were not given a required timeline but were asked to work with their staff to develop an implementation plan for Seattle's standards-based learning system. Principals also used the 15 Indicators as a reference for formative discussions with individual teachers.

The evidence of implementation of standards-based teaching and learning was reported by one principal as shown in Figure 5.2. Of particular note is the emphasis on evidence from both the classroom and school level, as

Figure 5.1   Indicators of Standards-Based Teaching and Learning

1. The district has developed clear statements of what students should know and be able to do.

2. Standards apply to all students with high expectations for their success.

3. The teacher knows how each lesson relates to district and state academic standards.

4. Students know what they are learning, what standards are related to it, and why they are learning it.

5. Standards are constant; instructional strategies and time are the variables.

6. Planning begins with standards rather than materials.

7. Practice activities are clearly aligned to standard(s) with the student as worker and the teacher as coach.

8. Students know how the teacher expects them to show what they've learned.

9. Students frequently evaluate their own work before the teacher does, using the same criteria.

10. Feedback to students is related to performance levels on standards, not based on comparison with other students.

11. Student performance data are used to revise curriculum and instruction.

12. The assessment system includes a balance of external tests for program evaluation and classroom assessments for individual student diagnosis and instruction.

13. Students have multiple opportunities to demonstrate achievement of standards.

14. Assessment of student achievement is consistent across teachers and schools, using common performance indicators.

15. Teachers work with colleagues to share and compare scoring of classroom-based assessments.

SOURCE: Used with permission of Joseph Olchefske, Seattle School District, Seattle, Washington.

well as communication with parents and community. This example of using district indicators and gathering classroom and school-level evidence demonstrates the three levels of collaboration that are illustrated in Figure 3.4.

Evidence of Reading Program Implementation

In Chapter 4, "The Reading Debate" was resolved through the use of a decision matrix. In another setting, two elementary schools housed in aging buildings were going to be merged and relocated into a brand-new structure. Both were Title I schools, both were involved in Reading First initiatives—but they had chosen very different approaches. The direction of the district was that the new school would select one of the federally approved programs and not have two different reading philosophies played out under the same roof. Proponents of each program had strong beliefs, and it was a time of stress. What brought them together was a vision of their desired future, focused on what would be

Figure 5.2   Summary of Schoolwide Standards Rollout

Classroom Implementation

- Visible posting of standards within the classroom and on hallway bulletin boards

- Grade-level/teacher calendars of standards covered, submitted to principal and shared with grade-level teams

- Use of Classroom-Based Assessments to include the following in first year: (1) At least one CBA for each strand of math, scored jointly by grade-level teams and results reported back to Math Goal Team for schoolwide data share; (2) Use of all reading and writing CBAs in every classroom; (3) Use of reading assessment notebooks utilizing at least two strategies from Bonnie Campbell Hill training

- Lesson plans include identification of targeted standards AND benchmarks

- Identification of and early intervention for students in lowest-achieving ranges of assessments

- Early K–2 reading/literacy focus with concentration on standards and reading continuum progress

- Math journals done in every class with writing emphasis on defending solutions to problems

- Visits to each other's classrooms or other school classrooms that are scoring well on Washington Assessment of Student Learning

- Bimonthly newsletters home to parents with emphasis upon curriculum and standards familiarity

---

Schoolwide Implementation

- Curriculum Night presentations focused on explanation of standards and assessments

- Development of report card alternative by Leadership team members and principal (Standards Student Report) for first trimester conference

- Emphasis on standards in every parent/teacher conference to include the following: (1) New written Standards Student Report, (2) sharing of District standards booklet, and (3) sharing of at least two pieces of student work as compared against scoring guides and anchor papers

- Principal communication about standards in bimonthly Principal Page newsletters as well as letter home regarding standards integration with parent/teacher conferences

- Use of Boeing Grant of $10,000 for further training in areas of scoring student work, using data effectively to formulate goals, visiting out-of-district classrooms using the state standards, establishing guidelines for effective math and writing journals, and attending national conferences on implementing standards

- Providing subs so that grade-level teachers can meet at least 3 half days to work on standards implementation plans, with minutes reported back to principal

- 100% of staff trained in Standards-Based Learning System, followed up with assistance from Central Support standards coach, and monthly meetings

- Principal will incorporate standards progression and implementation with each staff member during the evaluation process.

- Reworking teacher-prep schedule to provide more common grade-level meeting time for teachers

- Revision and reworking of Academic Achievement Plan to integrate and implement standards in all areas, to be accomplished by five strategic goal teams; every staff member is required to be an active member of a goal team; monthly meetings or as needed; minutes submitted to principal and other staff

- Technology support of standards in area of oral communication (i.e., hyperstudio projects) and publishing of writing, especially for spring Festival of the Arts

- Add half-time educational specialist to work with students above standard; set participation criteria using standards in state assessment and classroom

- Continue to align private and Weighted Student Formula budget to meet needs of EVERY student in getting them to standard and above; each grade level has specifically defined strategies as defined in the Academic Achievement Plan.

Community Implementation and Involvement

- Attend and present at fall Community Forum

- Publish news articles regarding standards implementation in neighborhood newspaper

- Student recruitment to include emphasis upon standards and assessments shared in January and February community visits

- Participate in events such as Rotary Principal for a Day and host other visitors to share our Standards Story

---

happening for teachers and students once Our Reading Program (ORP)—regardless of name—was identified:

When we have implemented ORP, teachers will

- Be engaging students in explicit reading strategies
- Be consistent in classroom procedures
- Be challenging students who need it and supporting students who need it
- Be enthusiastic and seeking to learn
- Be seeing student successes
- Be continuing to refine our practice

When we have implemented ORP, students will

- Be successful
- Love to read
- Read at or above grade level
- Support each other
- Be strategic readers (e.g., self-correct, problem solve)
- Be transferring skills and strategies through all their work

- Feel comfortable yet challenged
- Be receiving interventions when they struggle
- Use higher-level thinking skills
- Be moving from phonics foundation to using skills and comprehending
- Be proficient on the state test

We will all work together to support each other in reaching these outcomes.

These statements were created before staff began to analyze any specific program. This bold commitment of staff to become one and support each other has been a unifying force, as some learn a new program that is already familiar to others—and as some veteran users realize their practices may have "drifted" since their initial training. A year from now, these commitments will be the basis for providing evidence of implementation. Because the staff articulated outcomes for both adults and students, the needed evidence of impact on student performance is already foreshadowed.

Self-Evaluation of School Improvement Consortium

Readers of *Getting Excited About Data* (Holcomb, 2004) may remember a consortium of school districts that began to work collaboratively and strengthen their school improvement efforts and uses of data. Some districts were starting from scratch. Others had several years of training and work with a variety of models and processes. Each model had its own terminology, so it was dangerously easy to slip into arguments over semantics. The group developed Figure 5.3 to outline the seven components of their school improvement blueprint and provide a common vocabulary for discussion.

Four implementation indicators were provided for each of the seven components. The self-evaluation rubric was then used as a diagnostic tool, with each school marking the boxes that described its present status. It also served as a planning tool because it illustrated what the next steps should look like. The same rubric was marked each year to show the progress that had been made toward the "4" column. This demonstrated progress was part of the evidence that the consortium provided in its successful applications for continued funding.

Innovation Configuration Maps

Innovation Configuration (IC) Maps have been around since the early 1980s, when the developers of the Concerns-Based Adoption Model realized that trainers and change agents do not always provide a clear picture of what their program or recommended practice really looks like in operation. "When there is such confusion, principals and other facilitators may give conflicting signals, and teachers will create their own versions for the change as they try to understand and use the materials and/or processes that have been advocated" (Hall & Hord, 2001, p. 37). It's not that people don't want to do the right thing and do the thing right; it's that they have not been given clear images of what it looks like and sounds like when applied in their own context. So the innovation morphs into many different configurations, with every user thinking

Figure 5.3 School Improvement Consortium Self-Evaluation

	1	2	3	4
Structure	Consortium contact district coordination group	# 1 + School-level leadership teams (team in each building coordinating with district team); building-level planning	# 2 + Community component, formation of subcommittees for implementation	School leadership team is active and linked to district team; teacher involvement crosses grades and department lines
Profile	Awareness of use of profile at building level	Profile designed and data collected at building level	Data analyzed at building level with staff involvement	Data applied in goal setting and decision making
Mission	School mission statements exist but are not in alignment with the district mission statement	School mission statements are in alignment with district mission statement and/or beliefs but do not include full participation of shareholders	School mission statements are in alignment with district mission and/or beliefs and were developed with full participation of shareholders	School mission statements are in alignment and developed by shareholders and provide the direction and focus for decision making
Standards	Shareholders are aware of the concept of standards	Content performance standards are identified (math, language arts, social studies, science)	Curriculum and assessment are aligned with standards	Classroom instructional planning and assessment are standards referenced
Goals	Target goals are identified by school leadership teams	Working draft of goals developed through staff involvement supported by baseline data	Goals are measurable, performance based, data based, selected by full staff participation, and focused on student learning	Goals are measurable, performance based, data based, selected by full staff participation, focused on student learning, used to focus and consolidate resources and efforts; results drive the improvement plan
Plans	No comprehensive school improvement plan in place	Some elements in place; not clearly evident that there is a connection to student learning	All or most elements evidenced; site-based involvement; clear connection to student learning; staff development plans well developed	Strategies, timelines, and indicators of progress; strong evidence driven by profile; strong site-based involvement; clearly defined staff development activities; goals and timelines are specific, feasible, and occurring
Monitoring and Reporting	School complies only with mandates (e.g., state assessment)	Indicators are identified to monitor progress on each school improvement goal	Staff are engaged in regular review of progress indicators in the school improvement plan (internal)	Procedures for both internal and external reviews of progress are in place

that he or she has the right version and interpretation. "In addition, because teachers, like the rest of us, are always short on time, they will tend to reduce the amount of change and effort they have to invest" (p. 37).

Since new programs or practices are usually selected only after results they have demonstrated are checked (especially with the No Child Left Behind focus on scientifically based research and evidence), correct implementation is critical, or the documented results will not be achieved in the local setting. Student learning will not be maximized, the credibility of the initiators will suffer, and skepticism and low morale will carry over to inhibit the next change effort.

In short, an Innovation Configuration Map provides a clear description of what a new program or strategy is and is not. By describing a range of variations of use, it also provides a guide for increasing a user's effectiveness.

An IC Map is simply a table in which each row is a component of the program or strategy, and each column represents a variation in use. There is no set limit to the number of rows or columns. A component with four variations or levels of practice would have four columns, which might be labeled with numbers 1–4 or with terms like Highly Effective, Effective, Adequate, and Beginning. However, some components might have only three variations, or as many as five, or occasionally six. Thus, it is not necessary for all rows (components) to have entries in the same number of columns (variations).

An additional column, farthest to the right, would represent unacceptable use or nonuse, and could be labeled "Wrong Direction" (Richardson, 2007, p. 7). The developers of the two examples presented in Figures 5.4 and 5.5 did not include this column after discussions about their district and school culture and how the negative example might arouse resistance or evoke fear of use as an evaluation. This writer, like the originators, believes that there is great teaching power in a nonexample and that it should be clearly communicated that some practices are not appropriate or effective.

Purpose. The Innovation Configuration Map is a tool that educators can use to identify expectations about a new program or other innovation. Working on the IC Map can also help professional developers learn what the participants heard and understood from the training they received. Facilitators of work on IC Maps should emphasize that the IC Map is a tool for coaching and monitoring their own work and not for teacher evaluation.

When to Use. Ideally, an Innovation Configuration Map would be created during the planning stage, so that training would be developed to align with and focus specifically on the essential components of the new program or practice. In many cases when this is not done in the beginning, an IC Map can be developed after participants have received training in a new program or practice, and can be used to check for common understanding and to diagnose needs for further training and to demonstrate progress. The IC Map is also useful after initial stages to provide clarification or identify which components are going well and where additional support is needed.

Who to Involve. Hall and Hord (2001) recommend a group of 3–7 key people who can give concentrated attention to the task. Teachers and principals who are directly involved in implementation should be involved in developing the IC

Map. When this tool is new to the group, a facilitator with expertise in facilitation and experience with IC Maps should guide the work.

Materials Needed. Chart paper and stick-on notes are helpful for generating components and variations and moving them around as discussion continues. Resources from the National Staff Development Council may be useful, such as the August/September 2007 issue of *Tools for Schools,* which includes templates that can be copied.

Tips for Facilitators. The facilitator should take time to clarify the purposes of the Innovation Configuration Map and establish support for the importance of common language for understanding, consistency, and commitment.

The first step is to discuss the new program or practice and identify the main components that are part of it. These components become the rows of the IC Map, as seen in Figures 5.4 and 5.5.

The second step is to reach agreement on the ideal picture of implementation. The focus must be on *observable* behaviors or artifacts. Ask the group questions to prompt their thinking: What would it look like? Sound like? What would teachers be doing? These are the behaviors that need to be described. It may also be important to identify materials or artifacts, through questions like "What would be visible in the classroom?" and "What would students be using?" An IC Map for writing instruction might include references to written work being prominently displayed, students having draft books readily accessible, and so forth.

The descriptors of complete or ideal use of each component of the innovation are placed in the first column, so they are most prominent and are seen first. (This is the opposite of rubrics used for assessing student work, which move from left to right toward the best product.)

The third step is to identify practices for each component that are no longer acceptable or that would represent nonuse of the innovation. For example, an IC Map for implementation of a hands-on math program might include an item like "The cellophane has not been removed from the manipulatives kit." These indicators of nonuse or unacceptable variations are placed in the far right column.

Having established the two extremes, ideal use and nonuse, the group will think about variations that naturally occur and steps in growth from beginning to increasingly proficient use. These descriptors are placed in additional columns as needed, moving from ideal implementation to that which is unacceptable.

Once the group has agreed on the descriptions, the last step is to refine the statements by using parallel structure, which begins each descriptor with an action verb. The importance of this step is not just grammatical. The use of action verbs forces the group to be sure that they have focused on observable behaviors and reinforces the actions that implementers must take.

For Example: Implementation of Six-Trait Writing. This IC Map was developed at one school that was part of a districtwide writing initiative. A consultant from the regional education agency assisted teachers and administrators in reaching clarification about how they would assess their progress. Teacher collaboration increased as they developed a common language and realized that some teachers who were more confident and more advanced on the IC Map could help their colleagues.

Figure 5.4 Innovation Configuration Map: Six-Trait Writing

Essential Components of Implementing the Six-Trait Writing Approach Into Current Writing Instruction	Level 1	Level 2	Level 3	Level 4
Teacher demonstrates a thorough understanding of the six-trait writing approach	• Can articulate a rationale for the value and importance of six-trait writing approach • Uses a variety of instructional strategies that are appropriate to each of the six traits • Six-trait language is integrated into all curricular areas	• Can articulate a rationale for the value and importance of six-trait writing approach • Uses a variety of instructional strategies that are appropriate to several of the six traits • Six-trait language is integrated into several curricular areas	• Demonstrates an emerging awareness of the value and importance of the six-trait writing approach • Recognizes/accepts the six-trait writing approach as a schoolwide initiative • Six-trait language is used only in the context of writing	• Demonstrates an emerging awareness of the value and importance of the six-trait writing approach • Recognizes/accepts the six-trait writing approach as a schoolwide initiative • Six-trait language is used only in the context of writing
Effective instructional strategies are used to implement six-trait writing approach	• Continuously seeks and uses examples of writing from multiple sources to model the six traits (teacher's writing, newspaper, magazines, literature) • Embeds writing activities into daily lessons across all areas of the curriculum • Six-trait writing rubrics are routinely used to establish expectations and assess student writing	• Seeks and uses examples of writing to model the traits from more traditional sources (textbooks, basals, teacher writing) • Embeds writing activities across some areas of the curriculum • Six-trait writing rubrics are occasionally used to establish expectations and assess student writing	• Uses limited examples of writing to model the traits from other sources (computer-generated lessons, other teachers' lessons/ideas) • Writing activities are focused primarily on Language Arts • Six-trait writing rubrics are seldom used to establish expectations and assess student writing • Writing is assigned, not actively modeled or taught	• Uses limited examples of writing to model the traits from other sources (computer-generated lessons, other teachers' lessons/ideas) • Writing activities are focused primarily on Language Arts • Six-trait writing rubrics are seldom used to establish expectations and assess student writing • Writing is assigned, not actively modeled or taught

Teacher evaluates student data to monitor progress and revise classroom lessons to improve students' writing	• Consistently uses formal and informal assessments based on the six traits to document student improvement in writing and identify areas for growth • Consistently creates and revises lessons relevant to identified student writing needs • Engages students in analysis and assessment of their own and others' writing	• Frequently uses formal and informal assessments based on six traits to document student improvement in writing and identify areas for growth • Occasionally creates and revises lessons relevant to student writing needs • Engages students in analysis and assessment of their own writing	• Periodically uses formal and informal assessments based on the six traits to document student improvement in writing and identify areas for growth • Creates lessons based only on the curriculum • Student writing is assessed solely by the teacher	• Periodically uses formal and informal assessments based on the six traits to document student improvement in writing and identify areas for growth • Creates lessons based only on the curriculum • Student writing is assessed solely by the teacher
Teacher collaborates with colleagues to implement the six-trait writing approach	• Meets regularly with colleagues to discuss components of six-trait writing approach • Shares examples of student work • Offers lesson plan ideas • Willingly tries new ideas, offers and listens to constructive criticism about how to improve instruction	• Meets regularly with colleagues to discuss components of six-trait writing approach • Shares examples of student work • Listens to, but may not employ, new ideas or take into account constructive criticism about effective instruction	• Meets regularly with colleagues to discuss components of six-trait writing (only at required staff meetings) • Shares examples of student work (staff meetings only) • Does not contribute ideas for lessons • Not willing to try new ideas and has difficulty offering or accepting constructive criticism	• Meets regularly with colleagues to discuss components of six-trait writing (only at required staff meetings) • Shares examples of student work (staff meetings only) • Listens to contributions of others • Typically works alone to implement six-trait writing • Refrains from offering suggestions or accepting constructive criticism about effective instruction

SOURCE: Used with permission of Nana LoCicero, Roosevelt Elementary School, Kenosha, Wisconsin.

A Variation: Leadership for Change. Researcher Shirley Hord worked with the Gadsden School District in Arizona on development of professional learning communities and implementing change. When an innovation this complex impacts the behavior and responsibilities of many different groups, a separate IC Map can be developed to guide each group. In this case, specific attention was given to the role of principals and other leaders as they initiated, supported, and guided change. Figure 5.5 shows the IC Map that was developed to help leaders assess their roles, network with each other for support, and move their own practice forward—influencing, in turn, the teachers and the success of students.

IS OUR PLAN WORKING? EVIDENCE OF IMPACT

Figure 4.13 outlined the middle school team's plan for a mentor program. A collection of criteria, parent permissions, training plans, and minutes would provide the indicators that the plan is being implemented. But the goal was to improve student attendance and achievement, so reporting the work done by the adults is not sufficient to answer the question "How will we know we are getting there?" The success of the plan is determined by whether it has the desired impact on the students—in this case, whether students are in school more and whether being in school more is contributing to better performance.

In the "where are we now" phase of school improvement, data were gathered on student achievement to assess the current situation. The same data should be compiled annually to develop a longitudinal look at progress and can be portrayed in run charts.

When schools worked to identify "where we want to go," part of the effort was to take the major components of mission and belief statements and make them concrete with observable indicators. Chapter 3 provided the example of a school that wanted its students to become lifelong learners and needed to articulate what a lifelong learner looks like and sounds like at various ages. They brainstormed the characteristics of a lifelong learner that they would be able to see developing within their own students, even at an early age. They included things such as "gets interested in something," "goes to the library (or Internet) to learn more about it," "starts projects on his own," "tries to get other people interested," and "likes to figure out her own way to do it." But what if the instructional program is so prescriptive that a student doesn't have the chance to get interested in something on her own? What if trying to get someone else interested in your topic is considered cheating? What if figuring out your own way to do it doesn't match any of the boxes on the rubric? We need to be careful what we put in our mission statement, because then we have to demonstrate what we're doing to fulfill it *and* be sure we're not doing things that actually prevent it.

Another school faced a similar challenge from its mission statement, which included the phrase "prepared to live in a democratic, pluralistic society." It sounded great. But the staff was concerned about the reality of the rhetoric. The student population was quite homogeneous racially and economically, and staff members wondered if students were really aware of issues and needs outside their own environment. The observable behaviors that they decided to monitor were participation in student government, increased roles for students in shared

Figure 5.5 Innovation Configuration Map: Leadership for Change

The principal and other leaders . . . .

Desired Outcome	Level 1	Level 2	Level 3	Level 4

Create atmosphere or context for change	• Schedule time and place for staff reflection and collaborative work
	• Provide learning environment
	• Develop culture of learning
	• Develop staff's skills of collaboration:
	  o Modes of conversation
	  o Conflict management
	  o Decision-making models
	• Nurture leadership team skills
	• Activate leadership teams for learning
	• Monitor to ensure time is used well
		• Schedule time and place for staff reflection and collaborative work
		• Provide learning environment
		• Develop culture of learning
		• Develop staff's skills of collaboration:
		  o Modes of conversation
		  o Conflict management
		  o Decision-making models
		• Activate leadership teams for learning
			• Schedule time and place for staff reflection and collaborative work
			• Provide learning environment
			• Develop staff's skills of collaboration:
			  o Modes of conversation
			  o Conflict management
			  o Decision-making models
				• Schedule time and place for staff reflection and collaborative work
				• Provide learning environment

Develop and communicate a shared vision	• Identify purpose or school mission • Define values and/or staff beliefs • Engage staff in studying data to identify needs for improvement • Study and select new programs or practices to address the priority need for improvement • Create an IC Map that represents and communicates the new practice, the vision of change • Keep the vision visible • Revisit the vision periodically	• Identify purpose/school mission • Engage staff in studying data to identify needs for improvement • Select new programs or practices to address the priority need for improvement • Create an IC Map that represents/communicates the new practice, the vision of change	• Engage staff in studying data to identify needs for improvement • Select new programs/practices to address the priority need for improvement	• Engage staff in studying data to identify needs for improvement • Adopt new programs/practices to address the need for improvement

(Continued)

Figure 5.5 (Continued)

Desired Outcome	Level 1	Level 2	Level 3	Level 4

Plan and provide resources	• Gather staff information (SoC/LoU/IC) and relevant data
	• Use six strategies to develop an implementation plan that will achieve the vision
	• Identify resources needed and plan to access them:
	  ○ Currently available
	  ○ Needed as reflected in the vision
	• Establish timelines
		• Gather staff information (SoC/LoU/IC) and relevant data
		• Use six strategies to develop an implementation plan that will achieve the vision
		• Identify resources needed and plan to access them:
		  ○ Currently available
		  ○ Needed as reflected in the vision
			• Use six strategies to develop an implementation plan that will achieve the vision
			• Identify resources needed and plan to access them:
			  ○ Currently available
			  ○ Needed as reflected in the vision
				• Identify resources needed and plan to access them:
				  ○ Currently available
				  ○ Needed as reflected in the vision

Invest in professional development	• Gather and analyze student data (AIMS, mandated and district assessments) and teacher data (SoC/LoU/IC) • Use staff and student data to create adult learning activities • Create vision-driven action plan for professional development • Arrange for, schedule, and deliver adult learning activities • Establish timelines	• Gather and analyze student data (AIMS, mandated and district assessments) and teacher data (SoC/LoU/IC) • Use staff and student data to create adult learning activities • Create vision-driven professional development plan	• Gather and analyze student data (AIMS, mandated and district assessments) and teacher data (SoC/LoUt/IC) • Create professional development plan	• Create professional development plan

Check for progress	• Gather staff information
	  ○ SoC
	  ○ LoU
	  ○ IC
	• Include staff in interpreting data and determining needs
	• Develop a culture of continuous assessment
	• Celebrate small and large successes publicly and/or privately
	• Establish timelines
		• Gather staff information
		  ○ SoC
		  ○ LoU
		  ○ IC
		• Include staff in interpreting data and determining needs
		• Develop a culture of continuous assessment
			• Gather staff information
			  ○ SoC
			  ○ LoU
			  ○ IC
			• Ask staff what they need for implementation of new practices
				• Ask staff what they need for implementation of new practices

Provide assistance	• Schedule needed professional development:
	  ○ Large group
	  ○ Small group
	  ○ Individuals
	• Provide coaches and/or mentors
	• Review time and activities for collaborative work
	• Inventory resources, restock, and/or share
	• Revisit action plan and revise as needed
	• Celebrate small and large successes publicly and/or privately
		• Schedule needed professional development:
		  ○ Large group
		  ○ Small group
		  ○ Individuals
		• Provide coaches and/or mentors
		• Review time and activities for collaborative work
		• Inventory resources and restock
			• Schedule needed professional development
			  ○ Large group
			  ○ Small group
			  ○ Individuals

SOURCE: Used with permission of Olivia Elizondo Zepeda, Gadsden Elementary School District #32, San Luis, Arizona.

decision making, active participation in that year's county and state elections, and participation in community service projects. Students in civics classes became involved in identifying opportunities for student involvement, and students in math classes gathered the data on participation rates to show results. These school leaders realized that the existing culture of their school did not empower students to get practice doing the very things they wanted them to do as adults, so they had to alter some of their own roles and create new opportunities.

Gathering information on these indicators would become part of the monitoring stage as the school addressed the "How will we know we are getting there?" question. The tools that were introduced to display data in Chapters 2 and 4 are tools that can be used again and again throughout the process.

Many of us who learned and use Madeline Hunter's synthesis of theory and research related to effective instruction have difficulty saying the word *monitor* without adding *and adjust*. This is true for the implementation phase of school improvement. Although we needed specific action plans to set realistic timelines, acquire needed resources, and avoid overloading ourselves with too many complex efforts, those action plans must be considered "carved in Jell-O." If results cannot be observed or the changes we see are not the intended, desired ones, school leadership teams must acknowledge and address those facts. They will need to verify whether the action plan is being implemented as intended, and they may have to modify it on the basis of resources, unexpected barriers, and other needs that arise. They may need to reexamine whether the strategies selected for implementation should be changed. School leaders, however, must also use caution and guard against premature decisions to abandon a course before it has had time for a true test. The challenge is to strike a proper balance between flexibility and evolutionary planning on the one hand and patience and perseverance on the other.

Monitoring progress is not always a sophisticated and complicated endeavor. Sometimes principals agree to conduct business on the roof, kiss a pig, or sit in a dunking booth if students read a million pages—and parent volunteers construct a huge paper thermometer to count the pages that have been read. That is a way of monitoring progress that can motivate continued effort until the real results (higher reading scores) can be documented.

Middle School Evaluation Plan

John Bullen Middle School was a junior high for a very long time. As part of its transformation to a middle school housing Grades 6–8, the staff chose the Accelerated Schools model for school governance and comprehensive school reform design. The words in bold below represent how their journey might be recorded on Figure 1.1.

First, they spent a year and involved a broad range of shareholders in development of a vision and **mission** statement. Then they compiled their **school portfolio**, which included academic achievement data from the Iowa Tests of Basic Skills and the Wisconsin Student Assessment System, discipline data, and perceptual data from the Accelerated Schools Process survey. During the summer, the entire staff participated in the "Taking Stock" phase of the Accelerated Schools Process and discussed the data, using the inquiry process.

From the **concerns** that emerged, they identified four **priority goal** areas:

- Discipline
- Parent involvement
- Teaching and learning
- Communications

A cadre was formed to **study** each of these goal areas and recommend **strategies.** At this point, I became involved as the external coach and met with each cadre. That first visit was a little messy. People who had volunteered for the discipline cadre were entrenched in two camps, one for improving the new discipline plan and one committed to eliminating it. The parent involvement cadre included parents, but parents and teachers had quite different versions of what parent involvement should look like and who owned the problem. Some members of the communications cadre were carrying big axes to grind regarding the principal and central office. The teaching and learning cadre was the most harmonious group, but two big things were missing: Members weren't clear on their role, and they hadn't spent much time discussing the student performance data that were included in their school portfolio. So they didn't have answers for some of my initial questions:

- What specific area of student achievement is your focus?
- What is your leadership role in applying the training you've had in Dimensions of Learning?
- Where does introduction of the Schoolwide Enrichment Model fit with your overall instructional program and school reform design?
- What are the results you want to be able to report as a consequence of these strategies?

Each of these cadres had some problems to work through, but that is not a criticism. I was neither surprised nor disappointed. They were exactly where most groups are when they begin to work together! And they made rapid progress during that year. When I came back the next spring, they had reached agreement on the **strategies** they would recommend to the full staff. The discipline cadre had healed their conflicts and agreed to work on (a) consistent implementation of the Honor Level System and (b) improving the effectiveness of in-school suspension.

The parent involvement cadre had followed through on my recommendation to study Joyce Epstein's research and learn about the Parent Involvement Network through Johns Hopkins University. They had identified an ambitious agenda for (a) Parents in Education nights, (b) Lighted Schoolhouse activities, (c) a more reliable and current Calendar of Events so parents would know about the opportunities for involvement, (d) a directory of parents with interests they could share and ways they would like to volunteer, (e) a directory of teachers with their pictures and some personal information to help build connections with parents and students, (f) formation of a Community Action Team to deal with the issues that needed a broader coalition beyond parents, and (g) continuing with the Parent Teacher Student Association.

The teaching and learning cadre had studied the data and uncovered a need to expand the Learning Support Program so more students had access. They had also made the connection between the Powerful Learning component of Accelerated Schools and their plans for application of the Dimensions of Learning and use of the Schoolwide Enrichment Model in sixth grade. A Comprehensive School Reform grant from the state of Wisconsin provided resources for a significant group of staff to travel and receive in-depth training in all these designs.

The communications cadre had also prepared recommendations to (a) add a staff issues page to the Thursday bulletin, (b) identify staff liaisons and form a mediation team, (c) expand parent-teacher communication through technology such as classroom telephones and e-mail, and (d) include team-building activities in professional development plans.

Now they were ready for coaching on the action plans that would be needed. They were surprised at the dogged way we had to keep slugging through nuts-and-bolts questions such as these:

- And what would need to happen before that?
- How could you arrange time for that to happen?
- Then what could you *stop* doing with that time?
- Have you transferred all the steps you promised in your grant applications into these plans so your efforts are consolidated?

They were cooperative and worked hard because they realized that they had to present their recommendations to the rest of the staff. They knew that it would be hard to build strong commitment if they weren't ready with some preliminary answers to the "if we agree, how would it work" questions, so they really buckled down and hammered it out. They also said it was the hardest part of the process because "we like to procrastinate and leave the details for later." The words used here—*dogged, slugging, buckled,* and *hammered*—were their words as each cadre worked for a half day on their action plans and developed the main points for their presentation to staff. I left again, they went to their staff, and all the recommendations were accepted.

My next trip to Bullen focused on the **indicators** they would use in the evaluation plan they needed for their Comprehensive School Reform Design grant. I spent another half day with each cadre. We reviewed the applications they had written for every grant so we could be sure that every type of evidence that would be needed was included and would be gathered along the way. We didn't want to lose any possibilities of continued funding, nor did we want to have people scrambling for documentation at the last minute before filing the next application.

We also didn't want to pile on a lot of extra work to meet evaluation requirements, so we started by referring back to all the types of data they had at their disposal already. Figure 5.6 is the grid we constructed to represent their comprehensive evaluation plan, based on the "monitoring and evaluation" column of all the action plans. As noted at the bottom, it includes both qualitative and quantitative evidence.

One column has the heading "Targeted Methodology." This is where we reported specific types of data collection or analysis that would be needed to demonstrate the results of particular interventions and accomplishment of related goals. Every other notation or X on this grid represents evidence already available that

Figure 5.6   Middle School Evaluation Plan

Tools	Attendance, Sign-in Sheets	Fliers, Notices, Articles	Meeting Notes, Documents	Assignment Sheets in ISS	Staff Survey	Parent Survey	Student Survey/Interview	Targeted Methodology	Overall GPA Analysis	Overall Test Score Analysis	% Participation in Extracurricular Activities
Discipline											
Consistent implementation of HLS	X		X					Analysis of infractions by category			
Improving effectiveness of ISS				X				Improvement of grades and decrease of use by ISS users			
Parent Involvement											
P.I.E. nights	X	X						Parents come; grades up and homework up	X	X	
Lighted schoolhouse	X	X					X				
Calendar of events		X					X			X	
Directory of parents to volunteer			Directory X		X	X					
Directory of teachers' pictures and information			Directory X		X	X					
Community action team	To be developed in the future										
Continue PTSA	To be developed in the future										
Teaching and Learning											
Powerful Learning											
Application of Dimensions of Learning			Training participation X		X					Analysis by level	
Schoolwide Enrichment Model							X	Analysis by Friday attendance			
Expanded Learning Support			House plans X		X		X	Pre- and post-test		Analysis by level	
Communications											
Thursday bulletin with staff issues page			X		X						
Staff liaisons, mediation team	X		X		X			# of referrals and resolutions			
Technology for better parent-teacher communications					X	X		Homework completion			
E-mail; dismantle computer lab			X		X						
Team-building activities	X				X						
	Qualitative Measures							**Quantitative Measures**			

SOURCE: Used with permission of Blane McCann, John Bullen Middle School, Kenosha, Wisconsin.

could be gathered throughout the year, ready to attach and send away with grant reports and new applications—and also ready to publicize and celebrate at home.

High School Personalization

Earlier in the chapter, I referred to a panel discussion at a high school reform seminar. One of the speakers had described the principle of personalization and then reported his school's change to an eight-period day, and people had trouble seeing the connection. Contrast that example with the perseverance to move from general principles and ideals to congruent, concrete reality that is exemplified by the careful planning and conscientious monitoring described here.

The high school of 1,080 students reflects the diversity of urban Seattle and serves a large population of special education and English as a second language (ESL) students. The change process began when a core group of teacher leaders began to explore the Common Principles of the Coalition of Essential Schools (CES). After several years of cautious exploration and collegial dialogue, small forays and questions began to snowball into dramatic change.

The high school changed to a modified block schedule, created a school-wide mentorship program, required junior and senior projects and community service for graduation, and highlighted "personalization of education" as its greatest strength and most effective selling point with students and parents.

The personalization occurred through creation of heterogeneously balanced ninth-grade academies. Each academy housed 125 ninth graders, staffed by six teachers, realizing a student-to-teacher ratio of approximately 20:1. Students earned science, health, language arts, and social studies credit. Academic and behavioral standards applied to all students, and honors work could be arranged through individual student contracts.

Teachers collaborated during common prep time to encourage consistent policies and practices, flexible scheduling, strong communication links, and focused use of mentorships. Professional development time was spent on examining student and teacher work through five Critical Friends groups involving more than 85% of the staff.

The ability to forge schoolwide commitment around a set of principles and then define them in concrete terms and implement them is exceptional in itself, and the evidence of implementation has already been stated.

But the true purpose was to improve high school life for students, and evidence of impact was clear. Compared with ninth-grade statistics before the academies were implemented, freshman attendance increased from 84% to 92%, the average grade point average grew from 2.55 to 2.78, the dropout rate dropped from 6% to 2%, and discipline problems plummeted from 29% to 1%. Grades 9, 10, and 11 all demonstrated gains on the norm-referenced standardized tests given in the district.

Evidence of Student Learning

As shown in these middle school and high school examples, schools may have existing sources of data that can document the impact of school improvement on student learning and other student factors, like dropout rates and discipline infractions. Figure 5.4 shows how John Bullen Middle School had identified evaluation tools that would yield evidence of both implementation (e.g., sign-in sheets) and impact (e.g., grade point averages and test score analysis). As schools and districts have advanced through the years of No Child Left Behind, there has been a dangerously increased focus on state assessment results as the primary or only source of data being used to monitor student progress. Many authors have written lengthy articles about these dangers from sophisticated and statistical points of view.

I emphasize two very down-to-earth realities: First, the results from most state assessments are "too little too late"—it takes too long to get them, and the information is too general. The results come back months later, often not even in the same school year. (The worst I've encountered was a district in Illinois that had received the results from *last* year one week before the testing window opened for *this* year.) In Figure 5.7, the state test is illustrated as a floating bubble because it is not closely connected to the ongoing assessments that guide instruction, and because the timing is different across states.

Second, the results from state assessments are related to state standards in general but are not closely tied to the specific skills or benchmarks taught prior to the

Figure 5.7   Sources of Evidence: Pattern of Assessments

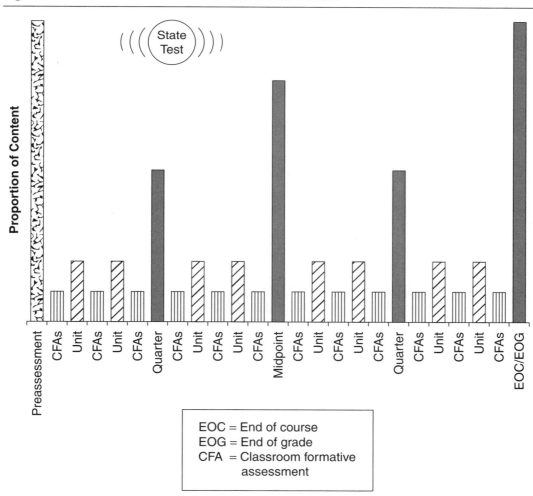

testing. For example, Wisconsin begins testing fourth-grade benchmarks in late October, so district curriculum mapping must study the assessment framework (test specifications) and move those benchmarks into third grade for instruction.

To be fair, the testing requirement of No Child Left Behind was not designed to be useful as feedback for teachers and students but to provide a basis for judging systems and applying sanctions. Practitioners and state leaders have simply tried our best to make it accomplish something more productive. We have looked for skills that are deemed most important by virtue of their weight in number of items or points, and have conducted item analysis when such information was available. Because of the high stakes connected to these tests, we use them as constructively as possible, but they are not sufficient, and in some cases are not even appropriate for the uses made of them.

Frustration with the high-stakes, standardized assessments have built into a crescendo of voices demanding assessment for learning, balanced assessment, formative assessment, short-cycle assessment, interim assessment, and on and on. Publishing companies have found a market niche for computerized tests that purport to be aligned with state standards and provide rather general levels of student progress over time, but not an indication of mastery of specific and essential skills that have been the intentional focus of most recent instruction.

Meanwhile, some proponents of professional learning communities have unleashed a new centralization-decentralization dilemma over development of common assessments. It seems logical that if a district has two large, comprehensive high schools, the assessment that verifies successful completion of Algebra I should be consistent for every student—regardless of the teacher or school—so that Algebra II can build upon it. Mike Schmoker's (2006) definition of the role of the central office for curriculum and instruction is helpful, stating that it should

- Assemble the evidence and start the dialogue around the importance of common curriculum, common assessments, and other fundamental elements of team-based learning communities
- Coordinate the development, by teachers, of common end-of-course outcomes and assessments in every course and subject area, perhaps starting with areas tested on state exams
- Establish procedures for grade and same-course teams to formally analyze annual achievement data, set measurable goals, and identify specific areas in need of improvement
- Ensure that each school sets a schedule for teams to meet, and establishes effective team meeting protocols and procedures for documenting the teams' focus and progress (pp. 156–157)

Figure 5.7 represents my vision of Lambert's (2003) concept of organizational reciprocity as applied to assessment for learning—and for having "real-time" data as evidence of impact. The complete figure represents a single content or subject area for the span of a course or grade level. As an example, we'll take the case of Algebra I when taught as a yearlong course. The four highest solid bars represent common assessments developed by teachers, and coordinated by the central office. They are the end-of-course (EOC) or end-of-grade (EOG) test, semester exam, and midterms. Their commonality is districtwide, to assure the degree of curriculum consistency necessary as preparation for the next level, in this case Algebra II. These district common assessments may be strongly influenced by materials included in a curriculum adoption, but choices should be made and appropriate local work done by those who provide the instruction—teams of teachers.

The first bar in Figure 5.7 is filled with dots because it represents pre-assessment, and I am not "solid" in my own thoughts on the topic. My hesitation is based on too many comments like "I have to do 3 weeks of review and pre-assessments, and then there's only about 3 weeks when I can teach before the state assessment starts." What I most urgently want to say is, *"Start teaching! If you're paying attention, you'll quickly spot those who are struggling, and then you can do some individual diagnostic work for more specifics."*

If the span of instructional time is a year, there are quarterly district common assessments. In Figure 5.7, each quarter is further broken down into 2- to 3-week periods, labeled as "unit" assessments. The amount of instructional time devoted to a unit of instruction should be based on the curriculum maps, which guide alignment of content and time and may vary from unit to unit. I have used 2–3 weeks for purposes of illustration, based on recommendations from both Tom Guskey and Doug Reeves about the frequency with which teachers should analyze information about their students' learning. The shorter, diagonally hatched bars represent the unit assessments that may be developed by teacher teams at the district level (especially in large districts) or by small groups at sites in departments, grade-level teams, professional learning communities, and so forth.

Between these unit assessments are the shortest sets of thin vertical bars that represent classroom formative assessments (CFAs). Multiple classroom formative assessments are brief and frequent. They consist of informal monitoring and quick observations that should be an integral part of the instructional process, such as short quizzes, examples performed by all students and checked by peers, and checklists used as teachers circulate during guided practice. Their purpose is to give students timely feedback and provide information for teachers to plan further instruction, to target students for tutorial support and other needed interventions, or to provide challenging enrichment opportunities.

THE PLAN AND THE PROOF

The previous chapters explore three key questions: Where are we now? Where do we want to go? How will we get there? This chapter has explored the question "How will we know we are getting there?" The emphasis has been on pre-planning how evidence will be gathered, so it can be reported as verification that implementation has occurred and that the effort is having an impact on student performance.

In *Students Are Stakeholders, Too!* (Holcomb, 2007), I chronicle a semifictionalized, composite case study of Knownwell High School, where students are "known well" and are authentically engaged in their school environment and in their learning. Their journey of change spans a 2-year period of time and includes the decisions reflected in Figure 5.8.

Figure 5.8 Knownwell High School's Improvement Plan

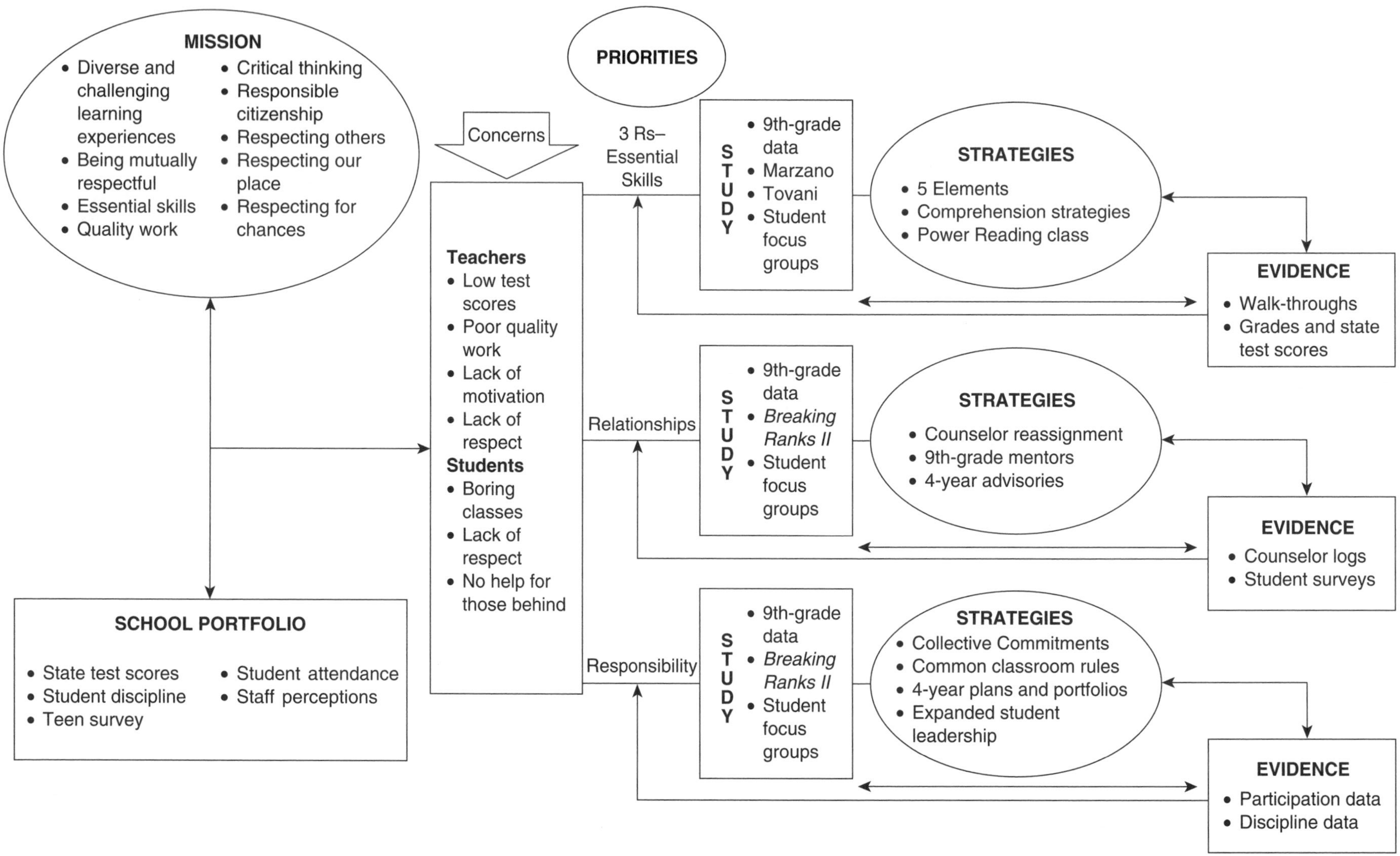

SOURCE: Reprinted from *Students Are Stakeholders, Too!* (p. 180), by E. L. Holcomb, 2007, Thousand Oaks, CA: Corwin Press. Copyright © 2007 by Corwin Press. Used with permission.

Figure 5.9 Knownwell High School's Proof of Improvement

***Priority Area:* Three R's (to provide diverse and challenging experiences, assure that all students master essential skills, and practice critical thinking)**

Strategies	Evidence of Implementation	Evidence of Impact

• Five Elements of Powerful Teaching
• Thinking strategies for reading comprehension
• Departmental help periods before/after school
• Teacher study groups for unit and lesson planning
	• Administrator walk-throughs show increasing use of Five Elements, ranging from 20% to 78%
	• Help periods attended by average of 15 students per period
	• All teachers trained in thinking strategies for reading; plans developed for protocols to work together on unit and lesson plans
		• Student survey shows use of Five Elements and some integration of thinking strategies
		• D/F lists reduced by 35%
		• Proficient on State Tests State Average
		  Reading 55% to 89% 72%
		  Math 42% to 72% 47%
		  Writing 55% to 83% 65%
		  Science 35% to 56% 36%

***Priority Area:* Relationships (in a mutually respectful environment)**

Strategies	Evidence of Implementation	Evidence of Impact
• Realignment of counselors by alphabet • Ninth-grade mentors • Advisories	• Letters to families that explained realignment and identified counselor • Mentor program established; met three times in August, once in September • Advisories incorporated into master schedule; being modified to 4-year configuration	• Discipline referrals for ninth graders down by 60% • Attendance rate increased from 91% to 95%

***Priority Area:* Responsibility (all students master essential skills, produce high-quality work, and practice responsible citizenship)**

Strategies	Evidence of Implementation	Evidence of Impact
• Expanded student government—House of Representatives • Collective Commitments and common classroom rules • Advisories • 4-year plans and portfolios	• House of Representatives established; 35 groups represented • Collective Commitments affirmed and published • Common rules identified and shared by mentors and teachers • Advisories incorporated into master schedule; being modified to 4-year configuration • Current ninth graders developed plans and started portfolios	• Discipline referrals for ninth graders down by 60% • Attendance rate increased from 91% to 95%

SOURCE: Reprinted from *Students Are Stakeholders, Too!* (p. 180), by E. L. Holcomb, 2007, Thousand Oaks, CA: Corwin Press. Copyright © 2007 by Corwin Press. Used with permission.

Answer Key

- Answering the "How will we know we are (getting) there?" question requires looking ahead to decide what evidence will be needed to document implementation and impact.

- Choosing research-based strategies does not guarantee success because results depend on consistent, accurate implementation. Innovation Configuration Maps are one of the tools that help practitioners clearly understand what it must look like and sound like, and how their practice must change.

- Evidence of implementation helps to assure that the adults follow through on the commitments of their school improvement plan, but the bottom line is improvement of student learning. A balanced set of large-scale, district and classroom assessments is necessary to provide evidence that staff efforts are really helping students.

The figure is shared here as an example of how Figure 1.1 can be completed to capture all the essential components of a comprehensive school improvement plan—on just one page.

The results of change displayed in Figure 5.9 are not fictionalized in any way. They are real improvements made at Bellingham High School. The center column captures the evidence of implementation by the adults in the school, while the right-hand column verifies evidence of impact on student learning. As we shall see in Chapter 6, the answers to "How will we sustain focus and momentum?" lie in a clear picture of the change(s) and depend on having evidence of progress to celebrate and renew energy and commitment.

6

Answering the "How Will We Sustain the Focus and Momentum?" Question

While writing the first edition, I watched on television while the city of Baltimore honored a hero. Baseball Hall of Famer Cal Ripken Jr. had broken Lou Gehrig's record of playing in 2,130 consecutive games. The numerals on the warehouse across from the diamond flipped to 2,131, and the crowd went wild. Cal just smiled and loped around the field as if he wasn't too sure what the fuss was all about. How did he reach that milestone? He just kept showing up for work. Along the way, he struck out at the plate now and then and recorded some errors in his position as shortstop. But he just kept showing up and doing his best. He knew how to sustain focus and momentum.

How can travelers on the road to school improvement develop that same tenacity? How do school leaders add momentum to the *M* of maintenance in RPTIM (Figure 1.1)? How does the innovation that was implemented in response to "How will we get there?" become institutionalized so that it is taken for granted as "just the way we do things around here"? Quality improvement users would say that you do so by repeating the PDCA cycle—now that you've checked what you've done, act on the information, and start again with planning. Those steps are important, but inadequate. They overestimate the power of technical processes and underestimate the power of the prevailing school culture. The scientific law that an object at rest tends to remain at rest is nowhere more true than in traditional organizations. Great leaders and great ideas have sparked new efforts that blaze briefly and sputter into oblivion because they are smothered by the overwhelming weight of the school culture. Lasting change requires reculturing, reshaping the norms of the organization—what the gurus of the early 1990s called "paradigm shifting." This chapter describes seven actions that are needed to sustain change:

- Understand and respond to reactions
- Continue training and coaching
- Cope with conflict
- Strengthen the culture of inquiry
- Support leaders and followers
- Shift from technical to adaptive
- Reaffirm organization values and commitments

UNDERSTAND AND RESPOND TO REACTIONS

Organizations are made up of human beings with vast prior experience and a wide range of personal needs and interests. To sustain a change effort, we must know how to recognize these needs and respond appropriately.

Children learn in different ways and at different speeds. In much the same way, adults adjust to change in different ways and at different rates. The Concerns-Based Adoption Model (CBAM) is based on studies of how teachers react to innovations. One component of the model identifies a developmental sequence of stages of concern through which people move as they accept and adjust to change. *Taking Charge of Change* (Hord, Rutherford, Huling-Austin, & Hall, 1987), published by the Association for Supervision and Curriculum Development (ASCD), describes the progression of concerns:

- Awareness
- Information
- Personal
- Management
- Consequence
- Collaboration
- Refocusing

Once individuals in the organization become aware of an impending or developing change, their first concerns revolve around wanting to know more about it and how they will be affected personally. As their questions are answered and they become willing to attempt the new practice, their concerns relate to how they will manage such logistics as time, materials, and record keeping. When these concerns of self and the task are addressed, teachers become more interested in how their use of a new practice is affecting students. More advanced stages of concern relate to sharing their new efforts with colleagues and using their own ideas to modify and improve the new practice. As part of CBAM, the researchers developed procedures for assessing the concerns of individuals within the organization.

Stages of Concern Questionnaire

The Stages of Concern Questionnaire (SoCQ) is a survey instrument that includes 35 items and requires only 10 to 15 minutes to administer. It can be scored by hand or by machine. The result is a profile that shows the intensity of each concern for that respondent. Average scores of groups or subgroups can be calculated.

Purpose. The SoCQ and the variations described below are designed to identify the most intense concerns felt by individuals and groups in the organization. This information is valuable in planning an organization's responses and support for its members.

When to Use. The formal SoCQ procedure is generally used when research or program evaluation is being conducted. It can also be used to provide diagnostic information during a change process. It can be administered several times during a year without losing its reliability.

Who to Involve. The SoCQ can be used with an entire school or district population in its machine-scorable form.

Materials Needed. The survey items and quick-scoring device are included in *Taking Charge of Change,* which can be obtained by contacting the ASCD. Respondents will need the survey form and pencils. For large groups, answer sheets that can be scanned and analyzed should be used.

Tips for Facilitators. The SoCQ itself is easy to administer, and the profiles produced from the results appear deceptively self-evident. The challenge is to interpret them accurately and respond appropriately. Study the descriptions in *Taking Charge of Change* carefully. If the SoCQ is to be used for formal program evaluation, the SoCQ manual and training in interpretation of SoCQ profiles should be acquired.

For Example: Cooperative Learning. After a number of training sessions, Anderson, Rolheiser, and Bennett (1995) made use of the SoCQ to document the experiences of teachers who were implementing cooperative learning. They discovered that the teachers surveyed seemed to cluster into three groups, which they called nonusers, tentative beginning users, and experienced beginning users. They identified nine concerns that were common to all three groups, although the concerns varied in intensity from group to group:

- Impact on teaching strategies
- Curriculum integration

- Time for implementation
- Student participation
- Individualization
- Student assessment and evaluation
- Student outcomes
- Collaboration with other teachers
- Quality of implementation

Because these concerns were felt by all participants, the authors were able to suggest alterations in the schools' staff development offerings that would respond and provide support for growth to the next stage.

A Variation: One-Legged Interviews. The SoCQ is the most formal method of identifying the concerns felt by participants in a change process. *Taking Charge of Change* also describes the use of face-to-face conversations in which the facilitator asks such simple questions as "How do you feel about _____?" and may follow up with more specific probes. This informal dialogue has been referred to as a "one-legged interview" because it should be concise enough to be completed before the facilitator would lose her balance if she were standing on one leg. To interpret the responses correctly, the facilitator must not interrupt and then must reflect on the entire conversation and analyze it holistically to assess the stage of concern being expressed.

Another Twist: Feedback Form. The authors of *Taking Charge of Change* also describe the use of an open-ended statement, such as "When you think about _____, what are your concerns?" Their recommendations are to regard this as more formal than the face-to-face conversation, encouraging respondents to answer in complete sentences. They also suggest two forms of analysis, first considering each sentence separately and then rereading and analyzing the tone of the whole response.

To use the open-ended statement for program evaluation or research, facilitators should read the authors' recommendations carefully and be thorough in their interpretation. I have found that even an informal, open-ended statement can provide valuable information for purposes of "quick and dirty" diagnosis and adjustments to staff development activities. I include an item such as "My biggest concern about _____ at this time is _____" on feedback forms at the end of training sessions. Although the interpretation can hardly be called scientific, I review the feedback forms with stages of concern in mind, which helps me make adjustments in follow-up sessions. It also indicates whether participants share common concerns or have a wide range of needs that will require a greater variety of responses.

CONTINUE TRAINING AND COACHING

A difficulty with every school improvement project I have encountered is that the schools spend too large a portion of their professional development resources on training before implementing a new innovation. The implication is that we can "front-end load" a process that takes years and requires individual movement through several stages of acceptance and use. The assumption is that adult learners can acquire new skills all at once, in isolation from practice, and can retain and retrieve them for use once the system has removed barriers and set them free to proceed. Conducting all the training at the beginning further ignores the reality that through the years, there may be considerable staff turnover. New people join the organization who were never introduced to techniques they will be expected to use. The quality management concept of "just in time" training is not a panacea but does respond to the adult learners' need for job relevancy and immediate application of the new learning.

Continued training should be of two types. Introductory or basic training should be repeated on a cyclical basis to include new staff members and those who may have attended earlier training but have not yet had a chance to implement it. For instructional approaches as complex as cooperative learning, interdisciplinary teaching, or learning styles, a sequence from basic to more advanced training experiences should be provided. These levels of training can respond to the needs of participants as they move through the stages of concern. Knowing that a higher level of training is available can also stimulate the progress of more cautious adopters.

Coaching is different from training and resembles the guided practice stage of instruction. Feedback is needed for those who are most active with the new technique, as well as those who are least skilled. The leaders need to refine and polish their practice because they are models for others and need to be sure they are providing accurate examples. Those least skilled, or most reluctant, need coaching to convey the expectation that they will continue to improve their art and craft in line with organizational goals.

The Coach in the Booth

I am currently involved in three types of coaching, all of which are important to continued success in a change effort. Later in this section, I'll describe coaching as providing feedback to principals. In another section, I'll talk about being a coach of support specialists who, in turn, coach teachers.

The most intense of the three coaching roles is that of external coach, which I described in the Chapter 5 story about John Bullen Middle School. This type of "critical friend" visits a school on a regular basis to review progress and feedback, present some "next steps" training or review and refresh previous training, and guide the actual work of application. In football, it's like the coach up in the booth who can see the big picture and provide feedback to the decision makers who are coaching on the sideline, where the action is. One of the teacher leaders at John Bullen Middle School wrote to me about my role there:

> You have shown us that you like and respect us. You have spent a lot of time with us carefully listening and probing with questions, such as "Do I hear you saying that . . . ?" Second, you have done a great job of staying objective. After listening and clarifying, you put our thoughts into some sort of graphic format that we have all agreed on and can use to stay on track in future.

This coaching role is quite different from training and from consulting.

A trainer engages learners in acquisition of new knowledge and skills and may provide suggestions for follow-up activities, but a trainer leaves. A consultant studies a situation and makes recommendations on how to solve problems or take appropriate action. The organization can choose whether to implement the suggestions. The consulting role is more customized and focused than training, but a consultant also leaves. A coach, on the other hand, is right there on the sidelines during the game, helping design the plays, giving the halftime pep talks, and enjoying the applause or enduring the loss along with the team.

The Sideline Coach

Another role of a coach who's right in the action is to provide feedback. As I was the central office administrator responsible for curriculum and instruction, my role with principals was one of coaching and support, not supervision and evaluation. For several years, principals in my district had been expected to work with their school leadership teams and develop documents called strategic plans, school improvement plans, and now (latest term) academic achievement plans. Their planning processes included developing the site-based budget, staffing package, and professional development plan. In previous years, their plans had been turned in to their supervisors, and copies were made and forwarded to the people in budget departments, human resources, special education, and compensatory education who were to verify that all compliance requirements had been met. But principals heard nothing in return unless some major issue was caught in the compliance review.

Group review and coaching made a tremendous difference. Under new leadership, all of the principals were asked to come (with members of their leadership team, if possible) and present their academic achievement plans to a panel that included the school supervisor and the others who had been nameless faces checking compliance in past years. Presenters were asked to talk about the collaborative process that was used to develop their plan, the data they reviewed and how the data guided their work, how their chosen strategies matched the needs of special populations, and so on. Through the dialogue, central office administrators gained a greater appreciation of school efforts, and school leaders received affirmation, immediate feedback, coaching on anything that needed to be revised, and suggestions for future consideration.

I asked several principals what they thought of this new process, and their answers were almost identical:

> It was nerve-racking to anticipate, and kind of intimidating until I started talking—but then it was really fun to have a listening audience that cared about my school and would understand what we're trying to do. And it was so much better than having our plans disappear into the "black hole at A & S [the Administration and Support Center]."

The Power of Coaching

Coaching is needed in all walks of life, and one of my favorite coaches in the world of sports is Mike Holmgren. I got curious about him when he was the quarterback coach in San Francisco and my football hero was Joe Montana. I started focusing more on Holmgren himself when I was a Wisconsinite, watching him smooth the rough edges off a Mississippi kid named Brett Favre and build the Green Bay Packers into Super Bowl champions. I was thrilled when he decided to come to Seattle a few months after I did—and occasionally claimed credit for his move. Maybe I find Mike fascinating because he was a high school history teacher—and now that he sports reading glasses along with his headset and clipboard, he really fits the image. My point in this example is that a coach is a teacher who gives feedback on performance and keeps track of whether the learning occurs.

One year, a player named Joey Galloway was a holdout (meaning he didn't show up at training camp), came back late in the season, wasn't very effective, and then left for the Dallas Cowboys. There weren't many broken hearts in Seattle. Most of the people interviewed on the street expressed a sentiment of "good riddance." But when I heard Coach Holmgren speak at our Seahawks Academy for middle school students who need a chance to turn around their lives, he was apologizing for having failed in that situation. People at the tables near me were saying, "Who cares?" or "Why should he feel bad about that?" But Coach Holmgren said, "My job has always been about building up people. If I lose somebody, I take it personally, whether it's a ninth grader, a high school senior, or a player." Coaching in the arena of school change is all about keeping people in the game.

That Mississippi kid Brett Favre has certainly stayed in the game. This season, he breaks records almost every time he hits the field. (As I write this final draft, one eye is on the Packers-Rams game and Brett just broke Dan Marino's record for yards passed!) But Favre recalls the firm coaching he received early in his career.

> Mike Holmgren never patted me on the back and said, "That's OK, buddy." There was never any of that. He laid into me every time. And I can't tell you how many times I came off the field and said, "I hate this guy." But as I look back, he meant more to my career than anyone. He was hard on me, but I see him now and I thank him for all those things. (Jenkins, 2007, p. F3)

The veteran quarterback knows his game—but he still goes straight to the bench after every plan to analyze the photos of plays, and he still gets coached. In fact, his current coach, Mike McCarthy, tricks him into *being* a coach as well. "I ask Brett questions on purpose just to make him talk. I know he knows the answer—make him talk, make him interact. It's more about the things that go wrong, because it's an opportunity for everyone to learn" (Jenkins, 2007, p. F5).

COPE WITH CONFLICT

It is in the nature of humans to differ, and from those differences, conflicts are bound to arise. One of the most popular topics for staff development in recent years has been conflict resolution. Unfortunately, the term *resolution* implies an unrealistic expectation that conflict can be eliminated and a mistaken assumption that the presence of conflict is a bad thing. I prefer to talk about "managing conflict" or "coping with conflict" because this acknowledges that a certain amount is unavoidable and that productive organizations often encourage it. Dynamic organizations are not populated by clones. "Groupthink" is a powerful killer of creativity. In fact, when writing about five principles of successful meetings, Bob Garmston (2006) included the need to "respect cognitive conflict by eliciting disagreements and respecting other viewpoints" (p. 1). He affirmed that "groups that discuss substantive differences of opinion produce better decisions, increased commitment, cohesiveness and follow-through" (p. 6).

Earlier in this book, I identified the "wrong" questions as being "How do we sell our plan?" and "How do we overcome resistance?" I like what Rick DuFour (Eaker et al., 2002) says about teachers with a "bad attitude" toward change. He reminds us that we all have attitudes shaped by our history and experiences. We have acted in certain ways, and to the degree that we repeat those experiences and get the same results, we develop attitudes. "Leaders who say, 'I need to change this person's attitude,' are trying to break into the cycle at the wrong point. . . . So the short answer to the question 'How can I change someone's attitude?' is simple: focus on his or her behavior rather than attitude" (p. 85).

I have personally witnessed and experienced the power of the next four techniques in helping groups cope with conflict by shaping responses to behaviors: Venn diagrams, Quick-Writes, Talk-Walks, and Go for the Green.

Venn Diagrams

A Venn diagram is simply a set of two or more circles. They are drawn to intersect, be concentric, or not touch at all, as a way of illustrating relationships. The name comes from the originator, mathematician John Venn, who specialized in logic.

Purpose. A Venn diagram can be used to illustrate complex relationships, display data, or generate discussion for problem solving and decision making. Venn diagrams help groups compare and contrast multiple sets of ideas or interests and are particularly valuable for demonstrating relationships that are difficult to describe in words.

When to Use. When members of a group are polarized and lack a sense of common ground, a Venn diagram can reopen communication and refocus the group.

Who to Involve. All members of the group, or parties to a conflict, should contribute to the Venn diagram.

Materials Needed. Paper and pencil are sufficient. Chart paper and stick-on notes are useful for constructing Venn diagrams that can be seen and discussed by larger groups.

Tips for Facilitators. Describe the purpose of a Venn diagram and present a simple example. Engage the group in determining how many circles will be needed and predicting how much they will overlap. Give instructions about writing their responses, one on each stick-on note. Small groups may sketch their own Venn diagram to share, or a large diagram can be developed as participants post their stick-on notes. Be flexible and add or move circles as the group's responses are compiled.

For Example: Character Education. To answer the "Where do we want to go?" question, a Venn diagram can be used to discover the common values and beliefs held by various shareholder groups. Each group (parents, teachers, community members, students) can meet separately and write its beliefs or interests, one per stick-on note. A large Venn diagram can be drawn with a circle representing each of the groups. The stick-on notes can then be placed in separate or overlapping areas of the circles. This communicates visually which values are shared by which groups. If even a few stick-on notes land in the centermost overlapping area, the group can see that there are shared values on which to build.

In many districts, members of the public are calling for renewed emphasis on character education, but they have diverse agendas as to what should be included. Some school leaders have courageously brought conflicting groups together to seek common ground. Figure 6.1 is a Venn diagram that illustrates the consensus reached.

Variations. Venn diagrams can be used during almost any phase of an improvement process. To answer the "Where are we now?" question, a group could use the circles to represent major forces or entities in the organization and how they relate to or influence each other.

Quick-Writes

A Quick-Write is similar to the informal stream-of-consciousness writing that is done in keeping a journal or log. A prompt is given, and participants are encouraged to record their thoughts as they emerge.

Figure 6.1   Venn Diagram: Topics for Character Education

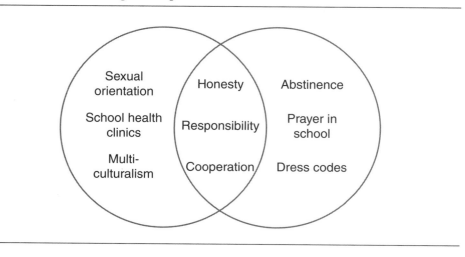

Purpose. The Quick-Write provides an opportunity for individual, reflective thinking about the topic or issue at hand.

When to Use. The Quick-Write can be used before initiating discussion about a complex or controversial issue. In this case, the purpose is to help participants clarify their own viewpoints and prepare words with which to express themselves before launching into position statements. The Quick-Write is also helpful as a tension reliever if a serious discussion is deadlocked or is becoming too inflammatory. Participants are asked to take a silent break and put their current position or issues into writing. This guides them to refocus and then reopen the discussion on a more positive note.

Who to Involve. When a Quick-Write is used to open discussion or deal with conflicts, all parties should be involved.

Materials Needed. Individual paper and writing tools should be supplied. Markers and chart paper should not be in evidence because Quick-Write participants are promised confidentiality.

Tips for Facilitators. Provide a writing prompt in the form of a sentence stem or heading. Assure participants that they are writing to clarify their own thoughts and decide how they can best express those thoughts to others. Their writing remains their own property, and they share only what they decide to after they have completed the activity.

For Example: Who Should Be in Charge? The district's site-based management advisory committee was meeting in an attempt to create better understanding between principals and representatives from some schools who felt that they were not being given enough authority in enough areas of school operation. Some of the parents and community members had complained to board members that principals were "holding out" and trying to retain control. Principals were upset and feeling threatened. Among themselves and to a few district administrators, they whispered that the district was "giving the ship away" and that it seemed unfair for them to be held accountable for their schools' success when the decisions were being taken out of their hands.

As an outside facilitator, I began the meeting by asking participants to do some writing on a form I had prepared. The blue sheets that I gave to principals had these headings:

I became a principal because I wanted to	Even though I knew I would have to
_____.	_____.

The green sheets given to parent and community representatives were headed as follows:

I want to be part of these decisions:	But not deal with these decisions:
_____.	_____.

When the participants had received their sheets, I asked them how much work time they would need, and I emphasized that they would be working independently. A time limit of 5 minutes was set, and they began to write.

When the time was up, I asked them to form groups with two or three blue sheets and two or three green sheets in evidence. Their instructions were to share their thoughts with each other. They could simply place their sheets on the table next to each other and make comparisons, or set their sheets aside and just express the overall feelings that emerged as they reflected on their roles in shared decision making.

Some groups looked at each other warily, and communication was slow to start. Other groups were able to candidly compare their feelings. They discovered that principals had worked hard to achieve administrative roles because they wanted to be instructional leaders. They wanted to work with teachers to improve instruction and wanted to be advocates for children. These were their primary motivators, despite their knowledge that they would have to deal with personnel issues, budget management, and paperwork for the organization. Parents and community members had indicated that they wanted to talk about what should be in the curriculum and how teachers should teach—maybe even evaluate teachers—but not be involved in firing them or in dealing with any element of "the bureaucracy." As they talked, the site-based management team members began to realize that they had been pushing to take over all the things that principals had seen as their real purpose and leave principals with only those tasks that were "the drudgery." Some principals began quietly to share how it felt to work for years trying to develop leadership skills and feel reduced to being a manager of the noneducational aspects of the school. This open discussion was the first step toward defining the roles of shareholder groups and clarifying the scope of site-based management for the district.

Talk-Walks

Talk-Walking is a technique based on the practice of "going on rounds" with students and colleagues in a teaching hospital. It adds the kinesthetic learning modality that is too often missing from the typical "sit and get" staff development workshop.

Purpose. Going on a Talk-Walk provides an opportunity for colleagues to exchange viewpoints in an informal atmosphere. It combines interaction with the stimulation of exercise and a change of scenery. The movement and change of environment are helpful in overcoming inhibitions and promoting a sense of well-being.

When to Use. A Talk-Walk can be helpful on many occasions. It can be used toward the end of a workshop to allow participants to discuss the implications of what they have learned and how they can apply it in their job role. It can also become an informal part of the school culture. Staff members can choose times to meet for both mental and physical exercise, combining a brisk walk with discussion of an article they have read or an idea they would like to try. Colleagues can use a Talk-Walk to seek each other's advice on a challenge they are currently facing. As a tool for coping with conflict, a Talk-Walk can provide a chance to ease a group out of a tense situation or nonproductive discussion by breaking participants up into smaller groups and moving them into another setting.

Who to Involve. Any group of two or three persons can engage in a Talk-Walk. In addition to workshop participants, variations have included teachers and students, or a principal and teacher(s). One friend of mine declares that a Talk-Walk is the only way she's ever found to get her teenage son to open up and communicate with her.

Materials Needed. The ideal environment for Talk-Walking is a place where participants can get outdoors and walk around the block or parking lot. Talk-Walking has also been effective in the confines of hotel corridors and conference centers. The main requirement is space to move out and away from the confines of the existing situation—both mentally and physically.

Tips for Facilitators. Set a time limit and a topic. Create a definite expectation that this is not just an extra break but a task-oriented activity. State the purpose clearly, such as "Come back with your analysis of why we are having difficulty with this topic and your recommendation of where we should go from here."

Use your own discretion about forming the dyads or trios for Talk-Walking. On some occasions, I have orchestrated the structure to get particular participants or groups talking to each other or to break up certain combinations that were sidetracking the whole group. Unless there is a specific reason for directing the structure of the groups, voluntary choices of partners are best.

For Example: Unsuspecting Recruits. It was a long, hot summer. I was one of several consultants hired to provide training for school leadership teams who would face new responsibilities under recent state legislation. Two weeklong institutes had already been held with good results. The in-state facilitators who were working with me had done a great job, the content had been well received, and the groups had left with the first draft of a school improvement plan in hand so they could complete it at their schools and submit it to the state in a timely manner. However, this Monday morning was totally unlike the others. When the state facilitators and I arrived, the people at the host school were friendly but had no knowledge about the supplies and materials we were expecting. Coffeepots had been packed away for the summer, and their whereabouts were unknown—always a bad sign. The participants arrived and were polite, but they seemed distant and wary. As I began the overview of the week and talked about the final product we would create by Friday, they became more tense. Their body language became rigid and hostile, and it was almost impossible to establish eye contact.

After struggling for nearly an hour, I decided to stop talking and introduce a short videotape. While I "huddled" with my co-presenters to analyze the situation, I watched the participants pass written notes and exchange nonverbal messages that seemed less than positive. My colleagues couldn't shed any light on what was happening, so I decided to take a risk and confront the situation. It didn't seem as if I had a lot to lose, because I'd never had them with me anyway.

When the videotape was over, I told them that I'd like to give them a chance to discuss the ideas in it but that I also needed their help. I described the feeling I had that we were not quite on the same wavelength and that I'd appreciate their suggestions on what might be done to create a better climate. I then described a Talk-Walk and asked them to come back in 10 minutes. By then, coffee would be ready, and we would take a 15-minute break (emphasizing that the walk was an activity, not a break). I asked them to either have the bravest member of their group talk to me during the break or give me an anonymous written note of feedback.

I wasn't sure how to interpret the enthusiasm with which they grabbed the opportunity to get together and move out, but they did accept the assignment. The feedback I received after the break was invaluable. They had been shocked at my opening comments that they were members of leadership teams and that we would be working together on improvement plans for their school. Many of them had been contacted just the week before and had been asked to attend a 5-day workshop. They were going to receive a stipend for attending, with an option of graduate credit, and the only prerequisite they knew about was that they were available. I asked them to set aside their confusion about their roles and learn what they could that day about the research on effective schools, while I sought clarification of their responsibilities.

That evening was spent on the telephone. Many calls flew back and forth to and from staff members at the state education department, local district administrators, my copresenters, and myself. We asked administrators from each district to come the next morning and meet with their participants to clarify the purpose of the workshop and their responsibilities that week and in follow-up with their schools. To their credit, every district cooperated, and the first part of Tuesday morning was spent in breakout rooms, laying the groundwork that should have been in place earlier. Some people dropped out and left. Those who stayed became one of the most cooperative groups I've worked with, eager to learn and fulfill their roles.

That Talk-Walk provided the tension release they needed and the information I needed with which to make changes in our relationship and purpose. I hate to speculate on what would have happened without it.

Go for the Green

Bob Garmston introduced this activity at a workshop called Premier Presentation Skills, which I attended several years ago. It is one of the most valuable techniques I have found for addressing conflicts and nonproductive behavior in groups.

Purpose. Go for the Green appeals to the senses through its use of color and metaphor. The purpose is to identify possible causes for nonproductive behavior and shift the focus from the problem behavior or the problem people to factors that can be changed more readily.

When to Use. Go for the Green can be used when groups, or the facilitators of a group, are aware of a behavior pattern that is interfering with their effectiveness.

Who to Involve. The entire group can be involved if the problem has been identified by the group as a whole. If only the facilitators or a few group members have become concerned about a pattern or situation, they can use Go for the Green to analyze it and develop strategies for dealing with it.

Materials Needed. To use Go for the Green, you will need large chart paper and black, green, and red markers.

Tips for Facilitators. Start with a red circle in the middle of the chart paper. Let the group know that you are using that color deliberately because there seems to be a situation that is "making them see red" or is "stopping" them from accomplishing their tasks. Involve the group in deciding on a label to designate the difficult behavior or situation, and write it in the circle. For example, the team described below was frustrated because team members continually engaged in side conversations and then didn't know what was going on in the discussion. Ideas had to be repeated for them, and time was wasted.

When the problem has been identified in red, switch to the black marker and write across the top of the page "Under what conditions would I . . ." Ask participants to think about reasons they might exhibit that behavior themselves. While they are thinking, switch to the green marker. As they share their thoughts, record them in green on diagonal lines going out from the red circle, like rays on a child's drawing of the sun.

Once the possible causes have been recorded, urge the group to "go for the green" rather than rave about the red. Talk about the various causes and how they might be changed or what accommodations could be made to decrease them.

Two aspects of this technique reduce conflict. By thinking about "why I might . . . ," critics who have complained usually realize that they've been guilty of the same behavior at some point. By going for the green, group members and facilitators often recognize ways in which their own planning (or lack of planning) has contributed to the difficulty.

For Example: Side Conversations. The leaders of the team were frustrated because it seemed as if they could never get anything completed in the time available for team meetings. Certain combinations of team members would sit together and engage in side conversations throughout the meeting. When their attention returned to the discussion at hand, they would ask people to repeat their statements. If the chairperson asked, "Have we reached a decision?" they would emerge and need a summary of what had happened and what the tentative conclusion was. The team leaders asked me for some idea of how to handle this problem, and I asked if they had a few minutes to learn a new group process technique. They were eager for a new tool, and I conducted a quick Go for the Green activity with them. Figure 6.2 shows the result.

Figure 6.2   Go for the Green: Side Conversations

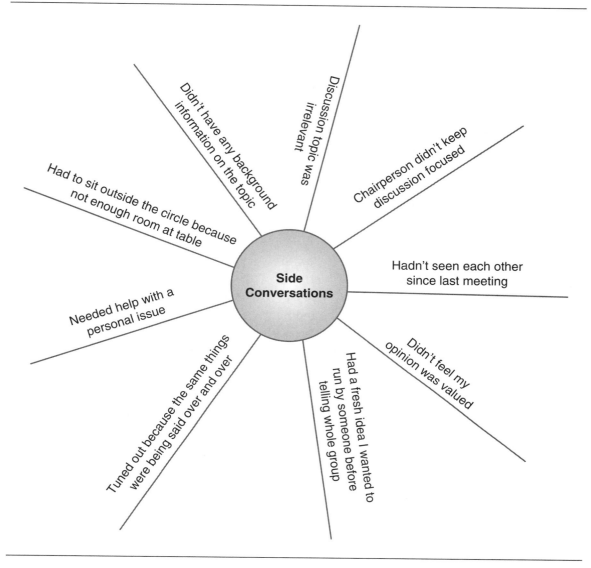

They looked at it for a while and asked if this was what I thought they should do with the group. I said they might want to use it at some time but asked them to look at it again and see if it gave them any ideas of things they might try first. They ended up with a list of strategies that matched the possible causes:

- Changing the room configuration so everyone could be around the same table
- Guiding the "side conversers" to other seats by setting up name cards on tables before the meeting
- Allocating a few minutes at the start of the agenda for participants to "check in" and focus on the purpose of the meeting
- Having a timekeeper monitor the agenda
- Calling on these participants for their viewpoints early in the discussion of each topic

The concerned participants decided to try these strategies first without confronting the behavior in the whole group. If that didn't work, they were going to ask me to do a Go for the Green and some other work on meeting behavior with their team. They didn't need to call.

STRENGTHEN THE CULTURE OF INQUIRY

This book was designed around a set of questions to convey that school change occurs through continuing cycles of inquiry: asking critical questions, seeking answers, proposing and testing solutions, and refining and renewing the process. It is the nature of books to start with a Chapter 1 and end after some sequence of content has been presented. The process of change and improvement is not that linear. It is cyclical but even more complex than a single cycle. At any given time, members of the organization may be engaged in studies of several aspects of the school or district. A more accurate visual image of continuous improvement is a corkscrew or Slinky toy, which consists of a series of spirals.

Action research is presented in this chapter to emphasize the importance of inquiry in maintaining the momentum of change and improvement. Several writers on action research describe stages of analyzing problems, collecting data, analyzing data, planning action programs, implementing programs, and evaluating the results. By that definition, this entire book describes a process that is continual action research.

Linda Lambert (2003) uses the term *reflective practice* to describe thinking about our practice—"how we do what we do—methods, techniques, strategies, procedures, and the like. Reflection enables us to reconsider how we do things, which of course can lead to new and better approaches to our work" (p. 7). After listing strategies like writing about practice (in journals or otherwise), peer coaching, debriefing, studying articles or books with peers, and reflection on the results of student interviews, she summarizes by stressing the deeper value in terms of creating the meaning that humans seek. "Reflection is our way of making sense of the world around us through meta-cognition" (p. 7).

Action Research

Action research is a method of participatory involvement in both individual and group learning. It is one of the few techniques that bridge the individuality of traditional staff development and the common effort of school improvement and organizational development. Action research expands the definition of teacher from deliverer of content to scholar of the processes of teaching and learning and investigator of the context of schooling. Participants in action research become more reflective practitioners and are also in a unique position to bridge the gap between K–12 and higher education.

Purpose. Action research is conducted for a number of specific reasons, but the overall purpose is to improve the teaching and learning process in the school. Because participants study topics, problems, or programs related to their roles and interests, action research makes inservice activities more relevant. Collegial relationships are strengthened, and the likelihood that what participants learn will be accepted by others in the school is increased.

When to Use. Action research is used constantly in a dynamic organization. Gathering data to better understand "Where are we now?" qualifies as action research to many writers. Investigating the possible causes of problems and concerns to decide "Where do we want to go?" and "How will we get there?" also qualifies as action research to some. Experts with the most rigorous definitions of action research place it in the context of piloting a new approach or program and evaluating whether it is working as well as intended or better than other practices. Because this book is written for active practitioners looking at real problems in their schools in the most timely and practical ways, I believe that all of these activities qualify as action research.

Who to Involve. The literature on action research describes three forms: individual, collaborative, and schoolwide. This book outlines a schoolwide process guided by a leadership team, in which the scope of the study encompasses the school as a whole, incorporates shareholder input, and develops action plans that affect all members of the organization. Individual action research can be conducted independently by teachers trying something new within their own classrooms. Collaborative action research involves members of the school staff working as peers. It may also include support and participation by district-level staff and university or college partners. Decisions about who should be involved will emerge when the action research question has been clearly stated and the audience for the findings has been identified.

Materials Needed. The necessary resources will vary greatly based on the purpose of the action research. They may include literature to review, technical support for gathering and analyzing data, or additional instructional materials to use with new teaching strategies.

Tips for Facilitators. One of the purposes and benefits of action research is to switch the ownership for change and improvement to the participants within the organization. To achieve this purpose, the role of the facilitator should be advisory and supportive, not central to the effort. As a "guide on the side," a facilitator can assist in important ways.

First, ask probing questions to help the individual or group frame the research problem or question accurately and specifically. The statement, "I want to see if cooperative learning really works" is a signal that such guidance is needed. Second, emphasize the need to gather appropriate data from which to draw conclusions. Third, discuss the purpose, methods, and data for the study to be sure that they are congruent.

Also, identify needs for outside expertise and enlist support. For example, if an action research project will include quantitative data analysis, it may be important to include a district-level or university partner as a consultant or team member. When deciding whether to pursue a university partnership, remember that a faculty member's reward system is based on conducting research that can be published. In many settings, professors are vulnerable if they spend too much time working with schools in a service capacity. No matter how dedicated they are to supporting the public schools, they will be most interested in projects that address general questions applicable to all schools, are grounded in a particular theory base, and involve rigorous use of data. If these are characteristics of your action research project, it would be wise to seek a higher education partnership. If your focus is primarily internal and pragmatic, expertise from the district or an intermediate service agency may be more appropriate.

Finally, consider the audience for the results of the project. If an individual teacher wants to see whether certain rewards he or she offers will increase the completion of homework assignments, that teacher is the only audience. If a teaching strategy or concept such as learning styles is being piloted by one group of teachers with the intent of testing it for possible schoolwide adoption, the audience is much broader, and the considerations are more complex. As a facilitator or coach, help the project participants anticipate the questions that will be asked by other staff members and be sure that the project will address them.

For Example: Cooperative Learning. Teachers in a junior high school were concerned about poor attendance patterns of their students. They discussed possible reasons for poor attendance at length. About the same time, some of them had been reading about student engagement in learning. A few others had attended a workshop on cooperative learning. They felt that use of cooperative learning might increase achievement and might seem more engaging to the students. Social studies teachers decided to work together and develop cooperative learning activities. Their goal was to have a cooperative learning activity every Thursday and see what would happen.

The data-gathering aspect of their project was overlooked at the time but eventually became an "aha!" event for the entire school. After a month or so, the guidance counselor reported at a faculty meeting that for some reason, school attendance in the seventh and eighth grades was showing an increase and was higher on Thursdays than on any other day of the week. He wondered if anyone was doing anything special on Thursdays. When the social studies teachers mentioned their experiment, the language arts teachers decided to test it further. They chose Tuesday as a day to use cooperative learning and consciously set out to have the counselor help them track the attendance patterns. At the time I lost contact with this school, the teachers had not yet determined the effects on student achievement, but they had certainly made an impact on student interest and stimulated discussion throughout the school.

Reflective Study Groups

Action research has many features in common with the following discussion of reflective study groups. People doing action research are sometimes called study groups, project teams, quality teams, or site councils. The more important word in this setting is *reflective*. These are small groups of persons who want more from staff development than "getting something new I can use in class tomorrow." These are members of the organization who want to think about implications and concerns, and consistency with goals. They are small groups who may meet during lunch once a week, for breakfast on the way to school, or in other environments they choose. They exist for a semester at a time, or they may go on and on. If they have not evolved in your school or district, they need to be initiated and nurtured because they are vital to the soul of the organization.

Purpose. Reflective study groups fulfill many purposes. They contribute to development of new knowledge bases within the school. They raise awareness of needs within the organization and provide feedback by pointing out discrepancies between practice and stated beliefs. Reflective study groups engage in a high level of professional dialogue that is similar to peer coaching. They study new literature and discuss its merits. They encourage each other to try new practices. Perhaps the most unique characteristic of reflective study groups is that members challenge each other with probing questions about their experiences: What happened? How and why? What feelings were created? What possible alternatives could be proposed? What plans could we suggest for next time?

When to Use. Reflective study groups can be formed and perform successfully when a climate of trust has been established among the participants and within the organization. Participants within the study group need to establish norms that anything may be questioned but that the questions must not be judgmental and that specific conversations are confidential. Decisions about communicating information and feedback to the whole school are made jointly and phrased objectively before being passed along.

Who to Involve. A rule of thumb on appropriate size for reflective study groups is three to seven participants. At the beginning, members of the group should be individuals with some common interests and prior experience working together as a foundation for the trust level that is essential. Thinking or learning style should be considered as well. With my apologies for this oversimplification, it appears that the concrete, linear thinkers do best or are most comfortable on action research teams with a specific design, whereas the more abstract thinkers contribute greatly to the process of reflection.

Materials Needed. Reflective study groups often begin as ways for colleagues to share things that they have read and learned and to get reactions from each other. Multiple copies of articles or books may be needed for this purpose. As study groups begin to focus on practices within the school and compare them with the best practices and new developments they read about, they may need access to various types of data and assistance interpreting them. One of the most important resources they will need is access to the ears of leadership as they identify new ideas and areas for possible improvement within the school.

Tips for Facilitators. A key role of the facilitator is to establish the norms of respect and confidentiality within the study group. You may be asked to help the group identify a theme for its study, acquire and assemble materials, organize meeting times, record main points made by the group, and provide guidance about how to share the group's new knowledge and ideas with the rest of the staff. It is unusual for all staff members to look on the work of reflective study groups as relevant and irresistible, so prepare them for and help them deal with staff reactions and resistance.

For Example: Lunch Bunch. Years ago, some colleagues and I formed what I believe constituted a reflective study group, although it did not emerge as a planned entity according to the suggestions given here. There just happened to be a bunch of us who belonged to the Association for Supervision and Curriculum Development and received its journal, *Educational Leadership*, every month. One day, we were lamenting about how hard it was to keep up with our professional reading and know how to share it with the rest of the school. This was before I knew anything about cooperative learning jigsaws, but we decided to divide up the contents of each issue, read our articles, and "sneak" over to McDonald's for lunch one day per week and talk about them. Others became curious about what we were doing and asked us to give them summaries of good information we found. Although we had no formal role, I believe we contributed to the learning of the organization.

Variations. Some study groups have tried to select excellent articles and make copies to put in everyone's mailbox, but they have been disappointed with the lack of reaction to them. Other groups have told me about two strategies that seem to work better. Rather than distributing the whole article, they prepare a summary on a 3″ × 5″ card that they distribute. The full article is then posted in several key places in the school, and group members invite anyone interested to talk to one of them about it or meet with them for breakfast on an appointed day.

Staff from another school told me about how they post an article on a large piece of bulletin board paper in the lounge. They highlight the main points so it can be rapidly skimmed, and they hang markers beside it. Casual readers leave "graffiti" comments about the article, which prompts others to read and react as well. The informal reaction energizes the thinking of the staff and sometimes generates ideas for consideration that are brought to the school leadership team and then presented to the whole faculty.

Another Twist: Lesson Study. A specific version of reflective study is practiced in Japan and Germany under the term "Lesson Study." Teams of teachers meet regularly to craft and refine lessons and teaching units in order to make them as powerful as possible in helping students master the concepts and skills from their initial introduction. Teachers deliberate over each step and its place in the sequence of the lesson, how much time to spend on guided practice, and how to assess and adjust based on student response. Their best lessons are shared in "lesson fairs" (Schmoker, 2006, p. 110). The best path to increased student learning is teacher learning about instruction.

SUPPORT LEADERS AND FOLLOWERS

Organizational change may be an oxymoron like jumbo shrimp. Organizations don't change as whole entities. They change as the people within them do, and those people don't change all at the same time. There are leaders; there are optimistic followers; there are pessimistic, reluctant followers; and there are some who don't budge at all. Those who lead the way—and those who readily join them—need support to weather initial resistance and continue their efforts. They need technical support to help get the actual work done. They also need the psychological and moral support of others who are and have been involved in the same situations.

Michael Fullan (2005) emphasizes the critical role of the district as the level where this support must originate: "[L]arge-scale reform requires pluralized leadership, with teams of people creating and driving a clear, coherent strategy," by which he means "high engagement with others in the district and plenty of two-way communication, which deepens shared ownership and commitment at all levels of the district." This commitment depends on "interactive feedback that comes from application and corresponding reflection and continuous refinement" (p. 67). All of these activities require dedicated time, or they get lost in the ongoing management concerns of the district.

Dedicate Time

When we define organizational capacity, the least alterable resource on the list is *time*, and the most frequent response when people are asked about barriers to change is *time*. Maintaining focus and momentum means dedicating time to them and protecting that time from other uses. When the Seattle School District launched its academic standards movement, it was clearly announced that the Summer Institute when teachers returned in August would be devoted completely to topics that related to the Standards-Based Learning System. Vendors who had given promotional presentations in years past were excluded. Sessions were scheduled for every type of teaching assignment and focused on teachers' roles in implementing standards and providing effective instruction to help students meet them. The superintendent compared the Summer Institute program to Henry Ford's guarantee of any color car you wanted as long as it was black. He said, "You can take a course in anything you want, as long as it's related to standards." This was strong modeling of the use of existing time in new ways that reflect desired practice.

Principals were later asked to share the ways in which they were dedicating time for their school's implementation of standards and academic achievement plans. They shared these ideas:

- Develop multiyear plans. You carry forward the goals you're still working on and just replace those that have been met. It keeps the momentum going.
- Put time frames on all the initiatives and work plans. For example, everything from the strategic plan says "2000–2005." That reminds people that we're still working on this, and it's not going to go away. It's a long-term thing.
- Keep the focus on a few main, highly visible priorities.
- Allocate all the staff development time that's in the district calendar for specific activities that are in the action plans.

- Rearrange the schedule so that study groups or action teams have common prep time.
- Reduce the class size at certain periods of the day by creating blocks when everyone is teaching reading and every adult in the school has a reading group.
- Develop a schedule and reserve a certain substitute teacher for several days a month. This gives continuity to students so that some work can be accomplished during the school day.
- Get two or three guest teachers to come on a certain day every month. They spend an hour and a half with each grade level, so those teams can meet.
- Be aware that there are multiple models of professional development, and it isn't just having speakers and workshops. Use the time and money for authentic, job-embedded, collaborative work.
- If you can't get subs, give stipends. It's not good, but it's better than nothing.
- For the money, take another look at summer. Teachers are much more productive on tasks such as developing curriculum or classroom assessments when they're refreshed and focused.
- Write grants so they *buy* time, not *take* time.

Above all, respect people's time by starting and ending as promised and keeping groups on tasks with clear outcomes. A person's time is one resource that cannot be replaced.

Celebrate

A major emphasis of Chapter 5 was the importance of identifying indicators to monitor, and gathering data to verify that an improvement plan is actually being implemented and is achieving the intended results. Those are technical aspects of change and accountability. In this chapter, the emphasis is on sustaining change and improvement as part of the culture of the organization. The indicators and data are just as essential, but for a different purpose.

Most of us are comfortable with the phrase "nothing succeeds like success" and mentally apply it to teaching students at the appropriate level of difficulty so that they will be successful and motivated to keep trying and make further progress. The same phrase and logic apply to organizational change. We can't keep on devoting energy above and beyond the call of duty without evidence that it is getting us somewhere. No school or district has the financial resources to provide extrinsic rewards commensurate with the amount of effort required to keep an organization focused on continuous improvement. We need evidence of progress to celebrate and rejuvenate our own energy.

Of all the roles I've held in schools and districts, the most rewarding was that of first-grade teacher. It was tough work, and I seemed to be very inefficient, as I was always the "last one out" after arranging learning centers and activities for the next day. But in no other role or setting have I been able to celebrate the same concrete evidence of accomplishment as when—one by one—a group of children turned into confident readers.

Terry Deal was one of the first to transfer his work on corporate culture to the context of schools, and any of his writing will be helpful. The work of Michael Fullan and Tom Sergiovanni refers to reculturing and the spiritual element of schools as organizations. When benchmarks are reached or milestones achieved, call on the staff members who love drama, the former cheerleaders, the social organizers, and plan unique ways to celebrate!

Provide Technical Support

Improving schools requires two sets of skills that few school leaders have had the opportunity to acquire in their graduate work or have seen modeled in their own experience. The first of these is knowing how to involve others in decision making. The other is knowing how to use data in appropriate ways to guide the decision making. School districts need to provide their leaders with training in teamwork and group process skills and give them access to external facilitators when they need help and encouragement working with groups. Technical support in gathering and analyzing data and access to individuals with the expertise for statistical analysis are essential.

Technical support is also a critical component of any major initiative in a school or district. When the Standards-Based Learning System (SBLS) was introduced in the Seattle School District, clear expectations were set for how principals would support teachers and how the district would support the schools. Principals' support for standards implementation was to include these activities:

- Know and show teachers how to use the SBLS materials.
- Coordinate time for collaborative planning and scoring.
- Keep the focus on priorities; don't allow distractions.
- Build a core of support and nurture teacher leaders.
- Observe for evidence of the 15 Indicators of Standards-Based Teaching and Learning (see Chapter 5).
- Engage all adults and hold everyone accountable.
- Align Academic Achievement Plan with standards and assessment priorities.
- Promote, model, and teach use of data.
- Address school climate issues from an academic perspective.

The district, in turn, outlined its support for standards implementation in these ways:

- Offer SBLS classes at a variety of locations and times to increase teacher access.
- Provide a team of support specialists who will come to schools and
  - Answer questions at staff meetings.
  - Teach models of standards-based lessons.
  - Observe in classrooms and provide feedback.
  - Facilitate collaborative planning and scoring of student work.
- Maintain the Standards Network so teachers can meet and share.
- Continue to align the instructional program (e.g., report card revision).

- Communicate answers to questions and new information through newsletters.
- Produce videotapes and materials for use in school-based but district-planned staff development.
- Maintain the focus on this initiative for several years so it will really happen.

The third type of coaching I mentioned in Chapter 5 involved my role with the cadre of standards support specialists who worked with teachers and principals on a regular basis. These teachers came directly from the classroom, so their range of coaching and facilitation skills varied depending on each person's prior experiences. We didn't have the luxury of a long retreat to practice our roles or funds to bring in a consultant for a Training of Trainers, so I coached their skills in small segments at our weekly staff meetings. Initially, we spent time role-playing situations they were encountering and asking for advice about how to handle them. Scenarios were introduced, such as a conflict between a principal and teacher regarding standards implementation. I played the role of the teacher, while one of the standards support specialists responded to the concerns and the other team members provided feedback. Role-playing was an effective way to help them learn strategies for dealing with conflict.

We also spent time discussing and developing concrete examples of the 15 Indicators of Standards-Based Teaching and Learning (Chapter 5). This included creating a standards-based unit and presenting it to a colleague. Explaining their planning process helped solidify their own understanding and provided mental rehearsal for the questions they would be asked at schools. As we debriefed on various sessions with school and community groups, we improved our presentation skills and developed a format for all workshop planning that included a standard for amount of presenter time and participant engagement time.

During a span of 8 months, I experienced the thrill of a coach who can observe the process as individuals develop personal skills and also grow as an interdependent team. That's the best part of being a coach—but also the worst part. The better you coach, the faster they grow, and the sooner you become nonessential. Now the coached are the coaches, and the Standards Network planning and facilitating are almost completely in their hands.

Facilitate Networking

School districts need to coordinate collegial support for their leaders. Access to e-mail as a quick, informal way to communicate within the district and with more distant colleagues should be provided to every principal encountering new challenges of school change.

Designating and coordinating mentor relationships is another form of networking that should occur through the district or professional associations. Just assigning a mentor is inadequate. Someone needs to be instrumental in setting times and places for mentors to communicate, helping them focus on needs and questions, and keeping the network active.

Teachers need networks, too. Classrooms are often places of isolation, and a school across town is sometimes as foreign as a school across the county or country. When three to five teachers from each school meet together, it is sometimes a unique experience just to be together with their own team members. When they reconfigure into grade-level groups that include colleagues from other schools, they get new ideas and energy. When they take materials and tasks back to their school for reflection and follow-up, they strengthen the communication loop between the district and the schools and among the schools across the district. Instead of a hierarchy of district committees to deal with such things as report card revision, this network provides a way to engage every teacher throughout the district who is interested in providing input.

The concept of networking has emerged in a powerful way in another setting. Earlier in this book, I described cuts in central office staff and a site-based approach to curriculum that resulted in a wide variety of reading philosophies and approaches in the district. However, Title I funds and Reading First grants were allowing more schools to staff a part- or full-time reading specialist in their building. The role of the district shifted to support through sponsoring a Reading Network. Through this network, reading specialists learn about best practices in other schools and gain new insights for their roles in their schools.

Open Space Technology

Open Space Technology is a specific form of collaborative learning or networking that was created by organizational consultant Harrison Owen (1997) when he discovered that people attending his conferences loved the coffee breaks better than the formal presentations. In its title, the word "technology" simply means that it is a "tool" or "method" for participation, not that it is a high-tech, electronic event. The words "open space" refer to a physical environment that is uncluttered and unstructured, as well as a mental set that must not be closed, but open to new ideas and perspectives. There is no keynote presenter or detailed agenda, and the facilitator's role is limited. Open Space Technology does not appeal to all, but it does offer something unique to those who want to experience a creative and open-ended learning or problem-solving experience.

Purpose. The purpose of Open Space Technology is to tap the expertise that already exists within individuals and the group, stimulate creativity, generate new ideas, discover shared interests, and propose or plan solutions to problems.

When to Use. Open Space Technology should not be used when there are tight parameters and predictable or "correct" outcomes that must be met. It is best used when there is a complex set of problems and priorities to be sorted out or when an organization is "stuck in a rut," needing fresh ideas and new approaches.

Who to Involve. All it takes is a group of interested and committed people who want to explore a theme or related set of issues. In order to have the necessary level of energy and a variety of voices, the group should be at least 20, and can extend to very large groups who would subdivide and meet in a variety of breakout rooms. Organizers should think of critical people and assure that they are invited, but participation must be completely voluntary. The decision to participate must be made with the understanding in advance that the event will be very open and unstructured. Participants who can "go with the flow" and are comfortable with ambiguity will enjoy the activity most. Some may be hesitant at first, but almost all will begin to relax and enjoy the free-flowing discussion.

Materials Needed. Organizers provide notification of a theme, but no advance agenda. The setting will require a large room, furnished with movable chairs, but no tables or desks. Large areas of wall surface (without doors, windows, and artwork) are needed, and permission must be obtained for posting signs and charts. Flip charts and markers will suffice for recording, although laptop computers can assist with compiling chart notes for future reference. Beverages and snacks should be available at the discretion or need of the participants, but no formal break occurs at any set time.

Tips for Facilitators. The primary role of the facilitator is to assure that a theme is identified that is specific enough to give direction but open-ended enough to allow for imagination and creativity. During the event, the job of the facilitator is to move about the open space to encourage participants, heighten expectations and energy for positive outcomes, and point out opportunities and new thoughts as they emerge. The facilitator must be able to suspend his or her usual sense of responsibility for productivity and outcomes and must be willing to trust the people and the process.

As indicated by no agenda and no formal break times, successful use of Open Space Technology requires uninterrupted time. It may last 2–3 hours on a single issue or problem, or extend up to 3 days if major decisions are to be reached, such as a strategic plan.

The activity begins with participants seated in chairs in a large circle. Each participant shares his or her name and reason for interest in the theme casually, without getting occupied in a formal ice-breaking exercise. After introducing the theme, the facilitator explains that the agenda is about to be created by the group, and the work will be self-managed according to the four principles and one law of Open Space. The four principles are

- Whoever comes will be the right people.
- Whatever happens is all that could have happened.
- Whenever it starts is the right time.
- When it's over, it's over.

The Law of Two Feet states that if you find yourself in a situation where you aren't learning or contributing, you should go somewhere else. It places responsibility on each person to accomplish what he or she needs to in order to feel the time was well spent. Participants are not required to stay with the same group and may even move apart for a while to reflect privately before rejoining a group.

After the introductions and explanation of the process, there is a time of quiet when individuals identify an issue or opportunity, give it a short title, write it on chart paper, and post it on the wall. When it appears that no one else is in the process of posting an issue or question, each participant stands up by his or her chart and announces the topic.

Others view the issues and decide where to go. If it is a multiday meeting with small groups in different locations, participants may sign the charts to indicate their interest. In most cases, the posters will be moved around the walls of the room, and groups will begin to form as people carry their chairs to the topics that appeal to them.

During the discussions, the facilitator rotates among the groups to see how things are going and what might be needed. When the time or energy has run out, all participants move back to the large circle. No one is required to speak, and when comments are made, they reveal the speaker's reflections rather than the traditional reporting out of all the items of the group discussions. (The complete list of items charted will be typed and shared with all participants.) The facilitator leads the group in going around the circle so that those who want to express closure are encouraged to say what was significant to them and what they propose to do as a result of the experience.

For Example: Sharing Current Issues. A few months ago, I attended an Open Space session at the conclusion of the fall conference of our state affiliate of the Association for Supervision and Curriculum Development. About 75 people remained for the purpose of learning, sharing with others, and reflecting on the content of several keynote presenters and a set of state initiatives. The initial topics that were identified by emergent leaders were Coaching for Teacher Effectiveness, Taking Best Practices in Grading and Reporting to School- and Districtwide Implementation, Response to Interventions, and Formative Assessment. The group discussing assessment was large, and the Law of Two Feet was implemented as a separate group split off to focus on Writing Assessment.

Figure 6.3 contains the notes that were typed from charts and shared on the organization's Web site. I have resisted the temptation to edit and refine the notes, so that you can see the variation in number and kinds of responses from the groups. Although fragmented, these notes have been perfectly adequate to refresh my memory about the discussions and remind me of action steps I intend to take, and colleagues with whom I will network further. I also learned that I can survive quite well—temporarily—without an agenda, a set of objectives, and an evaluation instrument, and that it's a refreshing change.

Active Listening

I recently worked with a principal who divided her time between three tiny, geographically remote schools. We talked about the uniqueness of her schools, and I asked her about her needs and ways the district could better assist her. She gave me a wistful look like that of a child staring through the window of a candy store, and I wondered whether I had created an expectation so great that I'd surely fail to meet it. But with a sigh, all she said was, "What I need most is someone to talk to about all this, but I guess that's not the district's job. I guess it's a personal problem." She was both right and wrong. It *is* a personal need, but it is also something the district should provide. Because her schools are

Figure 6.3 Open Space Technology: Chart Notes

Response to Intervention (RtI)

How to Implement an RtI Model

- Have teachers talk about why we are here—not special education but EVERY education issue.
- Give staff an overview of what RtI is.
- They (teachers) should identify what we are already doing that fits the RtI model.
- Need to think big (know where you are going) but start small
- Progress monitoring—how do we know it's working?
- Create a "personalized" schedule for each building in your district (Intervention Block).
- Make sure we are focused on the concepts, not the vocabulary.
- What staff do you have who can be used differently?
- Professional development to support teacher collaboration, etc.
- Find the boxes—think outside of them.
- Flexibility, flexibility! (Kids in groups, use of available staff, resource reallocation, etc.)
- Think student need, not student (or staff) label—"role release"

Coaching for Teacher Effectiveness

- Self-assess—autonomous
- Confidential
- Nonevaluative
- Establish trusting *relationship*
- Desired goal (versus happening now)
- Options—what could you do? Questioning
- Action Plan with next steps

Assessment

- Model formative assessments common to a grade-level team
- Have a meeting platform for teachers to collaborate.
- Identify essential learnings/targets to be measured by assessment—no more than 4–6.
- Assessment, whether considered formative or summative, is based on what users do with it—whether it's just a measure or if it is used to inform instruction.
- Connected essential qualities should be vertically aligned.
- Agree on targets/goals. (Needs to be common among grades/courses)
- Formative creation/review
- Bring samples of work/rubrics; e.g., bring writing assessment to use with a tuning protocol and then share feedback.
- Summative—identifies end-of-unit/quarter/semester targets
- Formative—identifies parts of summative and plans backward from end target.
- Frequent assessment *for* learning
- Difficult to have *both* common and formative—can't get immediate feedback and data may become unmanageable
- Staff meeting/professional development: share feedback of how teachers check for understanding—"How do you know if they know it?"
- Quick checks for teachers

Taking Grading and Reporting Best Practices to Schoolwide or Districtwide Implementation

- Send teams to experts.
- Read reference/best practices as school team.
- Pilot at one grade level, one level (elementary), or in one building.
- Add new to old; don't throw out baby with bathwater.
- Introduce electronic standards-aligned system for teachers. Organize by power standards (grade book).
- Seek parent response (Survey—parents, students, teachers).

- Public communication important—initial meetings, forums, etc,; Task Force reps.: parents, teachers, board members, administration.
- Consider consistency in terminology/language.
- ROOT IN MISSION!
- Align grading practices with other district initiatives.
- Do our grades accurately reflect learning of our students?
- Set mini-goals, long timeline.
- Recognize this is a *system* need and will take TIME.
- Acknowledge the issues (GPA, post-secondary institutions).
- Form focus groups (Regional/Discussion Boards) through ASCD to do these things.
- Consider recommendations to board for progress/policy revision.
- Aim for simplicity: standards vs. benchmarks (Maybe use benchmarks for trimester progress.).
- Start by giving teachers time and training to identify (20) essentials for their level/subject, then time to develop common formative assessments.
- Examine secondary-level work to engage in WHOLE-child teaching/learning; expose flaws/limitations of current grading practices.
- Start with something—separate behavior from achievement, use 4-3-2-1-0, etc.

Districtwide Writing Assessments

Questions

- Amount of time to implement
- What does it look like? (fit/with Lucy Calkins)
- Change writing rubric WKCE
- Bridge gap—classroom instruction to test results (standardized tests)

Answers

- Start with conventions
- Easier to agree per grade level
- Cannot rely on WKCE
- District writing assessment

District A

- Report scores to board
- Once a year—Spring
- 3rd, 7th, 11th
- Choose appropriate prompts—reevaluate each year.
- Pilot questions (prompts) with 2nd graders
- 45 minutes—select one day (no makeups)
- Direction sheet (code #, name), prompt, pre writing page, writing pages
- 4-point rubric, K–4, 5–8, 9–12, 2 days for all. Same rubric, different words
- After scoring, list trends in writing

District B

- Write Track $1 per student
- Computerized results reporting
- 6 traits
- Teacher assess/create prompts
- One day—score grade level
- Writing by hand
- Tracks learners
- The next year—teachers can use results as conferencing tool
- Hire subs
- Purpose: Writing achievement as a *system*

Steps

- Is your district CONCERNED and COMMITTED about writing?
- *Be ready* to move forward.

(Continued)

(Continued)

- *Decide* if you'll be using software help (i.e., Write Track).
- *Find out* what we're doing now.
- *Check out* what others have done and research practice.
- *Analyze* data.
- *Emphasize* ALL writing in ALL classes.

Summary

- We *solved* the world's problems, and the answer was adding *writing across the curriculum*! Imagine!!
- District writing *rubric* used in *EVERY* classroom
- *Long-term and wide-scale COMMITMENT!!*

---

different from the others in the system, she hadn't been able to find a mentor among her peers. I took on the role and found it mutually rewarding, as my job was also "one of a kind."

Purpose. In addition to needing a specific person to share questions and concerns with, principals and other school leaders need opportunities to practice their own listening skills and interact with a wider range of colleagues. I first learned about a group process called Active Listening Trios from friends in the California School Leadership Academy. Since then, I have seen it adapted by several facilitators for use in a variety of other settings.

When to Use. This group activity for active listening can be repeated every few months, focused on a common concern most relevant at that time. It can also be used after training in a new technique, to identify and respond to concerns about implementation.

Who to Involve. One or more groups of three people are needed who are willing to give each other 45 minutes of caring time. The process can be used to increase communication and understanding among groups of teachers, within school leadership teams, in adult-student interactions, and even in families.

Materials Needed. Active Listening Trios need a topic or concern as a focus and a timer to move the process along.

Tips for Facilitators. Begin by reviewing the characteristics of active listening:

- Using positive, open nonverbals
- Paraphrasing
- Asking probing questions
- Jotting down important points if the speaker consents
- Withholding advice until all the information is shared
- Hearing advice in full before reacting

Ask participants to form groups of three. There may be times when you structure the composition of the trios. For example, if a workshop setting includes people from several districts, I encourage mixed groups as an opportunity to share ideas from other areas.

Within the trios, have one person designated as *A*, another as *B*, and the third as *C*. Provide the focus for their conversation, and explain the following steps so they have a grasp of the overall sequence:

Round 1

A shares and explains; *B* and *C* listen with no comment.

B and *C* ask clarifying questions only (no statements); *A* answers.

B and *C* offer advice and suggestions; *A* listens.

Round 2

B shares and explains; *A* and *C* listen with no comment.

A and *C* ask clarifying questions only (no statements); *B* answers.

A and *C* offer advice and suggestions; *B* listens.

Round 3

C shares and explains; *A* and *B* listen with no comment.

A and *B* ask clarifying questions only (no statements); *C* answers.

A and *B* offer advice and suggestions; *C* listens.

Establish a time limit for each step (4 minutes seems to work well), and select an unobtrusive signal for when to move on. Move a marker along an overhead transparency or advance a PowerPoint sequence to provide a silent reminder of what to do next. Ask participants to stay with the process even if they can't think of any more to say at that step. Remind them of the importance of "wait time" to let both speakers and listeners process at a deeper level.

After the exercise has been completed, encourage participants to share

- What they learned about their problem and about listening in general
- How it felt to be listened to without interruption for 4 minutes
- How it felt to be silent and not interrupt for 4 full minutes
- How they might use this exercise in other settings

For Example: Family Fun. I conducted the Active Listening Trios exercise among a group of principals who responded to the prompt, "My biggest concerns about shared decision making are . . ." The activity was well received, the participants discovered that they had many of the same concerns, they generated good strategies for dealing with them, and several made commitments to keep in touch and marked dates in their calendars to establish a set time for communication.

A few weeks later, I unexpectedly encountered one of the participants in a shopping mall. He said, "You're the one who did the three-way listening thing, right?" I nodded, and he went on to tell me how he and his wife had used the same process with their teenager at home. He told me how embarrassed they were to discover that they had never spent even 4 whole minutes listening to his viewpoint on anything, and how much mutual respect had been gained as all three of them got equal time to share their feelings. They used this technique to turn family feuds into family fun.

In this chapter, we have explored the question "How will we sustain the focus and momentum?" Whether we create organizations that examine themselves and pursue continuous improvement depends, in large part, on how we treat those who carry the load on a daily basis. A critical aspect of leadership is nurturing the human resources of the organization through technical support, active listening, and caring responses.

SHIFT FROM TECHNICAL TO ADAPTIVE

Michael Fullan's name has been linked to the recognition that there will be predictable implementation dips during change processes. As schools and districts have worked to meet the No Child Left Behind demands for adequate yearly progress (AYP), they have noticed that change happens in fits and starts, not in linear fashion moving consistently upward on a graph. There are gains, and then there are plateaus. Fullan (2005) is helpful once again, advising us that when things plateau, it is time to switch from technical to adaptive approaches (p. 6). "[W]e need a radically new mind-set for reconciling the seemingly intractable dilemmas fundamental for sustainable reform: top-down versus bottom-up, local and central accountability, informed professional judgment, improvement that keeps being replenished" (p. 11).

The difference between technical problems and adaptive problems is described by Ron Heifetz (2003): "An adaptive challenge is a problem for which solutions lie outside the current way of operating. We can distinguish technical problems, which are amenable to current expertise, from adaptive problems, which are not" (p. 70).

Fullan (2005) continues, pointing out that "the set of strategies that brought initial success are not the ones—not powerful enough—to take us to higher levels" and that "we need a system laced with leaders who are trained to think in bigger terms and to act in ways that affect larger parts of the system as a whole" (p. 27).

Earlier in this chapter, the role of the district in providing networking opportunities was outlined. The initial charge of networks was to share best practices and successes. The new work of networks is to develop the broader vision of smart people by placing them in settings where they can feel associated with a larger system and grapple with more complex issues in critical and creative ways.

REAFFIRM ORGANIZATIONAL VALUES AND COMMITMENTS

Growth, change, improvement—these are easy words but hard work. Only our intrinsic values keep us dedicated to a cause that is difficult and unending. All of us have seen great programs come and go, not because they didn't have good results but because we got tired and returned to old ways that were not actually better—they were just easier.

In our personal lives, most of us would admit the tendency to get so caught up in the demands of our daily lives that we lose touch with our own values. In moments of stress, we hear ourselves say things or find ourselves doing things that are completely out of sync with our own ideals and beliefs. We discover we're driving just as rudely as everyone else in our city. We can't remember the last time we thought about our personal faith or the philosophy of education we brought to our work years ago. Or we realize we are not doing things—such as "random acts of kindness"—that we consider important and that we want our students, peers, and families to value. Sometimes we wonder how we got into such a state.

Just like individuals, organizations lose touch and lose their way when there is no time to reflect on the meaning of what we do each day. Dynamic organizations constantly reaffirm their organizational values and mission. Some ways to maintain this focus include keeping the big picture in sight and making conscious decisions about abandoning, synthesizing, integrating, or rejecting current and new practices.

Keep the Big Picture in Sight

In *Leadership and Sustainability,* Michael Fullan (2005) comments that the "perennial complaint that locals have is that they don't understand the big picture." It's important to respond quite literally—paint them a picture, display it prominently, and refer to it constantly as a reminder of the larger scope of specific events and activities, why they are being done, and where they fit in "the big picture" (p. 90).

We started back in Chapter 1 with an organizer that captured the components of the journey of change (Figure 1.1). Early in Chapter 5, I described using poster-sized versions of the organizer to diagnose the initiatives already under way in the school. Chapter 5 ended with a completed example of this "big picture" (Figure 5.8).

One school filled a huge bulletin board in its foyer with an arrangement of the separate components from Figure 1.1. Staff members created a beautiful scroll of their mission statement and displayed it on the top left corner of the bulletin board. In the lower left corner, they posted the executive summary of their conclusions from analysis of the data in their school portfolio. The priority goals they set were lettered in calligraphy on sentence strips. Strategies for each goal were connected by strings of yarn, which gave them the ability to connect several strategies to more than one goal area. Their combined master plan was illustrated with a series of laminated monthly calendars that highlighted the events from their action plans. Any visitor to this school knew what was happening and why. Any new idea or grant opportunity had to pass the acid test of proving where it would fit on that crowded, colorful bulletin board.

Abandon, Synthesize, Integrate, or Reject

There is a grave danger in learning too much about too many new things. The danger is that we can't do them all and still maintain the degree of focus that is needed to move the whole organization forward together. The phrase "organized **abandon**ment" has been used to encourage a process of looking carefully at existing practices and discontinuing those that are neither effective nor consistent with the values of the organization.

Another way to keep the organization focused is to be sure that similar projects and programs are **synthesize**d into a common effort. Especially at the district level, a function of organizational development is to "let the right hand know what the left hand is doing" and merge their efforts. For example, I once attended a principals' meeting where one of the curriculum specialists described a computer program he had set up to keep textbook inventory and how principals should handle "loaning" textbooks from building to building to maintain an accurate inventory. The audience did not seem appreciative of his efforts. Later, I learned that there was already a software system for keeping track of textbooks that had been developed by the media and technology division. These two projects needed to be synthesized and simplified so that principals could focus on their organization's core values of teaching and learning.

A third way to maintain the focus of the organization is to **integrate** multiple plans into one comprehensive master plan that can be displayed, referred to frequently, and monitored continuously. This is illustrated in Figure 1.1, where multiple action plans for implementation are combined into one master plan under the question "How will we sustain focus and momentum?"

"Asking the right questions" also applies to deciding whether it's really feasible to integrate some new initiative or program or grant opportunity that sounds attractive. The following questions have proved helpful for that purpose:

- What are the underlying values and beliefs of this project or organization?
- Do they fit ours?
- What outcomes are desired by these consultants or vendors or grant donors?
- Are they the outcomes we have already stated we want to achieve?
- What evidence is there that this works to achieve those outcomes?
- What steps, activities, and tasks are required to participate in this?
- Do we have committees or processes that already do that?

Dealing with aggressive vendors who have the perfect program to fit all your needs is sometimes like playing poker. You have to be able to call their bluff. Ask them about their values, beliefs, outcomes, and research before you tell them what yours are. A good salesperson is skilled at finding out what your needs are and using your own rhetoric as reassurance that the product will do the trick. Be proactive and prepared to outsmart the vendors who come to your door.

If a new initiative or program can't be integrated into what you're already set to do, the answer is simple—reject, reject, **reject.** This is true even of grants. If new money is going to create new work and make you less effective at what you're already trying to implement, you can't afford it. On the other hand, if the grant-funded activity can help you achieve your goals more effectively than what you're presently doing or if you're faced with an inescapable mandate, then it's back to the beginning of this section. What can you abandon to make room within organizational capacity for this wonderful new thing?

MAINTAIN ORGANIZATIONAL HEALTH

On the journey of change, there are many parallels between individual efforts and group adventures. Whether it's the athlete training for a marathon or the school improvement team building capacity to sustain the effort of veteran teachers struggling to incorporate new practices, similar advice is often appropriate: Stay hydrated. Pace yourself. Keep your eye on the finish line.

Take Rest Stops

The question "How will we get there?" includes development of action plans that contain time frames. When groups or committees work on action plans for the strategies related to the priority goal they were assigned, it is natural for them to "think big" and create ambitious plans that could exhaust all of the resources (time, energy, money) for that particular goal. An essential step for the leadership team as it compiles everything into the single master plan is to look critically at the "sum total" of all the action plans and ask an additional question: "How *fast* can we get there—and arrive alive?" In *Leadership and Sustainability,* Michael Fullan (2005) writes about cyclical energy and describes leaders as "stewards of organizational energy" (p. 35).

Monitoring and managing the energy of individuals and the system as a whole must be intentional during times of major change and high stress. Just as there are proper nutrients that can increase energy in an athlete, so also there are sources of energy creation in organizations. Fullan (2005) names five: moral purpose, emotional intelligence, quality relationships, quality knowledge, and physical well-being. He points out that there are "cycles of push and recovery" in organizations and warns district leaders about

> not aggravating the overload problem by piling policies upon policies, working on alignment so that the de-energizing effects of fragmentation do not take their toll, taking time out to review and consolidate gains, celebrating accomplishments, investing more resources as success accrues, and, of course, fostering the development of leadership at all levels of the organization and system. (p. 38)

Linda Lambert (2003) also writes about the "personal and collective ebb and flow" of energy in *Leadership Capacity for Lasting School Improvement:*

Even under the best conditions, some individuals burn out—not out of frustration and disappointment, necessarily, but out of exhaustion. By anticipating the possibility of burnout, school community members need to orchestrate energy by

- Guarding against low-priority initiatives that draw attention away from the essential work of the school
- "Gliding," during which time we consolidate and deepen our efforts
- Rotating major responsibilities so that no one person carries a major task for too long
- Letting individuals opt out of tasks occasionally when external or personal demands make it important to do so

- Keeping reflection at the center of practice
- Celebrating successes frequently
- Learning to occasionally say "no" (pp. 94–95)

In 2004–2005, my district developed a 5-year strategic plan that included 64 action plans with 33 identified for immediate attention. Major developments in the areas of curriculum and assessment were on the "do it now" list. After a year of development and 6 months of early implementation, many elementary teachers (who are generalists and deliver *everything*) and some elementary principals were on severe overload, asking for both "the big picture" (how does this all fit?) and some relief. In response, the common assessments that were being developed in reading and math were reduced in number, provisions for change in the gifted program were postponed for future implementation, mandated use of a new system for electronic grading and reporting was delayed, and other curricular changes were spaced out and integrated over the scope of a 7-year adoption cycle.

However, not all schools were feeling as much stress, and they wanted to keep moving forward—so the development work continues and those schools help us with "field tests," but the pace of mandated implementation has been adjusted based on realities of individual schools. At the district level, the superintendent's leadership team must engage in deep discussions about allowing rest stops while staying the course and continuing to support and stretch the most progressive leaders at the school and classroom level.

Have Regular Check-Ups at All Three Levels

That's why regular check-ups are needed at all three levels—to assure the ongoing strength of all the collaboration pictured in Figure 3.4. Fullan (2005) points out that

> districts need to take the pulse of student engagement, principal and teacher ownership and morale, parent and community satisfaction, and so on. . . .
>
> From our change process knowledge, we know that it is a mistake to abandon plans too soon when difficulties are encountered. One has to work through the implementation dips. But engaged districts know the difference between a dip and a chasm. When serious problems are experienced in a variety of situations and when they persist or get worse, involved districts pick up the cues early and act on them. . . .
>
> If they give in too soon in the face of conflict and fail to stay the course, they will not be able to work through the inevitable barriers to implementation. But if they show an inflexible commitment to a vision—even if it is based on passionate moral purpose—they can drive resistance underground and miss essential lessons until it is too late. (pp. 71–72)

One of the roles of the district is to create opportunities for schools (principals, teacher leaders) to network with each other and discover "the power of learning from a wider group of peers across schools . . . [which] has the double

Figure 6.4   Assessing the Instructional Focus of School Improvement Plans

This rubric is a tool for identifying and assessing critical attributes of School Improvement Plans that are most successful for improving instruction and student achievement.

1 = Current practices reflect very little of the criteria.

2 = Current practices include some criteria for some staff.

3 = All aspects of the criteria are present but not consistent for all staff.

4 = Exemplary implementation by all

The Process—Parameters	
1. It is clear to all parties that the School Improvement Plan will not be accepted unless it includes strategies that directly affect classroom instruction.	__/4
2. A designee of the district reviews the plan, provides feedback, and rejects the plan if it does not directly affect instruction.	__/4
The Process—Participation	
1. The overall school leadership team represents the roles and demographics of the school/community population, including parents, community, and students in Grades 4–12.	__/4
2. A data team helps identify significant/relevant data and prepares user-friendly visuals.	__/4
3. Study groups are formed to recommend strategies for each priority area. Classroom teachers are highly represented on teams for academic priorities (e.g., literacy and math).	__/4
4. Principal models instructional focus with continuing references to data and comments on instruction.	__/4
The Plan (Year 1)—Affirming Mission	
1. The statement of mission (beliefs, vision, etc.) explicitly accepts responsibility for the learning of all students.	__/4
The Plan (Year 1)—Analyzing Data Detail	
1. Specific skills with which many students struggle are identified from multiple data sources and multiple years.	__/4
2. Data on subpopulations of students are reviewed to identify unique needs.	__/4
3. Data are gathered to document current instructional practices and time allocations in areas of priority/concern.	__/4
4. Perceptual data identifies questions/concerns of stakeholders and the data team follows up with focus groups for clarity and collaboration.	__/4
The Plan (Year 1)—Setting Goals/Priorities	
1. Goals are specific, measurable, and set internally.	__/4
2. Goals reflect multiyear time frames (e.g., 3–5 years).	__/4
The Plan (Year 1)—Selecting Strategies	
1. Participants can state the link between each major strategy and data that substantiate the need for it.	__/4
2. Participants can state the link between each major strategy and the beliefs of the school.	__/4
3. Participants can state the link between each major strategy and proof of its potential to achieve desired results.	__/4
4. The combined set of strategies will serve *all* students *and* the unique needs of each subgroup of students. (See #1 and #2 under Analyzing Data Detail.)	__/4

(Continued)

Figure 6.4 (Continued)

The Plan (Year 1)—Selecting Evidence of Implementation	
1. Critical attributes of implementation are explicitly stated for each strategy (e.g., "Increase reading time to 90 minutes per day" is accompanied by guidelines for use of chunks of time to provide balanced language arts instruction).	___/4
2. Agreements are made about what data will be gathered, and by whom, to demonstrate fidelity of implementation.	___/4
The Plan (Year 1)—Selecting Evidence of Impact on Student Learning	
1. Formative/interim assessments are identified to balance large-scale assessments and inform instruction.	___/4
2. Time is identified for collaborative analysis of common assessments and discussion of instructional strategies to take place during implementation.	___/4
The Plan (Year 1)—Communication and Commitment	
1. A visual organizer/figure is created, displayed, and distributed to illustrate the main components of the plan for all stakeholders.	___/4
2. Staff members state the impact of the School Improvement Plan on their roles and affirm their individual commitments.	___/4
3. Roles of teacher leaders (e.g., department chairs) are clarified and are focused on instruction.	___/4
Implementation (Years 2 and 3)—Professional Development	
1. Time is reallocated as needed to provide training in new strategies and assure collaboration around instruction and assessment.	___/4
2. Other professional development initiatives are rejected or postponed to make successful implementation of identified strategies the #1 priority.	___/4
Implementation (Years 2 and 3)—Monitoring Implementation	
1. All staff members state key phrases of mission, priorities from the data, and major strategies under way.	___/4
2. Protocols (e.g., meeting notes) are used to assure focus and follow-up of teacher collaboration time.	___/4
3. Informal classroom visits (e.g., walk-throughs) focus on gathering evidence of implementation and provide data for celebration and support.	___/4
4. Staff members volunteer to share successes and are welcomed and applauded by peers.	___/4
Implementation (Years 2 and 3)—Monitoring Impact	
1. Common formative/interim assessments are given, analyzed promptly, and discussed collaboratively.	___/4
2. Whenever new data is received from external sources (e.g., state assessment), it is reviewed to compare to internal data and affirm existing plans and/or identify needs for revision.	___/4
Implementation (Years 2 and 3)—Sustaining Effort	
1. Evidence of implementation and impact is shared schoolwide and celebrated at regular intervals.	___/4
2. Major transitions and events in the school culture (e.g., start of school year) include review and renewal of commitment to the School Improvement Plan.	___/4
3. No new initiatives are undertaken without review of if, how, and where they fit within the School Improvement Plan.	___/4
TOTAL	___/140

Areas of strength for celebration:

Areas most in need of immediate attention:

advantage of accessing more ideas while increasing people's identification with a larger piece of the system" (Fullan, 2005, p. 70).

The importance of attention at all three levels is further underscored as Fullan (2005) continues: "When it comes to sustainability, each level above you helps or hinders—it is rarely neutral." He mentions the loss of time and momentum that has resulted from

> flying back and forth from centralization to decentralization. . . . Many jurisdictions have promoted (and some are still promoting) site-based management on the assumption that the local school is where it counts, so support should go directly to the school. In many cases, deliberate strategies from the state level have played down or bypassed the district. . . . If you have your systems hat on, you know right away that this is a mistake. You cannot omit any part of the system without paying the price. (p. 65)

The district role is indeed critical and was not explored in adequate depth in the two previous editions of this book. The major emphasis was, and still is, on schoolwide effort. But student learning is most dramatically affected by the quality of teaching and teacher-student relationships, so more attention has been placed on the classroom level and on curriculum and assessment issues related to instruction.

During the past year, I have had the opportunity to work with New Leaders for New Schools, a nonprofit organization focused on developing principals for urban settings. One of the products of that work was a rubric for assuring the instructional focus of school improvement plans. Figure 6.4 provides that framework for regular check-ups at the school and classroom level. Note that it represents a 3-year time frame, so it is not just a pre-assessment or an evaluation of the plan at the point when it's developed, but it continues to provide some checks as implementation rolls forward.

Serious travelers have a road map and stay close to the route they planned. They also keep the journey pleasant by taking rest stops and by checking fuel and oil levels regularly. We must embrace the same safety practices on our journey of school improvement.

Answer Key

- Answering the question "How will we sustain focus and momentum?" is most difficult because the struggle goes on forever and has so many facets. This question must be raised over and over, and organizational leaders must never assume that everything is going fine.

- Educators are human, and every frailty of humanity will emerge during the course of change. The Concerns-Based Adoption Model is powerful for helping leaders understand and respond to predictable concerns and conflicts.

- Conflict is unavoidable. Facilitators must be skillful with tools like Venn diagrams, Quick-Writes, Talk-Walks, and Go for the Green.

- The inquiry that occurred during the planning stage must continue throughout implementation as participants engage in reflective study groups and action research.

- When implementation dips occur and things get tense, leaders need to listen throughout the organization and maintain organizational health by adjusting pace and priorities as necessary.

7

Powerful Questions That Shape Practice

The previous five chapters focused on the five critical questions that guide the journey of change:

- Where are we now?
- Where do we want to go?
- How will we get there?
- How will we know we are (getting) there?
- How will we sustain focus and momentum?

The school improvement process served as the primary example for use of these critical questions and the tools and group activities that were provided. But the same questions guide change in any context. They can be applied at various levels in an educational setting for various purposes:

- Students developing their own goals and learning plans
- Teachers with different expertise working together in a classroom to support student learning
- Teachers with similar expertise and assignments working together to improve their skills and practice
- Teachers with different assignments working together to improve the schoolwide learning environment and culture
- Teachers, principals, and other shareholders working together to create a new vision for the future
- School representatives and district leaders working together to strengthen reciprocal relationships for planning, expectations, and support
- District leaders working together to model organizational learning and improvement

The same questions are also at the heart of organizational change in other settings, from businesses to hospitals to nonprofit organizations to churches to community clubs and causes. In fact, these five questions can also shape plans for personal and family goals, from weight loss to smoking cessation to shaping and managing the family budget. They are truly powerful, multipurpose questions.

This chapter emphasizes that they are not the *only* powerful questions and that the formalized improvement process is not the *only* means for shaping practice. Leaders—meaning every individual in an organization who observes, reflects, and expresses concern about conditions and outcomes—can increase their influence through effective use of questions. As leadership writers Warren Bennis and Burt Nanus (1985) have pointed out, "Leaders convey what really counts in an organization by how they spend their time, *the questions they ask,* their reactions to critical incidents, and what they reward" (emphasis mine).

Developing a concise, purposeful question requires careful thought. In fact, there are *questions* about developing a good question! What am I specifically trying to address and accomplish? Is this really an important issue or just a personal irritation? How will I word my question in a nonthreatening, affirming, but very clear manner? How will I use and react to the responses I get?

Lambert (2003) describes the formal school leader's powerful use of questions this way:

> [T]he principal must be nonjudgmental and use strategies such as reflective listening, pausing, and critical questioning to help others become self-directed leaders. "Somehow, when we talk it through, I hear myself think," said one suburban teacher about her principal. "She asks me a couple of pointed questions . . . and the minute she asks me those questions, I get it." (p. 119)

The questions in this chapter have been carefully worded, utilized in many settings, and refined. They have been successful in the vast majority of cases. They can be useful exactly as described, or they may be idea generators that help you refine your own powerful questions to raise issues and influence those around you, whatever your context or formal position title.

ENTRY QUESTIONS

Formal leaders, such as principals and central office administrators, are often assigned to positions in unfamiliar settings, sometimes with little background knowledge of the context, the individuals in the organization, or the history. The skillful leader is sensitive to the setting and seeks to learn about it firsthand. Even when directed to make changes and assured of full support, the leader should diagnose readiness for change and identify the changes that are perceived as needed by the individuals in the school(s) or department(s).

Emerging leaders also experience the unease of entering unfamiliar situations or roles. For example, a teacher who has had extensive experience elsewhere may be trying to find her place in a new setting and figure out how to contribute her expertise. A brand-new teacher with no experience may have more up-to-date training in an area like technology and want to help his colleagues without being labeled "that young upstart." A teacher who has been placed in a leadership role on a committee or project may realize she needs to challenge the thinking of her peers but fear risking her relationships.

The following simple questions—and your own variations—can be valuable to ask individuals and groups when entering a new setting or situation:

- *What's going well here that should be continued?*
  - ○ How can I learn about that?
  - ○ What can I do to support it?
- *What do you think needs to be improved or changed?*
- *How can I help or contribute to your goals?*

Another entry situation involves the need for leaders and coaches to understand the dynamics of collaborative groups and assure that they are constructive and productive. Whether they are called study groups, action research groups, critical friends, or professional learning communities, the emphasis must be on learning together to improve practice. Shirley Hord (2007) outlines these questions to ask when entering a professional learning community:

- *What are you learning in this group?*
- *Why have you chosen to learn about that?*
- *How are you learning it?*
- *How will your learning spread to others in your school?*

The responses serve two purposes: They describe what is occurring in the group, and they also provide evidence from which to assess whether this really *is* a community of professionals who are learning and improving their practice on behalf of student learning.

DATA-BOOSTING QUESTIONS

When I visit schools as a supervisor or for research, the teachers' lounge is not generally one of my planned destinations. On this day, though, my throat was dry, and I decided to patronize the vending machine and contribute to the proceeds for the student council. I paused with the door half open when I heard my name. "She's here again today, and you know what she's going to ask." Before I could close the door, I heard the sing-song reply, "Yadda, yadda, yadda, data, data, data—What's the most recent data you looked at, and what did you learn?" I was only slightly taken aback (40 years of experience may thin the hair but it thickens the skin) and then I became amused and pleased. My reaction shifted because I chose to interpret the comments as evidence that this faculty now knew some important things: what was important to me, what to expect from my visits, and that I would keep coming back.

Although leaders are encouraged to be flexible, members of an organization also need the security of knowing the leaders' priorities and observing a pattern of predictability. If they know where their principal stands, they also know what they can expect. Just as students will rise to the occasion when they have a relationship with a teacher and the teacher has clear, high expectations, most members of an organization will step up when they have a relationship with their leader and know what's expected. As in the Bennis and Nanus quote earlier in the chapter, these folks knew that I would ask the question,

- *What's the most recent data you looked at, and what did you learn?*

In some settings, where I have access to their actual data, my data-boosting questions will accompany an observation and be more specific:

- *Wow! I'm thrilled about the ____(results, gain, increase)____ that I see in this data from the ____(test, survey)____ . What did you do here that made this possible?*
- *Did you notice _____ when you looked at this data from the _____? What do you think about it?*
- *I'm puzzled by this data from the _____ because it doesn't seem to match with ___(other data, other source)___. What ideas do you have about it?*

These questions help to focus on specific data, while drawing out interpretations and reactions. They convey a presumption that the data have been reviewed, and they avoid "telling" what the findings mean or what action should be taken.

A third approach to data-boosting through questioning is this short and simple query:

- *What evidence can you show me?*

WALKING-AROUND QUESTIONS

The data-boosting questions can be used in groups, with principals, or just when walking around the school to observe and interact. Other questions that have been useful during informal visits are

- *What are you teaching?*
- *Which students have learned it?*
- *How do you know?*

That sequence illustrates the desired shift in focus from delivery of content to whether the targeted learning actually occurred for the students.

A variation on this sequence came to mind one day as I overheard a discussion about family involvement and communication. A parent in the group said, "Every afternoon, I ask my kids, 'What did you learn today?' And every time they say . . ." at which point the whole group chorused, "Nothing!" I wondered what the teachers would say to the same type of question, so I began to ask,

- What did your students learn today?
- What did _you_ learn today?

I have been pleased to discover that most respondents will need a moment to reflect, but when given that positive pause, they will mention something they noticed or thought about during that day. The point of a powerful question is not necessarily the answer itself—and certainly not a single, correct one. The point of a powerful question is to stimulate reflection and reasoning.

After using the question "What did _you_ learn today?" frequently, it dawned on me that I should apply it to my own practice and make a change in the notes I leave on teachers' desks or send by e-mail after making a school visit. I have always tried to express appreciation for the welcome I receive and reinforce the examples of good practice that I observe. More recently, I have begun to add something _I_ learned from being at the school.

At one school I visited, the principal arranged for me to use a conference room so I could be available to talk with teachers who knew I was coming and had some things to share with me. The conference room was on a narrow hallway in the main office area, directly across from the School Resource Officer (police liaison) and the Dean of Students. During short periods of time when I was not involved in conversation myself, I could overhear some of the exchanges between those adults and a sequence of individual students. I was impressed with the variety of styles and approaches they employed, depending on the student and the situation. And I was reminded of the realities of our student population and the situations that teachers face. My follow-up note did not focus on how well they were implementing the new mathematics resources, but on how much I learned and how important I realized school visits are for keeping district administrators grounded in reality.

A variation on the "What did _you_ learn today?" question has turned out to be very helpful to me in my role of workshop presenter. Many readers of this book also facilitate professional development and may struggle with the balance (or tension) between actively engaging participants and their prior experiences and yet having time to present and practice application of new knowledge and skills. Sometimes participants do not understand what the facilitator means by "a quick summary," or they tell an interesting tale that doesn't easily connect to the objective of the learning experience. I phrase the question this way and ask them to mentally rehearse their response:

- How have you done/used _____ (the topic of the workshop)?
- And what did you _learn_ from that?

I emphasize that the second question is the most important, and they need to focus on it as they rehearse. The rehearsal consists of 1 minute of silence in which they "talk inside their heads" to make sure their story will fit a 1-minute time limit. This helps to increase the focus and speed up the process of gathering knowledge and experience from the group. It also contributes to their own reflection, even if they do not share their stories aloud.

INSTRUCTIONAL QUESTIONS

The questions above focused on what students or teachers learned through their daily experiences and were phrased in past tense. I am concerned that we do not have more future-tense conversations about instruction. By that I mean groups of teachers working together to develop powerful lessons for initial instruction on complex concepts and skills.

In fact, some popular current versions of professional learning communities intentionally omit the question of instruction by urging schools to focus on what students should know and be able to do (standards), how to assess whether students know that, and what interventions to provide if students have not learned. Their emphasis is that it's about learning, not teaching, which is consistent with much of what I believe and have written. Unfortunately, by making no mention of the instructional design, there is a trend in implementation that I am sure does not match the intent. I am seeing a return to "pre-inclusion" practices that resemble "I taught it, I assessed them, and now I need somewhere to send them."

In Chapter 6, I added a segment on Lesson Study. Even if time is not available for the in-depth form of lesson study that occurs in countries like Japan and Germany, we must at least include this question in the collaborative work of teachers:

- *How can we teach this concept in the most powerful way and maximize the number of students who learn it the first time?*

I will be convinced that a true professional learning community exists when I see peers helping peers (Hord, 2003) as teachers collectively identify the most difficult concept in their course or grade, openly discuss how they have taught it, and review their students' levels of success. If at least one teacher has a high success rate, these teachers would observe each other, review each other's lesson plans, and proactively plan a powerful sequence of lessons that extend the *most* effective practices to *all* students in that grade or course. On the other hand, if all teachers in the group have done their best and students are not succeeding, a community of professional learners would seek out more teachers to assist them, whether in the form of district curriculum staff, external expertise, the library and Internet, or teachers in other schools with better outcomes. The best intervention is prevention of failure in the first place, so professional learning communities should share the most successful practices—from any source—in order to maximize students' success and minimize the numbers who need interventions. *Teaching* does matter.

STUDENT-WORK ANALYSIS QUESTIONS

The demands and threats of No Child Left Behind have resulted in the overuse and undercredibility of large-scale, standardized tests. As a result, vendors, consultants, and administrators have increased the discussion of formative assessment programs, products, and development processes. I have also written (Holcomb, 2004) about the need for a balance of large-scale and "up-close, real-time" assessments. What is more up close and in real time than the work that teachers routinely assign to students? And what needs more thought, reflection, and revision than the types of assignments we give, how we assess them, and how that turns into grades that in some cases determine destinies?

In recent interaction with a school's teachers, I was told how they were trying to do collaborative analysis of student work, but had been introduced to just one protocol with one or two questions and wondered if I could add some variety. I compiled this collection of questions in no particular sequence—just as examples from which they could choose, to stretch their discussion of student work:

- *What specific skills/benchmarks did we think this assignment would demonstrate?*
- *Does the assignment/assessment reveal what we need to know? Does it give us the information we need to provide feedback to our students?*
- *I think the strengths of my class are _____. How about yours?*
- *I see these as the needs of my students: _____. How about you?*
- *What instruction needs to occur to move my class (our students) to the next skill level?*
- *What patterns are we noticing?*
- *What commonalities do we see within a class? Grade level? School?*
- *What goals can I set for particular students? The class? Myself?*
- *How will the reteaching be different from the initial instruction?*
- *It looks like your students did really well. What did you do that helped your students succeed? What can we learn from each other?*
- *What interventions and enrichments are needed? How will we keep them connected to our classroom instruction and specific benchmarks?*
- *What specific steps will we take to offer these students (name them) help with this specific skill?*
- *What support do we need in terms of modeling, coaching, dialogue, and resources? How can we access it?*

My strong disposition is that schools should look first at assignments and assessments they already use. If those assignments/assessments don't provide useful information, the result should be changes in local assessment practices, rather than the purchase of yet more external tests to give.

LETTING-GO QUESTIONS

Travelers on the road to school improvement know that it is going to be a long trip with twists and turns and bumps along the way. But there are two things they should not have to experience: Their confidence should not be daunted nor their past efforts demeaned. A danger with initiating change for the future is that it can feel like an accusation that everything they have done before is somehow wrong. Two questions can be asked to affirm the value of prior experience before moving into a new phase:

- *Did it make sense then?*
- *Does it make sense now?*

The literature is full of discussion about assumptions, mental models, and paradigm shifts. A paradigm is an attitude or predisposition that governs our behavior, a perception held so strongly that it might not even be conscious, a filter through which we interpret everything around us. Our paradigms determine what we will consider right and possible.

We have inherited and absorbed attitudes from our past experience that are so strong, we may not know they exist. We have never questioned them because we are unaware of them. We just know that we get uncomfortable with some new ideas that "just don't feel right."

Some groups have found it helpful to start "letting go" by identifying things that have *not* changed about schools in the past 50 to 100 years. Some of the items that appear on a typical list are the following:

- 9 months of school
- Dismissal time about 3:00
- Grade levels
- Carnegie units for high school graduation
- Self-contained elementary classrooms
- Departmentalized secondary schools
- A, B, C, D, and F grades
- Separate tracks for college-bound and vocational students

The next step is to revisit those structures of schooling. The 9-month school year was linked to an agricultural economy, and we ask, "Did it make sense then?" The answer is yes. So—good for us! Why did we dismiss school about 3:00? The answer that eventually emerges is, "because factories ran a day shift that got out about 3:00." Did it make sense in the industrial period? Yes. Well, good for us again! What about Carnegie units? Where did they come from? Many people don't know that Andrew Carnegie pioneered the effort to identify some common standards as prerequisites that would put students on a more even playing field when they went on to a higher level of education. Did "Carnegie units" make sense in the days of rural schools to give them something to shoot for? Yes. Then good for us as public educators! Conduct similar conversations for the other items on the list and emphasize that those practices didn't emerge just by happenstance. They were responses to the needs of society—the shareholders—at that time. Encourage the participants to congratulate themselves and brag to each other about how public education was customer oriented even before that adjective was used.

When the celebration of pride dies down, pause and ask softly, *"Does it make sense now?"* Many groups act a little stunned by the question, but then they begin acknowledging that we do many things based on tradition, without thought about whether they still fit. They are also reassured when they realize that aspects of schooling we took for granted were once reforms themselves, based on the needs of a changing society.

Use of these two questions will not lead to overnight restructuring and will not make the change process itself any easier. But these questions can help groups become more conscious of the origins of our traditions while reasserting pride in our past experience. From there, they can move on to preserving the things that still make sense and considering ways to change the things that don't. At the least, it's a far more positive experience than sitting in an auditorium for 3 hours, listening to a proponent of some new method, and being told our practices are outdated and far behind every other developed country in the world.

HIRING QUESTIONS

Does anyone doubt that one of the most critical decisions for any organization is the selection of its leaders and staff members? Yet some may be surprised to find a segment here about hiring. It's usually described as a "management" thing, not an "instructional" thing. Well, if it is, then *management matters,* too. I have seen schools that were well-managed but academically low-performing. However, I have never seen a school become an academic high-performer without being well-managed.

Hiring the right people is essential, and there are inventories available to check the belief system of the candidate and screening procedures to check certification requirements (that they have met them) and criminal records (that they don't have them). The interview is still a critical piece, and articles and books have been written about questions that are appropriate and inappropriate, effective and ineffective. Here are two that have always been useful in helping me identify some critical characteristics in candidates.

- *Based on your background, select three experiences that were most relevant to the elements of this job description. Describe them—and tell us why you selected those.*

This question has greatly improved responses over the typical opening question of "Describe your education and experience." It prevents the lengthy response that sometimes begins with "Well, it all started on the day I was born . . ." It reveals whether the candidate has actually studied the job description. It also demonstrates whether the candidate can synthesize experiences and apply and transfer them from one setting to another.

A second critical question for candidates is this:

- *What is the connection between your work in this position and student success?*

This question has worked well for clerical and support staff as well as certified educators. For teachers, the last phrase may be changed to student achievement. In any setting, the link could be made to the mission statement of the organization. The bottom line is that schools and school districts exist to serve students, and everyone should be able to see how they directly or indirectly contribute to and are important to the core function.

TIME MANAGEMENT QUESTIONS

No one has enough time, but the challenges for principals are exceptionally complicated. More and more paperwork is required, while there are more and more challenges in the realm of "people work"—be visible, interactive, engaged with teachers, responsive to parents, personally knowledgeable of students, and on and on. Moreover, new tools (e.g., e-mail) have created expectations for immediate gratification on the part of the sender.

As a building administrator, there were two practices that greatly assisted me with balancing the time to be out and about and still be responsive to phone calls and e-mail. They involved teaching my secretary to ask two important questions when taking a message:

- *Dr. Holcomb spends most of the day with teachers and students. Would it be more convenient for you to meet with her before or after the school day?*
- *Dr. Holcomb spends most of the day with teachers and students. What number would work best to return your call between 4:00 and 5:00 this afternoon?*

Parents still got a response on the same day and had the opportunity to make an appointment with me. I certainly made exceptions for emergency circumstances, but this strategy helped me reduce the expectation for an immediate audience, provided a cool-down time in some situations, and shortened some of the telephone conversations since dinnertime was approaching. Most of all, it helped *me* hold myself accountable to get out and about and not get "caught" in the office when I said I was with teachers and students.

INVOLVEMENT QUESTIONS

Throughout the book, numerous admonitions and examples have underscored the importance of participation and involvement. Sometimes we neglect to include people because we just don't particularly enjoy their presence, and sometimes we just get busy and forget. In the case where we might be subconsciously excluding a person who seems difficult to us, these questions for reflection may be helpful:

- How much have I taken time to learn about this person?
- What assumptions could I be making that I should check out?
- How much listening have I done?
- Have I ever asked this person for feedback?

As a brand-new principal, I was appalled to discover that one of the teachers in my building thought I was a poor principal who "didn't like her or care about her." It was especially puzzling, since I considered her an excellent teacher and had never criticized her in any way. After some uneasiness, I finally decided to approach her with this question: "You know, you're not on the observation cycle this year, so I'm wondering if I have ever taken time to tell you what a wonderful teacher you are." Her immediate response was, "You're kidding! I didn't think you thought much of me." I was then able to tell her how sad that made me and ask her what I had done to make her think that way. She replied, "You come into the classroom often, and you always talk to the students and ask how they are doing and what they are learning. You never ask how *I* am." My desire to be an instructionally focused, student-centered principal had blinded me to the human needs of the adult in the room.

In the case of innocent forgetting to recruit participation, a succinct, multipurpose question to use is this:

- *Who else?*

A veteran principal, who was trying to make his own paradigm shift from benevolent dictator to a more shared approach, discovered that he needed constant reminders to include others. In his wallet, on his daily calendar, and above the door where he would see it as he left his office, he placed the two words *"Who else?"* When he analyzed a situation and prepared to "share decisions" by announcing what he had decided, those signs were his prompts to think about who else should have a voice. They reminded him to consider who else might have expertise to share; who else would be affected by the decision; and above all, whose cooperation was essential to making the decision work. By concentrating on these visual reminders, the experienced principal found himself receiving compliments from parents and staff on his new leadership style.

Organizations change as people within them change. That's one reason for the emphasis on participation and involvement in the study and planning phases of school improvement. Another reason is that organizational change is far too difficult and complex for one leader to be able to make happen on her own.

In *Leadership and Sustainability*, Michael Fullan (2005) points out two aspects that are needed to build capacity: mechanisms for teachers to work together daily and development of leaders that replicate themselves (p. 69). In an earlier book (2003a), he stressed that "Ultimately, your leadership in a culture of change will be judged as effective or ineffective not by who you are as a leader but by what leadership you produce in others" (p. 137). The leader must always be asking, *"Who else* has the potential to develop into the next even-better leader?"

THE COMMITMENT QUESTION

There's another version of the "who else" question that we need to revisit frequently when we are tired, frustrated, discouraged, and wondering why we ever got into this situation in the first place and whether it's worth the effort to keep trying. We need to answer those questions *with* a question:

- *Who else . . . if not me?*

If I don't model perseverance, who else will? If I don't have the emotional intelligence to understand and manage my own emotions, motivate myself, and demonstrate empathy and interpersonal effectiveness, who else will model it for the adolescents in our care? If I don't model continuous personal improvement, who else will care about continual professional and organizational improvement? If I don't reach out to meet our constituents halfway, who else will see the need to do so? The "Who else?" question can be a powerful tool in our own self-talk and motivation as leaders. It's all about commitment to the journey of change.

Early in the book, I pointed out that there are ramblers and there are travelers. The ramblers will wind up where they will and probably won't remember how they got there. The travelers will probably reach their destination, especially if there are rest stops and information booths along the way. As leaders, change agents, and group facilitators, we staff the rest stops and information booths. If we provide adequate support and accurate guidance, the travelers are more likely to be interested in taking another trip, pursuing yet another destination of improvement.

The ultimate travelers are the astronauts who broke the space barrier and who now make shuttle missions seem almost routine. I remember the first step on the moon, I held my breath with the rest of the country during the *Apollo 13* mission, and I watched the *Challenger* disaster and tried to explain it to my students. So I was eager to visit the Kennedy Space Center with my husband and three nieces. My most powerful memory is of the Mission Control room, where I watched in fascination as green panels lit up to simulate the countdown toward launch—and chills went through me as one panel flashed repeatedly, COMMIT—COMMIT—COMMIT. I realized how irrevocable that decision was for the astronauts and thought about the courage of those who had taken that risk. And, as usual, I thought about commitment to school change.

The second highlight of the tour was seeing the shuttle *Columbia* sitting on the launch pad being prepared for the next mission. The timing was significant because this was to be the first mission with a female commander. My nieces and I reveled in the knowledge that somewhere in a building we passed on the bus, Lieutenant Colonel Eileen Collins was getting ready to make history. She would be responsible for the heaviest and most expensive payload ever: NASA's 25-ton, $1.5 billion Chandra X-ray Observatory. Gina, Kacie, Danielle, and I talked about the importance of their math and science education and physical health and having lofty goals and how much more they would be able to do than my generation or my mother's. And, as usual, I thought about school change—and wondered if their schools have changed enough to deliver on their dreams.

Back home a few days later, I watched the launch of the STS-93 shuttle mission. There were moments of anxiety as an electrical short knocked out some computers for the main engines and an instrument display in the cockpit failed. Following the launch, tiny leaks caused the engines to run out of fuel seconds too soon to reach the exact desired orbit. As commander, Collins remained calm throughout the mission and completed the release of Chandra on schedule, with all systems functioning perfectly.

A short time after, I was preparing to leave for the office when I overheard the TV announcer say that Lt. Col. Collins was to be Katie Couric's next guest on the *Today* show. Having set her up as a role model for my nieces, I wanted to see her and hear what she had to say. Couric asked Collins whether she was afraid when things started going wrong and how she made the decision to continue with the launch.

The answer was simple. This courageous woman said something like this:

First of all, I didn't have time to be scared. We train so thoroughly and have a plan for everything that my mind was just running through the plan and preparing to do whatever came next. Second, we have total faith in the support teams on the ground who are monitoring every system very carefully and would not put us in harm's way. So—no—I wasn't scared, and it was an easy decision to commit to launch.

The conversation took me back to that moment in the Mission Control simulation when the flashing green panel signaled the moment of no turning back. And, as usual, I thought about school change. Those statements by Lt. Col. Collins sounded like answers to the question of how we get people to commit to school improvement. We need plans. We need training. We must provide plenty of support. Our principals and teachers need to know both that we are monitoring *and* that we won't put them in harm's way.

These are the conditions that replace fear with faith to commit to the shared journey of school change. If we don't have the courage to make that journey, there are young men and women who will never reach the destination of their dreams. Godspeed us all.

Answer Key

- The use of carefully worded questions can be a powerful tool for leaders to use to focus their organizations on priorities and shape practice, such as use of data- and research-based instructional strategies.
- Instructional leadership is key and rests on a foundation of effective management. Management matters, too. The right questions can assist with hiring and balancing demands on time.
- Participation and collaboration are critical. "Who else?" questions are important reminders to help leaders increase involvement.
- Questions for reflection can help the leader maintain his or her own focus and commitment.

References and Further Reading

Anderson, S. E., Rolheiser, C., & Bennett, B. (1995). Confronting the challenge of implementing cooperative learning. *Journal of Staff Development, 16,* 32–38.

Bennis, W., & Nanus, B. (1985). *Leaders: The strategies for taking charge.* New York: Harper & Row.

Bolman, L. G., & Deal, T. E. (1994). *Becoming a teacher leader: From isolation to collaboration.* Thousand Oaks, CA: Corwin Press.

Bonstingl, J. J. (1992). *Schools of quality: An introduction to total quality management in education.* Alexandria, VA: Association for Supervision and Curriculum Development.

Darling-Hammond, L. (1994, November). *The current status of teaching and teacher development in the United States.* Background paper prepared for the National Commission on Teaching and America's Future.

Darling-Hammond, L. (1996, March). The quiet revolution: Rethinking teacher development. *Educational Leadership, 53*(6), 4–10.

Deal, T. E., & Peterson, K. D. (1999). *Shaping school culture: The heart of leadership.* San Francisco: Jossey Bass.

Eaker, R., DuFour, R., & DuFour, R. (2002). *Getting started: Reculturing schools to become professional learning communities.* Bloomington, IN: National Educational Service.

Epstein, J. L., Sanders, M. G., Simon, B. S., Salinas, K. C., Jansorn, N. R., & Van Voorhis, F. L. (2002). *School, family, and community partnerships: Your handbook for action.* Thousand Oaks, CA: Corwin Press.

Evans, R. (1996). *The human side of school change: Reform, resistance, and the real-life problems of innovation.* San Francisco: Jossey Bass.

Fullan, M. G. (1993). *Change forces: Probing the depth of educational reform.* New York: Falmer.

Fullan, M. G. (1999a, December 6). *Change forces at the millennium.* Presentation at the National Staff Development Council Annual Conference, Dallas, TX.

Fullan, M. G. (1999b). *Change forces: The sequel.* Philadelphia: Falmer.

Fullan, M. G. (2003a). *Leading in a culture of change.* San Francisco: Jossey Bass.

Fullan, M. G. (2003b). *The moral imperative of school leadership.* Thousand Oaks, CA: Corwin Press.

Fullan, M. G. (2005). *Leadership and sustainability: System thinkers in action.* Thousand Oaks, CA: Corwin Press.

Fullan, M. G., & Stiegelbauer, S. M. (1991). *The new meaning of educational change.* New York: Teachers College Press.

Garmston, R. J. (2006). The five principles of successful meetings. *The Learning System, 1*(4), 1, 6, 8.

Garmston, R. G., & Wellman, B. (1999). *The adaptive school: A sourcebook for developing collaborative groups.* Norwood, MA: Christopher-Gordon.

Goodwin, B., & Dean C. (2007). Three school improvement mistakes (and how to avoid them). *Changing Schools, 55,* 3–4.

Hall, G. E., & Hord, S. M. (2001). *Implementing change: Patterns, principles, and potholes.* Boston: Allyn & Bacon.

Hall, G. E., & Hord, S. M. (2006). *Implementing change: Patterns, principles, and potholes* (2nd ed.). Boston: Allyn & Bacon.

Heffner, E. (2007, October 15). Seattle schools changing course. *Seattle Times.* Retrieved October 20, 2007, from http://seattletimes.nwsource.com.

Heifetz, R. (2003). Adaptive work. In T. Bentley & J. Wilsdon (Eds.), *The adaptive state* (pp. 68–78). London: Demos.

Holcomb, E. L. (1991). *School-based instructional leadership: Staff development for teacher and school effectiveness.* Madison, WI: National Center for Effective Schools.

Holcomb, E. L. (2004). *Getting excited about data: Combining people, passion, and proof to maximize student achievement.* Thousand Oaks, CA: Corwin Press.

Holcomb, E. L. (2007). *Students are stakeholders, too! Including every voice in authentic high school reform.* Thousand Oaks, CA: Corwin Press and National Association of Secondary School Principals.

Holly, P. (1991). Action research: The missing link in the creation of schools as centers of inquiry. In A. Lieberman & L. Miller (Eds.), *Staff development for education in the '90s: New demands, new realities, new perspectives* (2nd ed., pp. 133–157). New York: Teachers College Press.

Hord, S. M. (1997). *Professional learning communities: Communities of continuous inquiry and improvement.* Austin, TX: Southwest Educational Development Laboratory.

Hord, S. M. (2003). *Learning together, leading together: Changing schools through professional learning communities.* New York: Teachers College Press.

Hord, S. M. (2007, December 2). *Professional learning community: What really is it?* Presentation at the National Staff Development Annual Conference, Dallas, TX.

Hord, S. M., Rutherford, W. L., Huling-Austin, L., & Hall, G. E. (1987). *Taking charge of change.* Alexandria, VA: Association for Supervision and Curriculum Development.

Isaacson, N., & Bamburg, J. (1992, November). Can schools become learning organizations? *Educational Leadership, 50*(3), 42–44.

Jenkins, C. (2007, September 29). Favre holds youngsters accountable. *Capital Times* (Madison, WI), F3–F5.

Johnson, D. W., & Johnson, F. P. (1994). *Joining together: Group theory and group skills.* Boston: Allyn & Bacon.

Katz, N. H., & Lawyer, J. W. (1994). *Resolving conflict successfully: Needed knowledge and skills.* Thousand Oaks, CA: Corwin Press.

Koch, R. (1998). *The 80/20 principle: The secret to success by achieving more with less.* New York: Doubleday.

Kotter, J., & Cohen, D. (2006). *The heart of change: Real-life stories of how people change their organizations.* Boston: Harvard Business School Press.

Lambert, L. (2003). *Leadership capacity for lasting school improvement.* Alexandria, VA: Association for Supervision and Curriculum Development.

Lewis, A. C. (2002, March). School reform and professional development. *Phi Delta Kappan, 83*(7), 488.

Loucks-Horsley, S., & Stiegelbauer, S. M. (1991). Using knowledge of change to guide staff development. In A. Lieberman & L. Miller (Eds.), *Staff development for education in the '90s: New demands, new realities, new perspectives* (2nd ed., pp. 15–36). New York: Teachers College Press.

Louis, K. S., & Kruse, S. D. (1995). *Professionalism and community: Perspectives on reforming urban schools.* Thousand Oaks, CA: Corwin Press.

Marzano, R. J. (2003). *What works in schools: Translating research into action.* Alexandria, VA: Association for Supervision and Curriculum Development.

Marzano, R. J., Pickering, D. J., & Pollock, J. E. (2001). *Classroom instruction that works: Research-based strategies for increasing student achievement.* Alexandria, VA: Association for Supervision and Curriculum Development.

McLaughlin, M. W., & Talbert, J. E. (1993). *Contexts that matter for teaching and learning.* Stanford, CA: Center for Research on the Context of Secondary School Teaching.

McManus, A. (1992). *The memory jogger for education: A pocket guide of tools for continuous improvement in schools.* Methuen, MA: GOAL/QPC.

Olson, L. (2007). More power to schools. *Education Week, 27*(13), 23–26.

O'Neill, J., & Conzemius, A. (2006). *The power of SMART goals: Using goals to improve student learning.* Bloomington, IN: Solution Tree.

Owen, H. (1997). *Open Space Technology: A user's guide.* Potomac, MD: Berrett-Koehler.

Reeves, D. B. (2000). *Accountability in action: A blueprint for learning organizations.* Denver, CO: Advanced Learning Press.

Richardson, J. (2007). Focus groups zoom in close on school district's concerns. *Tools for Schools, 9*(1), 1–3, 8.

Rosenholtz, S. (1989). *Teacher's workplace: The social organization of schools.* New York: Longman.

Schmoker, M. (2006). *Results now: How we can achieve unprecedented improvements in teaching and learning.* Alexandria, VA: Association for Supervision and Curriculum Development.

Scholtes, P. R. (1988). *The team handbook: How to use teams to improve quality.* Madison, WI: Joiner.

Senge, P. (1990). *The fifth discipline: The art and practice of the learning organization.* New York: Currency Doubleday.

Sergiovanni, T. J. (1994). *Building community in schools.* San Francisco: Jossey Bass.

Sparks, D. (2006). Appeal to the heart as well as the head. *Tools for Schools, 9*(4), 1–2, 4.

Supovitz, J. (2007). Why we need district-based reform: Supporting systemwide instructional improvement. *Education Week, 27*(13), 27–28.

Treisman, U. (2007, August 15). *Emerging strategies for inspiring math teaching and learning.* Presentation at Olympic Educational Service District, Bremerton, WA.

Tuinstra, R. (2007, October 15). Bellevue school district is losing its leader. *Seattle Times.* Retrieved November 8, 2007, from http://seattletimes.nwsource.com.

Wood, F. H. (1989). Organizing and managing school-based staff development. In S. D. Caldwell (Ed.), *Staff development: A handbook of effective practices* (pp. 26–43). Oxford, OH: National Staff Development Council.

Index

CORWIN PRESS

The Corwin Press logo—a raven striding across an open book—represents the union of courage and learning. Corwin Press is committed to improving education for all learners by publishing books and other professional development resources for those serving the field of PreK–12 education. By providing practical, hands-on materials, Corwin Press continues to carry out the promise of its motto: **"Helping Educators Do Their Work Better."**